FATAL NEGLECT: The U.S. Government's Continuing Failure to Protect American Citizens from Terrorists

Table of Contents

Part Four: The War on Terror at Home

Part Five: What the Future May Hold

Conclusion

FATAL NEGLECT

**The U.S. Government's Continuing Failure to Protect
American Citizens from Terrorists**

**A Special Report Produced By:
Judicial Watch, Inc.**

**Larry Klayman
Chairman and General Counsel**

**Thomas Fitton
President**

**Managing and Contributing Editor
Chris Farrell**

**Contributors
Irene Garcia, Brandon Millett, Wesley Millett
Cristina Rotaru and Russell Verney**

Judicial Watch, Inc., a non-partisan, public interest group organized under Section 501(c)(3) of the Internal Revenue Service Code, investigates and prosecutes government corruption and abuse. For more information visit the Judicial Watch Internet site at: www.JudicialWatch.org, or contact:

Judicial Watch, Inc.
P.O. Box 44444
Washington, DC 20026

Toll Free: 888-JW-ETHIC

e-mail: info@judicialwatch.org

FATAL NEGLECT: The U.S. Government's Continuing
Failure to Protect American Citizens from Terrorists.

Cover design by Jennifer Millett-Barrett
Text design by Shirley Gromen

Dedication

In Memoriam

On the first anniversary of September 11, 2001,
this book is dedicated to the thousands of Americans who lost
their lives and, sadly, the untold others who will follow because
of our government's **Fatal Neglect**.

Foreword

By:

Larry Klayman, Esq.
Chairman & General Counsel
Judicial Watch, Inc.

Anyone who reads, watches television or listens to talk radio knew it would happen. It was only a matter of time. The experts and non-experts have all said – starting with a report in the *Economist* in the annual 1990 edition – that a major terrorist attack on American soil, probably even nuclear or biochemical, would occur in the near future. Indeed, to deflect attention away from his own problems at the height of the Clinton scandals, the former commander-in-chief even predicted it, laying out a scenario not far afield from what occurred on Tuesday, September 11, 2001, a day that will more than live in infamy.

We must mourn the dead and wounded. The time is one of national reconciliation and pride. (One of my friends, Barbara Olson, was killed in the terrorist attacks.) America must remain united, perhaps now more so than ever. And we must support our president, George W. Bush, his cabinet and advisers. We will learn in the days, months and years ahead what we are made of: Are we the "Monica Lewinsky" generation – or more akin to our forefathers, who overcame great hardship to fight for, form and mold a great nation?

Our country is at war. Our adversaries, both foreign and domestic, have infiltrated where we live, where we work and where we play. The enemy is among us. At current estimate, thousands of Islamic radical terrorists have been allowed entry into the United States. We cannot forget that our leaders must be held accountable for failing the American people. However, we are also to blame for not demanding more from them. It took time for Osama bin Laden and his terrorist comrades to infest our major cities and towns here and around the globe. This did not occur overnight. The American government and its European and other "allies" allowed this to happen, with little to no clarion call to those unsuspecting citizens, who themselves neither keep informed nor have any interest whatsoever in matters reaching beyond sports, pop culture and personal gratification – the "me" generation.

Government corruption does not extend simply to bribery of politicians and judges. It concerns much more. It stems from a basic

i

dishonesty of the ruling elite to not tell the truth, the full truth, to the people. Of course, telling the full truth requires that public officials accept the consequences of their truth telling. If the people are fully informed, of course, their votes may not be cast in a way that would result in their election and re-election; thus the "phenomenon" of politicians painting a rosy picture.

Eight years of Clinton scandals, and consequent deceit and criminality, worked a cancer on the body politic of the United States. Because of the weakness of his government – indeed one impeachment was not enough – the former president could neither tell the truth, nor take or marshal any concerted action to begin preparations and planning for days like September 11th: To the contrary, to boost his own popularity and deliver the "goods" to the American people for votes, he and his wife (ironically now New York's senator) usually pretended that all was well, all the time using our money for social welfare programs that would help ensure their administration's longevity. They even released Puerto Rican terrorists from prison when Mrs. Clinton needed votes for her New York Senate campaign. And, of course, she also took large campaign contributions from Muslim groups, some of which have terrorist connections.

The nation's armed forces were decimated and its Federal Bureau of Investigation and Central Intelligence Agency allowed to either decay, or become the "yes" men of a dishonest chief executive and first lady. As a result, no real planning was made to prepare for, much less fight, what any informed individual knew was the real challenge of the 21st century: global terrorism. Indeed, the Clinton-Gore administration, by accepting political bribes in the form of campaign contributions from rogue terrorist states like China and collaborating with the master terrorist, Fidel Castro, over Elian and other issues, furthered the likelihood of massive terrorist activity by turning a blind eye to its benefactors – communist and other regimes with whom the Clinton-Gore administration felt a romantic kinship. And, the Republicans did not have the guts to do what they needed to do: drive the criminals from office and into prison cells.

"Clinton corruption" left us unprepared to prevent the bloodshed of September 11th. Bribed by the forces of evil, it is no wonder the Clinton-Gore administration looked the other way rather than prepare the nation for this horrific future. If the former president, as he liked to crow, would build the bridge to the 21st century, it was the "Bridge Over the River Kwai."

Many of those who understood the situation voted for George W. Bush – not because they revered his intellect, background or professed conservative credentials – but because the alternative of four (and perhaps eight) more years of national security neglect held grave ramifications. At least a "President Bush," many reasoned, would surround himself with top-notch advisers, like Vice President Cheney, who had helped orchestrate and "win" the Persian Gulf War. I was one of those many who voted for then-Governor Bush for this very reason, even though I was disillusioned about his stated lack of commitment to bring the Clintons and other dishonest politicians to justice.

But no sooner than having been sworn-in, the new president not only reaffirmed his lack of interest in taking concrete steps to clean up government corruption, but he also set out – in his "compassionate conservative" way – to prove that he, like Clinton, was interested only in "soccer mom issues." Cosmetic education and Social Security reform, and tax rebates, dominated public discourse as the nation's defenses and security apparatus were allowed to continue to atrophy. Indeed, to pay for the new compassionate conservative social welfare and tax rebates, the defense budget was even to be trimmed. Sure, there was talk of missile defense, but this was years away. The terrorist threat, with which Vice President Cheney was assigned, was put on the back burner, as the Bush-Cheney administration and its cheerleaders would boast about how the new commander-in-chief was performing "above expectations." It was only a matter of time before the cancer which grew during the Clinton-Gore administration metastasized, and turned deadly malignant.

On September 11th, the world witnessed the terrifying events of planes crashing into the World Trade Center and Pentagon. I, myself, experienced the panic and pandemonium on District of Columbia streets as I rushed home to my family. As government and private sector workers fled for their lives, I could not help but think, so much for the experts whom I had voted for as a cure to eight years of Clinton neglect of our national security. Why were we so totally unprepared?[i]

How could 19 individuals, some of whom were already on FBI and CIA watch lists, be allowed to board airplanes at Dulles and Logan Airports? Why were Washingtonians not formally advised through our national emergency broadcast system that a plane was headed in their direction, as Vice President Cheney was safely deep below The White House? Why were D.C. police uninformed that there even was a crisis, other than what they could glean from watching television? Why were there no emergency evacuation plans? (Even members of Congress and White House staff were left to fend for themselves, as they fled buildings in near total hysteria.) Why did we have to lose over 3,000 lives?

On the national television talk shows and other media, our leaders have feigned ignorance of the likelihood that domestic aircraft could have been used as bombs. Have they not read Tom Clancy's books? Were they not aware that other terrorists who, while in custody, provided intelligence about this during the first World Trade Center bombing trial? And why did they ignore explicit intelligence reports by line FBI agents predicting the events of September 11th?

Yes, we have mourned and the country has pulled together. We must unite, and our people have no choice but to follow the lead of the President of the United States. But, we must never forget that our politicians and government officials have not only withheld the full truth from the populace, but have been grossly negligent and reckless. For Clinton and company, their criminality and corruption were largely responsible. For Bush and his new administration – albeit for a short eight months – it was a desire to focus almost exclusively on social giveaways, to boost popularity ratings following the contested Florida election. In any event, our leaders let us down.

To not tell the full truth, to delay implementation of necessary measures to protect our country and to paint a rosy picture for political purposes are forms of government abuse. Indeed, the primary function of the government, as mandated by the Constitution, is to protect the people from foreign and domestic tyranny. But because of years of inattention and recklessness, we must live with the consequences of likely even more severe and perhaps fatally catastrophic terrorist acts on American soil, where millions could be killed and maimed. Even worse, the confidence with which we have to fight this new war – the confidence that our leaders are giving us the facts, all the facts – is sorely shaken. Perhaps this is the biggest casualty of September 11th.

Yes, I am a patriot and I love my country, but no matter how deep my loyalty to the President of the United States and the nation, I will not stop demanding answers for what happened and, above all, also demanding government honesty and accountability. Only in this way can we quickly correct what went wrong and then successfully fight and win the war against terrorism.

---

[i] See: Gilbert Gail, "At the Airports: Risks & Security Detected, Debated For Many Years"; Bradley Graham, "Pentagon Unprepared for Something We Have Never Thought Of," Washington Post, A-1, Sunday, Sept. 16, 2001; and Steve Twomey, "District Unprepared To Cope With Attack," Washington Post, A-1, Monday, Sept. 17, 2001.

FATAL NEGLECT: The U.S. Government's Continuing Failure
to Protect American Citizens from Terrorists

Part One: U.S. Intelligence and Law Enforcement

American Intelligence and the Attacks of September 11th

"It was an intelligence debacle, a colossal failure of intelligence."[1]

Sen. Richard Shelby of Alabama

"It is a lamentably common practice in Washington and elsewhere to shoot people in the back and then complain when they fail to win the race. The loss of so many lives in New York and Washington is now called an 'intelligence failure,' mostly by those who crippled the CIA in the first place and by those who celebrated the loss of its invaluable capabilities." [2]

Tom Clancy, Novelist

"There is no such thing as 100 percent intelligence, particularly in the field of counterterrorism. What you get are snippets of intelligence, which you have to piece together. You are very lucky if you get intelligence about when, where and how." [3]

Stella Rimington, former head of
Britain's MI5 Security Service

Past Is Prologue

"What did the government know, and when did it know it," has become a familiar refrain to Americans seeking accountability from their government in any number of scandals, tragedies and foreign policy "events" of the post-Nixon era. The deepening skepticism and cynicism of the public in general and the elites of the Fourth Estate towards the government and its intelligence and other agencies manifested itself within days of the September 11th attacks. Many Americans wondered how, with an intelligence budget of no less than $30 billion dollars per year, the United States was unable to detect and prevent the September 11th attacks. Indeed, seeking to deflect blame and the concomitant political fallout, Bush-Cheney administration and Congressional officials claimed to have no clue in advance about the tragedy.

Senator Dick Lugar, a member of the Senate Foreign Relations Committee and the Select Intelligence Committee, was commenting within a week of the attacks that, "There certainly were no (warning signs) available to the members of the intelligence committee, I attend the meetings regularly and there were no indicators."[4]

But were there? In February 2000, Director of Central Intelligence (DCI) George Tenet provided the following testimony before the Senate intelligence Committee:

> Osama bin Laden and his global network of lieutenants and associates remain the most immediate and serious threat. His organization is continuing to place emphasis on developing surrogates to carry out attacks in an effort to avoid detection, blame and retaliation.

One year earlier, in 1999, Tenet testified in the same forum that:

> Osama bin Laden is still foremost among these terrorists, because of the immediacy and seriousness of the threat he poses. Everything we have learned recently confirms our conviction that he wants to strike further blows against America. Despite some well-publicized disruptions, we believe he could still strike without additional warning.

Placed in the context of the serial bombing campaign begun in 1995 against U.S. facilities in Riyadh, Saudi Arabia, in 1996 at the "Khobar Towers," our embassies in East Africa (August 1998) and the USS Cole (October 12, 2000) was there a true intelligence failure, or was there an unrealistic attitude of continental invulnerability and a near total void in planning what is now known as "Homeland Security?" Perhaps both existed.

Taking things a step further, one must ask if the American public was even remotely concerned with terrorism before September 11th. Terrorism issues or policy questions did not factor much in the 2000 general election. With few exceptions, the press did not aggressively pursue terrorism stories. The last decade of bombings against American interests should have served as an explicit and dire warning of things to come, yet were seen as unfortunate, isolated incidents. On September 9, 2001,

4

Secretary of Defense Donald Rumsfeld threatened a presidential veto if Congress shifted $600 million from ballistic missile defense systems to counterterrorism programs. Attorney General John Ashcroft's Justice Department budget submission of September 10, 2001, increased funding in 68 law enforcement programs – none dealt with counterterrorism.[5] The American people, their government and its intelligence agencies were asleep at the switch – period.

Beginning May 16, 2002, the Washington press corps, some members of Congress, and others were whipped into a furor over The White House's disclosure that President Bush was cautioned last August that Osama bin Laden might be planning a hijacking. The response to the disclosure has been characterized as politically motivated opportunism; bureaucratic finger-pointing; anti-Bush press sensationalism; an exercise in 20/20 hindsight; and by some, as a legitimate quest to uncover the important background facts that accurately depict the state of affairs within our government. In a televised damage control effort on May 16, 2002, National Security Adviser Condoleezza Rice said the government had received numerous reports of terrorist threats last summer, and emphasized that the information seemed general and pointed toward potential attacks overseas. On May 17, 2002, President Bush defended himself against critics' suggestions that he ignored warning signs of the September 11th attacks, saying "I would have done everything in my power to protect the American people" had he known of Osama bin Laden's plans.[6]

In fact, the information President Bush received in the August 6, 2001, briefing had been public for months. The Federal Aviation Administration (FAA) published a report called "Criminal Acts Against Aviation" on its Internet site in 2001 (before the hijackings) that warned that although Osama bin Laden "is not known to have attacked civil aviation, he has both the motivation and the wherewithal to do so." The report added, "Bin Laden's anti-Western and anti-American attitudes make him and his followers a significant threat to civil aviation, particularly to U.S. civil aviation." Both American Airlines and United Airlines, which each lost two planes on September 11th, acknowledged receiving Federal FAA alerts and periodic security information bulletins, but no specific warning of a hijacking threat.[7]

What became "news" and stoked the political controversy over the intelligence failure was the inability of The White House to explain why it took eight months to reveal that the CIA had raised the specific possibility of a hijacking by al Qaeda, even in conventional terms, that were not specific or predictive of the nature of the September 11th attacks.[8]

The second factor in play during mid-May 2002, was the existence of the FBI's so-called "Phoenix memo," from an FBI agent who identified a disturbing pattern of flight training by Middle Eastern males.[9] How the Bush-Cheney administration and the Bureau handled the Phoenix memorandum, warning that Osama bin Laden's followers could be training at flight schools, dominated news reporting and talk shows.

On the heels of the "Phoenix memo" came the disclosure of a 13-page typed letter written by Colleen Rowley, a Special Agent and counsel in the FBI's Minneapolis field office, who alleged obstruction and apathy on the part of FBI headquarters staff in pursuing the investigation of the so-called "20th hijacker," Zacharias Moussaoui, and a pattern of misleading public statements by FBI Director Robert Mueller concerning stalled inquiries leading up to the September 11th attacks. The shockwaves of the botched flight school leads from Phoenix and Minneapolis have done much to shape the discourse concerning the government's poor articulation of what it has done leading up to the September 11th attacks, and how its current course of action will protect and defend the American people.

The Bush-Cheney administration has also not explained how capturing Osama bin Laden, or destroying the Taliban and al Qaeda in Afghanistan, Pakistan and elsewhere will stop existing, semi-autonomous terrorist cells from operating in Western Europe and North America. One terrorist can still inflict enormous damage – killing or injuring thousands. Has the U.S. government been forthright with the public? What can Americans expect and plan for?

Are the September 11th attacks an "isolated incident," an aberration that has now been fully addressed and permanently corrected? Have we sufficiently "won" the "War on Terror" to easily revert back to our comfortable, pre-September 11th way of life? NBC's Tim Russert asked Senator Richard Shelby of the Senate Intelligence Committee what we should expect:

| MR. RUSSERT: | "Do you expect another terrorist strike in the United States?" |
| SEN. SHELBY: | "Absolutely. I hope not. I'd like to tell you otherwise. But I believe there will be a terrorist attack." |

During the week of May 19, 2002, and thereafter, Bush-Cheney administration officials echoed Senator Shelby's remarks.

The current dire predictions call for accountability. How did we get here? Who is responsible? Not a single senior Bush-Cheney administration official, department head or agency chief has been called to account, formally reprimanded or fired for what happened on September 11th. ABC News reported that Cofer Black, who has run the CIA's counterterrorism center for the past three years, has been moved out of the post.[10] Cofer Black is hardly a "household name," and certainly not a decision-maker with the political "horsepower" of DCI George Tenet. Rather than a senior, responsible official, the press has been offered an interim sacrificial lamb who may or may not be culpable for failing to detect and deter the terrorist attacks. Tenet and his staff are portraying themselves to the media as "taking action" so the public can sleep well.

There is a vacuum of both personal and official responsibility in American government. In many other Western constitutional republics or democracies, the political consequences of the September 11th attacks would have resulted in wholesale firings within a Cabinet, or perhaps even the fall of an entire government. For the last 20 years, Americans have listened to government officials talk about "accepting responsibility" for tragedies, negligence and abuses of power, but rarely are there any substantive results. It is as though merely saying the words themselves equates with actually bearing the weight of the action and all of its attendant consequences.

During the Clinton-Gore administration, then-Attorney General Janet Reno presided over, among other things, Waco, the Oklahoma City bombing and the forced deportation of Elian Gonzalez to Communist Cuba. Reno likewise claimed to have "followed the evidence" on a string of scandals that dealt with everything from Democratic Party campaign finance abuses, the sale of U.S. trade mission seats, transfer of high technology to Communist China in exchange for campaign cash, and the deplorable personal behavior and serial perjuries of then-President Clinton. Despite this sorry record of "law enforcement" Janet Reno remains one of the longest serving Attorney Generals in U.S. history, in large part because she inoculated herself from press criticism by being quick to "accept full responsibility." Now, Attorney General John Ashcroft of the Bush-Cheney Justice Department has adopted a policy of near total secrecy over his post-September 11th actions, perpetuating the crisis of confidence in the nation's highest law enforcement office.

The public is owed detailed explanations and full accountability from their public servants. Or, the same thing may happen again.

The State of American Intelligence

There are a number of criticisms of government intelligence operations typically leveled by members of Congress and the Washington DC think tank analysts that specialize in intelligence and security matters. They are not necessarily new or innovative. In fact, they are old arguments that are resurrected periodically and re-hashed in a cyclic process dating back to the Civil War era. Over time, the technical aspects of the arguments have become more complex, just as the means of intelligence "collection" have become increasingly sophisticated. The arguments for and against aggressive intelligence collection are part of the see-sawing arguments of America's "split personality" on intelligence matters. Seventy years ago many American intelligence operations were closed down on the orders of Secretary of State Henry Stimson. His rationale: "Gentlemen do not read each others' mail." No one feels that way about Osama bin Laden today.

Some analysts believe the several agencies dealing with various forms of intelligence information, or "INTS" (e.g. imagery intelligence – IMINT, human intelligence – HUMINT) are duplicative, and spend too much of their time, money and energy engaging in petty "turf wars," designed to protect their information niche, rather than aggressively pursuing our foreign foes. In some cases, each of the military services and a handful of civilian intelligence agencies all target and collect intelligence information on the same foreign intelligence objective. In such cases, it is virtually guaranteed that none of the agencies share their reporting with each other.

As a result of September 11th, it is now universally accepted that the most effective intelligence collection discipline for counterterrorism operations is HUMINT. The very essence of an Islamist terrorist organization's operational strength is its capacity to conspire. The conspiracy insures operational security, unit cohesion, mission focus and clean lines of communication and command. Countering the terrorist threat means penetrating the organization, learning their plans, and identifying the perpetrators so they can be neutralized. This is an incredibly demanding and dangerous mission for the American case officer and the intelligence "asset" recruited to penetrate the organization. Speaking at Duke University in April 2002, James Pavitt, the CIA's Deputy Director for Operations (DDO), the agency's top case officer, said the following concerning al Qaeda:

> The terror cells that we're going up against
> are typically small and all terrorist
> personnel . . . were carefully screened. The
> number of personnel who know vital

information, targets, timing, the exact
methods to be used had to be smaller still. .
. . Against that degree of control, that kind
of compartmentation, that depth of
discipline and fanaticism, I personally
doubt—and I draw again upon my thirty
years of experience in this business—that
anything short of one of the knowledgeable
inner-circle personnel or hijackers turning
himself in to us would have given us
sufficient foreknowledge to have prevented
the horrendous slaughter that took place on
the eleventh.[11]

Sadly, CIA practice has been to assign case officers on overseas tours for an average of only three years – barely enough time to truly get comfortable in the operating environment, let alone penetrate a terrorist cell.

Many "operators" – the intelligence case officers and special operations warfare soldiers/sailors/airmen/marines involved in actually conducting the intelligence gathering and reconnaissance missions – point to mid-level bureaucrats and staff officers within the intelligence "colossus" as the principal obstacles to accomplishing important missions, because they are "risk averse."

Vincent Cannistraro, the former CIA counterterrorism chief, faults the agency "for not penetrating al Qaeda – for not even trying." He calls its response to the terrorist challenge "very passive." "The job is to *deter* terrorism," he says, "not make arrests after the action."[12]

The cautious corporate culture within the CIA is partly the result of poor morale, attributed in some measure to a perception of the agency's reduced importance and relevance during the Clinton-Gore administration, when then-President Clinton stopped receiving routine presidential intelligence briefings. In a two year period, former President Clinton met one-on-one with then-CIA Director R. James Woolsey a grand total of two times. The CIA's poor morale was also rooted in the devastating debacle of the Soviet mole Aldrich Ames, who was unmasked in 1994. Elsewhere in the Federal government, the CIA's "customers" were more interested in focusing the agency's post-Soviet era collection capabilities on economic spying, nuclear proliferation, the war on drugs and other priorities.

While intelligence professionals are often anxious to achieve a "big win" in the intelligence war, politicians are often not willing to take chances in an unforgiving political and press environment. Robert Baer, a veteran CIA case officer, may have expressed it best:

> Whether it was Osama bin Laden, Yasir
> Arafat, Iranian terrorism, Saddam Hussein,
> or any other of the evils that so threaten the
> world, the Clinton-Gore administration
> seemed determined to sweep them all under
> the carpet. Ronald Reagan and George
> Bush before Clinton were not much better.
> The mantra at 1600 Pennsylvania Avenue
> seemed to be: Get through the term. Keep
> the bad news from the newspapers. Dump
> the naysayers. Gather money for the next
> election – gobs and gobs of it – and let
> some other administration down the road
> deal with it all. Worst of all, my CIA had
> decided to go along for the ride. [13]

Contributing to this grim environment was the steady politicization of the intelligence organizations and processes that stressed Gramscian psychological techniques featuring "sensitivity awareness" and "diversity" seminars. *Insight* magazine reports:

> Intelligence professionals are forced to attend
> sensitivity-training classes and do role-
> playing skits to conform to politically correct
> social themes. Another CIA official adds,
> "The management wasted countless
> thousands of hours by making all of us sit
> through workshops to make politically
> correct diversity quilts." Pieces of fabric were
> distributed to CIA employees on which they
> were instructed to sew, draw or glue art,
> photographs and slogans reflecting
> "diversity" themes dictated during mandatory
> sensitivity seminars. "Can you imagine
> being a manager and having your staff say,
> 'Sorry, I need to take off an hour to work on
> my diversity quilt?' It just scalds me." He
> estimates that the quilting workshops and
> seminars cost the CIA more than 20,000
> hours of employee time. The diversity quilts
> are on display inside CIA headquarters." [14]

The fact that psychological techniques, meant to achieve "passive revolution," and derived from the theories of Marxist philosopher Antonio Gramsci, were, and presumably still are, actively part of the CIA's in-service professional development program is mind-boggling. Even more disturbing is that the same program of politically correct sensitivity training is pervasive throughout all branches and departments of the federal government. Within the U.S. Army, the program is known as "Consideration of Others," using small group interaction "to inculcate a sensitivity and regard for the feelings and needs of others, we must institutionalize this program in order to maintain a climate of dignity and respect."[15]

In a corollary to the sentiments of the intelligence "operators," many analysts and staff on Capitol Hill realize that the so-called Torricelli Rules, imposed by former DCI John Deutsch, have unreasonably restricted intelligence operations. The Torricelli Rules, named after U.S. Senator Robert Torricelli, forbid the recruitment by the CIA of any person with a criminal or human rights violation record.[16]

In 1995, Senator Torricelli, a New Jersey Democrat, and then a congressman, came to the aid of Jennifer Harbury, an American whose husband was a communist guerrilla from Guatemala named Efrian Bamaca. Bamaca and his Cuban-sponsored comrades were responsible for terrorist attacks across Central America and threatened the lives of U.S. citizens living and working in the region. Bamaca "disappeared" in the early 1990's at the hands of Guatemalan security forces.

In March 1995, Torricelli held a press conference alleging that a Guatemalan colonel, a paid asset of the CIA, was responsible for the disappearance of Bamaca and an American citizen. Torricelli assigned responsibility to the CIA, and accused the agency of murder. Deutsch fired the CIA's Latin American division chief and adopted recruitment and reporting rules – drafted by the Leftist organization Human Rights Watch and endorsed by Guatemalan guerrillas – as the new CIA operational standard.

The Torricelli Rules unreasonably restricted CIA case officers from recruiting foreign persons with a criminal or human rights violation record. The types of persons, organizations and activities that the CIA is charged with gathering information about are often unsavory, violent and/or criminal. The persons associated with those types of intelligence "targets" are normally not characterized as "boy scouts." In order for the CIA to be able to collect timely, useful intelligence there are occasions when they simply must engage the services of persons who would otherwise be classified as undesirable.

The term of DCI Deutsch was also characterized by the diminution of both HUMINT operations and offensive Counterintelligence (CI) operations (so-called "double agent" operations). Deutsch favored technical collection means – typically Signals Intelligence (SIGINT) and IMINT. Since September 11th, almost every person with a television set is now familiar with the term HUMINT, thanks to a steady stream of news analysts, "experts" and commentators who uniformly decried the United States' poor state of affairs in that field.

> "Many of the same people who are charging intelligence failures – particularly in Congress – knew for years that our (human intelligence) element was being badly underfunded. They did nothing to fix it,' said Anthony Cordesman, senior fellow at the Center for Strategic and International Studies. 'Not enough agents, there isn't enough money for training agents, and many haven't even visited the areas they are supposed to monitor,' says Cordesman."[17]

In a classic example of the CIA's desperate scramble to correct years of neglect and indifference, an October 4, 2002, article from the *States News Service* reported: "The agency's recruitment center has posted notices that it is in particular need for specialists on the Middle East, Asia, and Africa and international economists focusing on financial vulnerabilities, analysis, and illicit finance. The agency is also seeking foreign language instructors in Arabic, Dari/Pashtu, French, Persian (Farsi), Russian, and Spanish."[18]

CIA veterans Bob Baer and Vincent Cannistraro both stress the need for intelligence officers to spend less time with their foreign counterparts and more time in the field gathering their own intelligence. The recent state

---

• Ironically, Senator Torricelli was "severely admonished" by the Senate Ethics committee in July 2002 for taking bribes from a New Jersey businessman, David Chang, taking official actions to benefit chang, including contacting government officials, writing letters to other governments and letting chang and his representatives attend meetings between the senator and government officials from other countries.

of affairs within the Clandestine Service of the CIA had foreign-posted case officers increasingly relying on "liaison contacts" with host nation security and intelligence services as the source for intelligence information reported back to CIA headquarters. While there are certainly situations and circumstances that are best-suited for liaison contacts, the CIA is, in those circumstances, essentially relying on the reporting of the foreign intelligence service rather than obtaining the intelligence information from its own vetted and operationally tested sources, under their own control. Both men feel that overseas case officers were more likely to spend their time waiting for sources to walk through the door than to leave U.S. embassies to develop intelligence sources and information independently.

Cannistraro has stated, "Sitting back passively collecting information from liaison services from allied countries, whether it's Saudi Arabia or Pakistan or Jordan, . . . you're subject to intelligence collected by a third country on a subject you should be able to collect firsthand," he said. Although there are some places where U.S. agents cannot gain firsthand intelligence, Cannistraro said, "When we're totally dependent on another country, as we were, for example on Pakistan, then you're hostage to the political situation in that country, with disastrous results."[19]

Amidst the now frantic calls for a renewed national HUMINT effort, it bears repeating that it is nearly impossible to penetrate small, disciplined, conspiratorial organizations like al Qaeda. Most of the operatives are personally known to one another, or related by blood or marriage. Finding a reliable U.S. citizen able to achieve such a penetration is equally daunting. The number of Americans that are genuinely bilingual and bicultural – capable of living like natives in the Middle East as well as Central and South Asia – is exceptionally small. That is why aggressive U.S. intelligence case officers – in both the CIA and the Defense HUMINT Service – rely on foreign agents, some of whom may have "unsavory" pasts.

Overseeing CIA operations since the spring of 1997 is Clinton-Gore administration appointee George Tenet. Inexplicably, he is the only Clinton-Gore cabinet member to have retained his position in the Bush-Cheney administration. Two weeks after the September 11th attacks, President George W. Bush traveled to CIA headquarters to show his support of Tenet.

"George and I have been spending a lot of quality time together," Bush said at their press conference. "There's a reason. I've got a lot of confidence in him, and I've got a lot of confidence in the CIA."

Perhaps so, but that does not answer sufficiently the critics in the media, in Congress and across the nation who seek full, personal accountability. In retrospect, the American people would come to ask whether they themselves should have had confidence in the Bush-Cheney administration, specifically Tenet. The American people are owed and deserve a full accounting. While focusing on the terrorist enemy and being a "team player" will suffice for the first few months of what President Bush has predicted may be a decades-long war, a full and complete *post mortem* must be forthcoming. It will undoubtedly uncover indicators that existed in advance but that were obscured or contradicted by other evidence.

On February 6, 2002, DCI Tenet appeared before Senate Intelligence Committee and stated that September 11th "was not the result of failure of attention and focus and discipline and effort. We have been at war with al Qaeda for over five years."

Under close and critical questioning by Sen. Richard C. Shelby (R) of Alabama, Tenet bristled and aggressively defended the CIA. During the hearing, Tenet claimed that the CIA had penetrated al Qaeda before September 11th, but that the terrorists' operational security concerning the deadly plot was so closely held among the Islamists, that the secret planning for the operation resided "probably in the head of three or four people."

Tenet closed his statement before the Senate Intelligence Committee saying, "We welcome the committee's review of our record on terrorism. It's a record of discipline, strategy, focus and attention." Tenet should get his "review," if not by a Congressional committee, than by the media and Judicial Watch.

HUMINT was not alone when it came to operational restrictions. The 1978 Foreign Intelligence Surveillance Act (FISA) placed strict limits on the operations of the country's main electronic eavesdropping agency, the National Security Agency (NSA), within the United States. In order to preclude some of the "wiretapping" and "bugging" abuses made famous by the FBI's "COINTELPRO" and "Garden Plot" operations against radicals of the 1960's and early 1970's, a court was established to review and certify requests for electronic surveillance and concealed monitoring in national security crime investigations. The USA Patriot Act, a set of anti-terrorism measures passed in October 2001, relaxed the standards for obtaining intelligence warrants, requiring that foreign intelligence be a "significant," rather than "primary," purpose of the investigation. The system is still prone to abuse, as evidenced by a May 17, 2002, opinion by the FISA court that oversees the Justice Department and FBI. Justice and FBI officials supplied erroneous information to the FISA court in more than 75 applications for search warrants and wiretaps, including one signed by then-FBI Director Louis J. Freeh. Authorities also improperly shared intelligence information with agents and prosecutors handling criminal cases in New York on at least four occasions. The former FISA court chief justice, U.S. District Judge Royce C. Lamberth, documented the Justice Department's and FBI's abuse of powers in his ruling, and was so angered by inaccuracies in affidavits submitted by FBI agent Michael Resnick that Resnick was barred from ever appearing before the court, according to the ruling and government sources.

Another challenge to the U.S. SIGINT collection program comes in the form of "collection volume." The amount of electronic information "vacuumed" from the skies 24 hours per day, seven days a week, is staggering. At some point, all of that information must be reduced to a form wherein a human being can review and analyze the contents of the raw intelligence. Certainly, computers are enormously helpful to the NSA in categorizing, sorting and processing the information collected from a wide variety of platforms around and across the globe. "Human intervention" requires the evaluation of data and a decision. Being able to quickly identify **the** single piece of information necessary to complete the jigsaw puzzle of intelligence information developing from all intelligence information sources is akin to trying to take a sip from a fire hose.

There is now public knowledge of at least one instance wherein the NSA intercepted and recorded a conversation in Arabic, before the September 11th attacks, in which the participants discussed, in general terms, a major operation planned for that day. However, the information was not translated until after the attacks, because NSA analysts were simply too swamped and overwhelmed with data.[20]

And of course, it is "sexier," and therefore easier, to sell a brand new satellite collection platform – worth millions of dollars in defense contracts – to congressmen with defense plants in their home districts, than it is to get funding for NSA to hire 100 Farsi-speakers to actually listen to, translate and analyze the intelligence information. Each of the agencies and the "INTS" faces program budget obstacles similar to this example. Meaningful, reliable intelligence analysis is neither easy nor cheap. There is no quantity versus quality formula at play.

Additionally, our intelligence agencies are heavily weighted towards "current operations" analysis and research support. The United States has historically been extremely week at long-term analysis – those programs that take the five and 10 year view of trends, capabilities and intentions, rather than the more fashionable and high-tech "real time" downloads portrayed in popular cinema. "Instant gratification" is not a hallmark of serious intelligence analysis and forecasting. It is, however, a big part of the American psyche and culture, and to a certain extent it explains how we could track the movements of Soviet ballistic missile submarines in "real time," and know what Gorbachev was having for dinner, while simultaneously failing to predict the collapse of the Soviet government.

Ironically, the often unheralded excellence of American intelligence can actually work against itself in successfully identifying a surprise attack. Richard Betts, Director of the Institute of War and Peace Studies at Columbia University, and a member of the National Commission on Terrorism has noted: "There are often numerous false alarms before an attack, and they dull sensitivity to warnings of the attack that does occur. Sometimes the supposed false alarms were not false at all, but accurate warnings that prompted timely responses by the victim that in turn caused the attacker to cancel and reschedule the assault – thus generating a self-negating prophecy."[21]

Betts continues: "The point is that intelligence can rarely be perfect and unambiguous, and there are always good reasons to misinterpret it. Some problems of the past have been fixed by the technically sophisticated system we have now, and some may be reduced by adjustments to the system. But some can never be eliminated, with the result being that future unpleasant surprises are a certainty."[22]

The CIA's public relations rehabilitation has already begun. *Newsweek's* Evan Thomas was given unprecedented access to detailed paramilitary operations information and CIA officers in a story for the magazine's April 29, 2002, edition. Thomas' news article reads more like a movie script, and paints a portrait of a newly invigorated "special activities" group (the CIA's, until recently neglected, paramilitary force). Thomas caveats his glowing report with an escape clause, "While some intelligence experts remain gloomy, most agree that the CIA is making gradual headway against a very difficult foe. One major terrorist attack, of course, could make even that carefully hedged assessment sound like so much wishful thinking."[23]

Apparently, the Bush-Cheney administration could not agree more with Thomas' cautionary remark. Hard on the heels of the bitter criticism the Bush-Cheney administration faced in mid-May 2002, for failing to disclose details of an August 6, 2001, intelligence briefing that mentioned al Qaeda and the possibility of aircraft hijacking, Vice President Cheney, FBI Director Robert Mueller and Secretary of Defense Donald Rumsfeld went on a "doom offensive." During interviews on the news shows of Sunday, May 19, 2002, Vice President Cheney warned that a strike is "almost certain" and "could happen tomorrow, it could happen next week, it could happen next year." The following day, Director Mueller added warnings that a walk-in suicide bombing like the ones that have terrorized the Israelis is "inevitable" in the United States. Defense Secretary Rumsfeld, in testimony before a Senate Appropriations subcommittee on May 21, 2002, stated that state terrorism sponsors such as Iran, Iraq, Syria, Libya and North Korea are developing weapons of mass destruction – nuclear, chemical and biological devices – that will certainly be supplied to terrorist groups for use against the United States. "They (terrorists) inevitably will get their hands on them and they will not hesitate to use them," Rumsfeld said.[24]

By all appearances, the Bush-Cheney administration did not want to be subjected to the criticism and scrutiny of the prior week, and chose to initiate a press offensive that heightened and highlighted the number, type and severity of terrorist warnings and threats confronting the United States. How else can the Bush-Cheney administration explain Homeland Security Director Tom Ridge's saying his office had not raised the nation's formal alert status in light of the new terror warnings issued by administration officials? Ridge refused to increase the alert status because the intelligence on possible attacks was "too vague." Unfortunately, it appears the Bush-Cheney administration's "doom offensive" was less about a sincere effort to protect the American public from terrorist acts of violence than it was to protect politicians from criticism and pressure. It seems designed to blunt inquiries into the U.S. intelligence community, the Bush-Cheney administration, and to inoculate themselves from further criticism, should there be more terrorist attacks on U.S. soil. The administration went to great lengths to announce the warnings, made no change to the nation's alert status and provided no context, advice, or even encouragement to the public over the Memorial Day weekend – a sadly ironic fact.

The remarks of Messrs. Cheney, Rumsfeld and Mueller are extraordinary and actually raise additional, deeply disturbing questions about the war on terror, rather than merely providing important warnings to the public. Columnist Helle Dale of the *Washington Times* responded to Director Mueller's defeatist admissions that "We will not be able to stop it, it's something we all live with," by asking, "Can anyone imagine Winston Churchill telling the British in 1940, 'The Germans are coming and there's nothing we can do about it. I wish I could be more optimistic, but I suggest you get used to the idea.'?"[25]

Ms. Dale goes on to point out that the rest of the world – including terrorists – are listening and reading, *via* the airwaves, Internet and newspapers, to Messrs. Cheney, Rumsfeld and Mueller's forecasts of inevitable death and destruction for the United States. Al Qaeda, Hamas,

Hezbollah and Saddam Hussein must be very encouraged. Ms. Dale closes her editorial by recommending that Director Mueller be given a copy of Mr. Churchill's speeches, or look for a less demanding job.

Overlooked Indicators & Missed Opportunities

The following chronology traces the major, publicly available, terrorist-related incidents pointing to the attacks of September 11th:

- A 1990 New York City murder should have been the first warning that Islamist terrorists were organizing to kill in this country, but police said the gunman, Sayyid Nosair, had acted alone. This Egyptian-American's shooting of the Jewish extremist Rabbi Meir Kahane was the first missed opportunity in the war against terrorism. The FBI had seized Arabic language tapes and documents from Nosair's apartment, but the material was not inventoried or translated for years. It was only then that detailed bomb making instructions were discovered, as well as pictures of New York landmarks, including the World Trade Center. The material also made it clear that Nosair was part of a network of terrorists who for years had been planning attacks to kill large numbers of civilians. The FBI also learned that Nosair's defense had been paid for by Saudi millionaire Osama bin Laden.[26]

- December 1994 – Algerian terrorists hijack a plane with the intention of crashing it into the Eiffel Tower. The attack is thwarted when French police storm the plane, which had been forced to land in Marseilles.[27]

- 1995 – After uncovering Ramzi Yousef's "Bojinka" plot for an al Qaeda-linked terrorist cell to blow-up planes over the Pacific Ocean, Philippine authorities alert the FBI that Middle Eastern pilots may be training at U.S. flight schools with the intention of launching suicide hijacking missions against federal buildings. Philippine investigators also found evidence targeting commercial towers in San Francisco, Chicago and New York City.[28]

- In 1996, the F.B.I. asked officials in Qatar for assistance in apprehending another alleged accomplice of Yousef, Khalid Shaikh Mohammed, who was then believed to be in Qatar.

18

According to the FBI, Mohammed was involved in a conspiracy to "bomb U.S. airliners" and was also believed to be "in the process of manufacturing an explosive device."[29]

- Sudan, a nation on the U.S. list of sponsors of terrorism, had expelled Osama bin Laden in 1996 at the urging of the U.S. government. Then Sudan sent a message through American businessman Mansoor Ijaz. They appeared willing to share information on al Qaeda. Sudan's intelligence chief showed Ijaz some files on al Qaeda. Ijaz delivered the message personally to the National Security Council (NSC) and members of Congress.[30]

- There was a disturbing inconsistency in the terrorism "policy" of the Clinton-Gore administration that is demonstrated by examining terrorist bombings. After the bombings of the embassies in Africa in 1998, President Bill Clinton signed a series of orders secretly authorizing the use of lethal force to capture or kill Osama bin Laden. According to intelligence sources, there were three occasions since 1998 when the United States had information about bin Laden's location, but the Clinton-Gore administration was not willing to risk losing American lives to capture him.

- September 11, 1999 – A federal report entitled, "Sociology and Psychology of Terrorism: Who Becomes a Terrorist and Why?," warned that al Qaeda may be planning to hijack an aircraft and plow it into the Pentagon in response to the 1998 U.S. strike against terrorist camps in Afghanistan. The report, created for the National Intelligence Council and shared with federal agencies, said: "Suicide bomber(s) belonging to al-Qaida's Martyrdom Battalion could crash-land an aircraft packed with high explosives (C-4 and Semtex) into the Pentagon, the headquarters of the Central Intelligence Agency (CIA), or The White House." Created from open-source government records, the report says that Ramzi Yousef and Abdul Murad, conspirators in the 1993 World Trade Center bombings, had admitted to plotting to bomb CIA headquarters.[3]

- In late December of 1999, a group of al Qaeda terrorists armed with knives hijacked an Indian airliner and diverted it to Kandahar, Afghanistan.

- Also in December of 1999, Ahmed Ressam, an Algerian, is arrested with false identity documents, explosives and timing devices while crossing the Canadian border into Washington state. His goal was reportedly to destroy Seattle's Space Needle during the millennium celebrations.

- The Clinton-Gore administration treated the first World Trade Center bombings, the suicide attack on the USS Cole, and Ahmad Ressam's attempt to blow up the Los Angeles airport on New Year's Eve 2000, as criminal investigations rather than acts of war. A decision was made to adopt the "loose networks" theory of terrorism.[32] This theory, never before pursued in American law enforcement or intelligence circles, held that major acts of terrorism were carried out by shifting, amorphous groups whose existence was unknown until the moment of their strike. Somehow, American intelligence and law enforcement adopted, simultaneously, two conflicting theories of terrorist *modus operandi*. The traditional state-sponsored model of trans-national, conspiratorial, criminal terrorist enterprise made room for the new "loose network" theory. The Clinton-Gore administration's conflicted policies, once translated and implemented in the field, added to the already confused state of affairs in the neglected world of counterterrorism.

- ABC News learned that a month before September 11th the CIA received intelligence that bin Laden's right-hand man, Dr. Ayman Zawahari, was at a medical clinic in Yemen. But the Bush-Cheney administration rejected the plan to pick up Zawahari and bring him to the United States for trial because they could not be "100 percent sure" that it was Zawahari.[33]

- In January 2000, members of Osama bin Laden's network met in Malaysia. Among them were men later identified as plotters of the attack on the USS Cole anchored at a port in Yemen. The CIA failed to put those men, Khalid Al-Mihhar and Nawaf Alhazmi, on a terrorist watch list for another 18 months even though a surveillance video linked them to al Qaeda. Both slipped into the United States undetected. Once on the list, the FBI failed to find al-Mihhar and Alhazmi. Despite being sought by the FBI, there was no system in place to alert the airlines that the men were "wanted," before the two hijackers boarded American Airlines Flight 77 that would crash into the Pentagon on September 11th.

- Beginning in December 2000, and continuing through the spring of 2001 there was an increase in intelligence "traffic" indicating that bin Laden's al Qaeda terrorist group was planning an attack[34]

- The summer of 2001, marked a period of intense concern over imminent terror action by al Qaeda. Intelligence "I&W" – indications and warnings – were voluminous and frustratingly non-specific, but nonetheless, a heightened state of alert was ordered at a number of U.S. Government facilities. Barton Gellman of the *Washington Post* detailed the alert in his report of May 17, 2002, entitled "Before Sept. 11, Unshared Clues and Unshaped Policy":

> On July 5 of last year, a month and a day before President Bush first heard that al Qaeda might plan a hijacking, The White House summoned officials of a dozen federal agencies to the Situation Room.
>
> "Something really spectacular is going to happen here, and it's going to happen soon," the government's top counter-terrorism official, Richard Clarke, told the assembled group, according to two of those present. The group included the Federal Aviation Administration, along with the Coast Guard, FBI, Secret Service and Immigration and Naturalization Service.
>
> Clarke directed every counterterrorist office to cancel vacations, defer non-vital travel, put off scheduled exercises and place domestic rapid-response teams on much shorter alert. For six weeks last summer, at home and overseas, the U.S. government was at its highest possible state of readiness — and anxiety — against imminent terrorist attack.

* * *

On June 22, the military's Central and European Commands imposed "Force Protection Condition Delta," the highest anti-terrorist alert. The next day the State Department ordered all diplomatic posts to convene emergency action committees. The CIA, including the Rome station chief, said the most probable targets included the U.S. Embassy in Italy, the Genoa summit of the Group of Eight leaders in July, and the Vatican — a threat that caused Bush to change the venue of his meeting with Pope John Paul II to the papal summer residence at Castel Gandolfo outside Rome.

On July 3, Tenet made an urgent special request to 20 friendly intelligence services, asking for the arrest of a list of known al Qaeda operatives.

As late as July 31, the FAA urged U.S. airlines to maintain a "high degree of alertness." All those alert levels dropped by the time hijackers armed with box cutters took control of four jetliners on the morning of Sept. 11.

- French intelligence did identify and warn the CIA about a French Algerian, Zacarius Moussaoui. They passed on a thick folder outlining his radical Islamic connections, but in August, 2001, the FBI failed to fully investigate Moussaoui or pursue his connections despite the suspicions of a flight instructor in Norman, Oklahoma.[35]

While much ink and many hours of television time have been spent on discussions about "connecting the dots" of the intelligence tips available before September 11th, the proximate cause of the intelligence failure is communications failure. The CIA has had a National Counterterrorism Center ever since 1986. It is a joint operation with members of the CIA, the FBI and other national security organizations sharing information gathered overseas or from foreign sources. The intelligence is not simply shared, but analyzed, data based, and acted upon – all from what analysts like to call a "fusion center." **No such organization existed for domestic intelligence and counterterrorism law enforcement purposes prior to September 11th.** It's just that simple. The left hand did not know what the right hand was doing – domestically. For example, the FBI never told the CIA it had arrested Moussaoui on August 16th. The CIA was running name traces and requests for assistance through French intelligence liaison contacts for someone in the custody of the FBI. Neither the FBI nor the CIA told The White House anything about Moussaoui. There was no central clearing house – no fusion center – where actions could be coordinated, information shared, analysis and data basing conducted. In hindsight, this complete void in domestic intelligence seems painfully obvious, but prior to September 11th many would have had grave reservations concerning the infringement of civil liberties by the formation and operation of such a domestic intelligence apparatus.

Reorganizations and Remedies

Tragedies such as September 11th have a way of changing our perspective concerning defense, domestic security and law enforcement investigative techniques. As an example, let us briefly examine the utility of the so-called "random searches" instituted at airport security checkpoints. In blind adherence to political correctness, security administrators insist that no type of "profiling" should or will be used to screen passengers. So, the septuagenarian grandmother of Nordic stock, flying home to Minnesota from visiting her grandchildren in Ohio, is subjected to the same level of scrutiny as all other passengers. The identities and demographics of the September 11th hijackers and al Qaeda members are well known. They are all Middle Eastern males between 20 and 35 years old. Certainly that does not exclude or exonerate all others from meriting special scrutiny, but Grandma Lundquist and her nail file should not unduly distract the security checkpoint.

So, now that there is a USA Patriot's Act and several billion dollars in Congressional appropriations available, what will the federal government do? Argenbright Security, the troubled firm that employed criminals as airport security screeners, still runs the checkpoints at five major airports. *USA Today* reports that the Transportation Security Administration has still failed to fix vulnerabilities in jet cargo screening that allow for bombs to be planted without detection.

A strange combination of lack of professionalism, ineptitude and cronyism seems to pervade the entire matter of homeland security. To top it off, the very Director of the new agency, the Office of Homeland Security, former Pennsylvania governor Tom Ridge, possesses no counterterrorism or intelligence credentials, and his only "relevant" qualities are his service in the Army and a friendship with President George W. Bush. Despite being charged with coordinating the activities of 70 government agencies and receiving the president's "full support," Mr. Ridge has apparently spent his first nine months trying to get a phone number, office address, Internet web site, and developing a color-coded terrorism threat warning system, while avoiding Capitol Hill committees who wanted his testimony.

Before the announcement of the creation of a Department of Homeland Security, there was some hope that a domestic intelligence fusion point could be created within the old "Office of Homeland Security." Since President Bush's announcement of his intention to create a new departmental cabinet level position, more questions have been raised than answers offered concerning organization and responsibilities. Creation of a new government department raises the bureaucratic and appropriations stakes in both the executive and legislative branches of government. The unfortunate consequence of this major reorganization is that it does very little, if anything, for speeding critical intelligence information to the users who need it now.

---

[1] Michelle Mittelstadt, "Signs Were There - In Pieces; Intelligence Agencies Failed To Put Scraps Of Information Together," *The Dallas Morning News*, October 6, 2001.

[2] Tom Clancy, "First We Cripple The CIA, Then We Blame It, "*Wall Street Journal*, September 18, 2001.

[3] Christopher Andrew, "There Is No Such Thing As Full Intelligence," *The London Times*, September 17, 2001.

[4] Sean Higgins, "U.S. Spies Hammered By Criticism In Wake Of Surprise Terror Attack," *Investor's Business Daily*, September 18, 2001.

[5] Frank Rich, "Thanks for the Heads-Up," *New York Times*, May 25, 2002.

[6] Christopher Newton, "Bush Defends Hijack Warning Reaction," *Associated Press*, May 17, 2002.

[7] Ina Paiva Cordle and Jay Weaver, "Two Airlines In Sept. 11 Attacks Say They Got No Specific Warnings," *Miami Herald*, May 17, 2002.

[8] David E. Sanger and Elisabeth Bumiller, "No Hint of Sept. 11 in Report in August, White House Says, But Congress Seeks Inquiry," *New York Times*, May 16, 2002.

[9] The Phoenix memo is discussed within the context of the FBI's counterterrorism operations, below.

[10] *ABCNews*, "Bush on Defensive," May 17, 2002, http://abcnews.go.com/sections/us/DailyNews/warningmemo020517.html.

[11] Maxim Kniazkov, "Top CIA Official Warns Next Terror Attack Unavoidable," *Agence France Presse*, April 28, 2002.

[12] Stephen F. Hayes, "Why Does Tenet Have Tenure?; Clinton's CIA Chief Is Alive and Well As A Bushie," *The Weekly Standard*, October 29, 2001.

[13] Rober Baer, "See No Evil: The True Story of a Ground Soldier in the CIA's War on Terrorism," Crown Publishers, New York, 2002, page 266.

[14] J. Michael Waller, "Blinded Vigilance," *Insight,* October 15, 2001.

[15] Department of the Army, "Consideration of Others Handbook," Introduction: A Leadership Imperative, http://www.odcsper.army.mil/default.asp?pageid=29f, June 4, 2002.

[16] Scan Higgins, "U.S. Spies Hammered By Criticism In Wake Of Surprise Terror Attack," *Investor's Business Daily*, September 18, 2001.

[17] Sean Higgins, "U.S. Spies Hammered By Criticism In Wake Of Surprise Terror Attack," *Investor's Business Daily*, September 18, 2001.

[18] Jim Geraghty, "Terror Attacks Mean Long Days, Sleepless Nights at the CIA: Life at the Central Intelligence Agency Has Been Turned Upside Down Since Sept. 11," *States News Service*, October 4, 2001.

[19] Steve Hirsch, "Patching the Cloaks, Sharpening the Daggers," *The National Journal*, April 27, 2002.

[20] Pierre Thomas and Martha Raddatz, "A Big Warning," *ABC News,* June 7, 2002, http://abcnews.go.com/sections/us/DailyNews/911conversation020607.html.

[21]   Richard Betts, "Fixing Intelligence," *Foreign Affairs*, January 2002.

[22] Ibid.

[23] Evan Thomas, "A Street Fight," *Newsweek*, April 29, 2002.

[24] John J. Lumpkin, "Rumsfeld Says Terrorists Inevitably Will Get Chemical, Nuclear or Biological Weapons," *The Associated Press*, May 21, 2002.

[25] Helle Dale, "Too Bad About The Bombers; Is the FBI Director Really Up To The Job?," *Washington Times,* May 22, 2002.

[26] Laurie Mylroie, "Study of Revenge: The First World Trade Center Attack and Saddam Hussein's War Against America," AEI Press, Washington, DC, 2001, pages 10-32.

[27] Michael Hirsh and Michael Isikoff, "What Went Wrong," *Newsweek*, http://www.msnbc.com/news/753689.asp?cp1=1, May 21, 2002.

[28] Maria Ressa, "U.S. Warned In 1995 Of Plot To Hijack Planes, Attack Buildings," *CNN,* September 18, 2001, http://www.cnn.com/2001/US/09/18/inv.hijacking.philippines/index.html.

[29] Seymour M. Hirsch, "Mixed Messages," *The New Yorker*, June 3, 2002.

[30] Mansoor Ijaz, "Clinton Let Bin Laden Slip Away and Metastasize; Sudan Offered Up The Terrorist And Data On His Network. The Then-President And His Advisors Didn't Respond," *Los Angeles Times*, December 5, 2001.

[31] John Solomon, "1999 Report Warned of Suicide Hijack," *The Associated Press*, May 17, 2002.

[32] Mylroie, pg. 2.

[33] Deborah Amos and Chris Bury, "Missed Signals: Did Anyone See It Coming?," *Nightline, ABC News,* February 19, 2002

[34] Bill Gertz, "For Years, Signs Suggested 'That Something Was Up'," *The Washington Times*, May 17, 2002.

[35] See: Chapter 2, "The FBI: Failures Compounded By Lies"

The FBI: Failures Compounded by Lies

The FBI has been just as discredited as the CIA by its inability to provide warning of the terrorist attacks. Prior to September 11, the FBI, under its new director Robert Mueller, was struggling to recover from its own espionage scandal, the uncovering of Robert Hanssen, a mole for both the Soviets and Russians at the very heart of U.S. counterintelligence operations. As discussed later, in June 2001, *Washington Times* writer Jerry Seper reported that Hanssen passed secret software to the KGB that the Russian intelligence service passed along to al Qaeda, potentially enabling bin Laden to detect and monitor U.S. efforts to keep track of him.

The FBI, after all, is responsible for domestic counterterrorism measures, and many of the hijackers had lived in the United States for years. The Immigration and Naturalization Service had trouble just putting together a list of the hijackers and their visa dates – and that was after the attacks. Those are major problems that have little to do with the CIA.[1]

In a Cox News Service article by Rebecca Carr, three anonymous FBI officials claimed, "The FBI's counterterrorism effort was strengthened after bombs exploded at the American embassies in Kenya and Tanzania on August 7, 1998, killing 234 people and injuring thousands more."[2]

Indeed, apparent steps were taken. In October 1999, then FBI Director Louis J. Freeh* and Attorney General Janet Reno created a new counterterrorism division. Unfortunately, the Freeh/Reno response has proven to be a meaningless gesture, intended to deflect political and media heat. The FBI was not committed seriously to conducting and supporting pro-active terrorism countermeasures, whether as intelligence operations or as criminal investigations.

The Freeh/Reno response was symptomatic of a number of uncoordinated individual counterterrorism initiatives that received support in the late 1990's. Overall, the effort lacked a program architecture, a unified, coordinated policy or sufficient long-term funding. "Counterterrorism," for the FBI and other government agencies, meant issuing "strongly worded" press releases, accepting enormous emergency appropriations from Congress and, unfortunately, doing very little to help investigating agents in offices around the country. Little changed in the way the International Terrorism Unit at FBI headquarters did business. Reports came in from the field and were filed without analysis or information sharing.

The Story of Special Agent Robert G. Wright, Jr.

The case of FBI Special Agent Robert G. Wright, Jr., illustrates the FBI's refusal to accept fault and correct their dereliction of duty in the field of counterterrorism. Special Agent (SA) Wright is the only FBI agent in history to use the civil forfeiture laws to seize approximately $1.4 million dollars from the HAMAS terrorist organization operating in the United States. Despite this impressive success, the FBI has gone out of its way to block Wright's investigations and prevent him from telling the terrifying truth about terrorist operations in the United States.

The corporate culture within the FBI has been more concerned about protecting and preserving the organization's image and status than addressing terrorist acts that kill Americans. Special Agent Bob Wright repeatedly pressed FBI leadership within the Chicago Division and at the FBI headquarters to pursue leads and open additional cases similar to the HAMAS case – against terrorists operating within the United States.

SA Wright learned, among other things, that not-for-profit organizations were being used by the U.S.-based HAMAS terrorist group as front organizations in the United States to recruit, organize, train and support HAMAS terrorist operatives and to plan and carry out terrorist attacks. Indeed, many of the terrorist subjects were business owners and/or leaders of HAMAS not-for-profit organizations. Logically, then, as SA Wright concluded in 1995, following the money trail and seizing terrorists' assets would be the means of neutralizing this terrorist threat.

However, criminal investigations of known and suspected terrorists residing in the United States, such as the aforementioned HAMAS operatives, were not desired by the FBI's International Terrorism Unit.[3] Indeed, there existed a concerted effort on the part of agents conducting counterterrorism intelligence investigations to insulate the subjects of their investigations from criminal investigation and prosecution. The motive for this conduct is simple and quite disturbing. By preventing the current subjects of their intelligence cases from being investigated and prosecuted for known criminal activities, some of which involved international terrorism, these intelligence agents avoided the new and additional work that would be required to open and pursue criminal cases. Indeed, once these agents opened an intelligence case, they would "milk it" for years, not taking on any additional work. These intelligence agents regarded SA Wright and others who agreed that criminal cases should be opened to halt the criminal activity that threatened the American public's health and safety as a threat to their "job security."

There was virtually no effort by the International Terrorism Unit to neutralize known and suspected terrorists residing in the United States. The result was that, at great risk to the American public, the FBI allowed foreign-born terrorist operatives, such as the perpetrators of the September 11th attacks, to engage in illegal activities in the United States while FBI intelligence agents gathered information about these operatives, purportedly for analysis and future action in the event that a terrorist act ever occurred. Indeed, in 1994, when SA Wright complained to his supervisor that the FBI was merely gathering intelligence so they would know who to arrest when a terrorist attack occurred, his supervisor surprisingly agreed that this was true.

The FBI's conscious failure to undertake criminal investigations of suspected terrorists in the United States was further shown when managers from the FBI headquarters' (FBIHQ) Counterterrorism Division met with the Joint Terrorism Task Force (JTTF) in Chicago and admitted to SA Wright that no one at FBIHQ reviewed or attempted to link all the reports filed by the FBI field offices regarding terrorist activities in the United States. It was further conceded that the field office reports were merely filed and maintained at FBIHQ for future retrieval in the event that an act of terrorism occurred. Regrettably, the largest obstacles to SA Wright's criminal investigation efforts of the HAMAS enterprise in the United States were the management of the Chicago field office and the FBIHQ Counterterrorism Division in Washington, D.C.

Nonetheless, in 1995, SA Wright initiated corollary "Act of Terrorism" criminal investigations, against FBI management wishes. Through his investigations, SA Wright uncovered information that the aforementioned not-for-profit organizations were being used to recruit and train terrorists and fund terrorist activities in the United States and abroad, including the extortion, kidnapping and murder of Israeli citizens.

SA Wright's successful investigation, code named "Vulgar Betrayal," led to the June 9, 1998, seizure of $1.4 million of funds destined for terrorist activities. This seizure was the first occasion that the U.S. government utilized the civil forfeiture laws to seize terrorist assets in the United States. The seized funds were linked directly to Saudi businessman Yassin Kadi. On October 12, 2001, Yassin Kadi, a.k.a. Yassin Al-Qadi, was designated by the U.S. government as a financial supporter of Osama Bin Laden. According to a U.S. government source, Kadi provided $3 million to Bin Laden and his al Qaeda organization.

Despite the unqualified success of SA Wright's investigation, FBI management failed to take seriously the threat of terrorism in the United

States. FBI management intentionally and repeatedly thwarted and obstructed SA Wright's attempts to launch a more comprehensive investigation that would identify terrorists, their sources and methods of funding before they attacked additional U.S. interests, killing more U.S. citizens. The FBI's lack of support for SA Wright's "Vulgar Betrayal" investigation was obvious to his new supervisor in April 1998, when the latter wrote, "Agent Wright has spearheaded this effort despite an embarrassing lack of investigative resources available to the case such as computers, financial link analysis software, and a team of financial analysts. Although far from being concluded, the success of this investigation so far has been entirely due to the foresight and perseverance of Agent Wright." Indeed, in 1999, SA Wright purchased some of the much needed equipment and software from his personal funds because he was unable to obtain the necessary funding and support from the FBI.

Worse yet, it appears that FBI agents in the Chicago field office intentionally withheld information vital to SA Wright's investigation. One such incident involved a relief supervisor who was one of the most outspoken critics regarding opening criminal investigations on terrorist subjects. Specifically, in 1997, SA Wright began an investigation of two known HAMAS terrorists residing in the Chicago area named, Shareef Alwan and Razick Saleh Abdel Razick. SA Wright asked this particular relief supervisor whether he had any information concerning the two terrorists. The relief supervisor replied that he did not. SA Wright then spent several weeks investigating the whereabouts of these terrorists. One afternoon, SA Wright and another FBI agent were in the office discussing whether to contact someone who could help locate the terrorists. Overhearing who they were going to contact, the relief supervisor realized SA Wright was going to discover that he had lied and withheld vital information about the terrorists from SA Wright for years. The relief supervisor then disclosed that he knew one of the terrorists had been arrested overseas in 1995, as a result of his terrorist activities. The relief supervisor then admitted that he had placed the copy of the arrested terrorist's 1995 statement in an obscure location where no one would find it.

Ultimately, on August 4, 1999, FBI management removed SA Wright from the "Vulgar Betrayal" criminal investigation. Shortly thereafter, the FBI closed the "Vulgar Betrayal" investigation.

In August 1999, SA Wright began writing a manuscript which outlined his efforts to investigate known terrorist threats against U.S. national security and the FBI's efforts to thwart this investigation. SA Wright finished the final three pages of the 500-plus page manuscript titled,

"Fatal Betrayals of the Intelligence Mission," two days after the September 11th attacks.

When SA Wright became an FBI agent, he signed an "Employment Agreement" that expressly requires FBI employees never to divulge, publish or reveal information from investigatory files of the FBI or any information relating to material contained in the files, or disclose any information or produce any material acquired as a part of the employee's official duties or because of the employee's official status without the written permission of the FBI Director.

However, FBI employees may utilize the FBI's pre-publication review program to seek permission to publish material, even material critical of the FBI. Indeed, no objection to disclosure or publication by a current or former employee is to be interposed solely because a work is critical or disparaging of the FBI, the Government or its officers and employees. In addition, no objection is to be interposed solely because of errors in the work. The reviewers' major concern while reviewing the work should be the protection of the substance of information which could be expected to damage national security if disclosed.

The FBI employee's work must be submitted to the Office of Public and Congressional Affairs (OPCA) for the Director's consideration at least 30 business days in advance of the proposed disclosure. OPCA coordinates the pre-publication review process for the Director. OPCA is required to prepare the FBI's response to each request for pre-publication review "not later than thirty (30) business days" after the request and all related materials are received by the FBI. The 30 business day time limit is a result of case law that states that any longer period of time would unreasonably restrain the employee's First Amendment rights to free speech.

Over 70 days had elapsed when SA Wright, fed-up with the FBI's attempts to mislead the Congress and the American people, filed a lawsuit in the U.S. District Court for the District of Columbia.[4] SA Wright could no longer tolerate the FBI's cover-up of its criminal negligence in pursuing terrorists within our own borders.

On May 10, 2002, the day after SA Wright was forced to file suit in order to protect his rights and make the important effort to tell the truth to the American public, the FBI finally responded to SA Wright's long overdue pre-publication review requests. Despite the fact that SA Wright had carefully documented all of the material in his book using unclassified, "open source" material (e.g., public documents, newspapers and professional journals), the FBI's position was: "We cannot, therefore, authorize public dissemination of this material in its entirety at this time."

On May 30, 2002, SA Wright, with Judicial Watch Chairman Larry Klayman, President Tom Fitton and co-counsel David Schippers held a press conference at the National Press Club in Washington, DC. SA Wright became the first FBI agent to go before television cameras and "blow the whistle" on the FBI's negligence, willful failures by supervisory agents to provide leadership and direction, as well as deliberate bureaucratic foot-dragging and intransigence for the purposes of preserving the *status quo* and "not rocking the boat." At the press conference, SA Wright, through his Judicial Watch counsel, made another stunning revelation concerning dereliction of duty in an active counterterrorism investigation with financial ties to Osama bin Laden by an active, Muslim FBI agent

The Muslim Agent

In the spring of 1999, SA Wright received a call from an FBI agent in Dallas who advised Wright that a friend of his worked as an accountant for a company whose president and vice president SA Wright had served with Federal Grand Jury subpoenas. The Dallas agent also advised Wright that the accountant was concerned about harming his pending application that he had submitted to the FBI to become a translator. Through the course of SA Wright's investigation, he had determined that the accountant's employing company had received financing from a known terrorist financier and a U.S. government-designated HAMAS terrorist. The Dallas FBI agent, the accountant and the company officers mentioned above are all Muslim.

According to the Dallas agent the accountant had inquired of him if he should quit his employment, as it appeared there was a criminal investigation underway. The Dallas agent advised that he had consulted with a Dallas Police Department detective assigned to the Terrorism Task Force, and the Case Agent in the Dallas FBI office working on the HAMAS investigation. The Dallas agent stated that the police detectives' files contained intelligence and investigative information from SA Wright's cases.

A few weeks later, SA Wright received another call from the Dallas agent. The Dallas agent advised that he had been telephoned by the accountant, who stated that the president of the company was aware of his (the accountant's) relationship with the Dallas agent. The president inquired if the accountant could arrange a meeting between the Dallas agent and the company president regarding SA Wright's investigation. The accountant then mentioned his concern to the Dallas agent that <u>funds the accountant was transferring overseas on behalf of the company may have been used to</u>

<u>finance the embassy bombings in Africa</u> (the bombings were committed by bin Laden's organization). In addition, the accountant recounted unusual events following the receipt of SA Wright's Grand jury subpoenas. One of the unusual events the accountant mentioned was the secretive travel and meeting of an associate from a Middle Eastern country who met with the president and vice president of his company and then returned, without contacting the accountant. The accountant considered the Middle Eastern visitor a friend and normally they would have taken time to have dinner and spend time together.

The Dallas agent asked SA Wright if he desired him to meet with the company president. SA Wright told the Dallas agent that he wanted him to have the meeting and to wear a concealed recording device ("a wire"), to record what transpired. SA Wright reported this development in his case to his supervisor, and then went to the United States Attorney's Office, which concurred that the wire would be of great interest in the development of the investigation. When SA Wright returned to his office, his supervisor advised him that the Dallas agent was not going to wear the wire, and that Wright should forget about it.

While back at the U.S. Attorney's Office on other investigative matters, one of the Assistant U.S. Attorneys ("AUSAs") brought up the Dallas agent wearing a wire. The AUSAs still wanted the Dallas agent to wear a wire to meet with the company president, so a conference call with the Dallas agent and his supervisor was arranged.

The AUSAs expressed to the Dallas agent the importance of the investigation and the purpose of the wire. The Dallas agent stated that he would only record the individual (the company president) if he told him that he (the Dallas agent) was wearing a wire. One of the AUSAs told the Dallas agent that they would get a meeting location and wire it, so that the Dallas agent would not have to wear the wire. This was not acceptable to the Dallas agent, who then proposed placing a tape recorder on a table and then speaking with the company president. When that technique was dismissed as unacceptable, the Dallas agent advised that he would meet the company president alone and make an official written report, as he had done before in response to a similar request from the FBI's Tampa office.

The AUSAs asked the Dallas agent what was at the root of his continuing objections to either wearing a wire or having the meeting placed wired when he met with the company president. The Dallas agent advised that he feared for his safety. When he was told that the FBI would protect him, the Dallas agent said he did not trust the FBI to protect him. The AUSAs continued to ask why the Dallas agent would not wear a wire and he stated, "A Muslim does not record another Muslim."

Thereafter, the Dallas supervisor concluded the telephone conference. The AUSAs conferred with their boss, the U.S. Attorney for the Northern District of Illinois, who spoke with the then-SA in Charge ("SAC") of the Chicago Division, Kathleen McChesney.

Meanwhile SA Wright telephoned FBIHQ and spoke with the Acting Unit Chief of the International Terrorism Unit and explained what had just transpired with the AUSAs and the Dallas agent. The Unit Chief's first reaction was that SA Wright "would have to understand the Dallas agent's perspective." SA Wright disagreed strongly with the Unit Chief and explained that they had both taken the same oath and it was their duty as FBI SAs. The Unit Chief told SA Wright that he had a good point. Shortly thereafter, SAC McChesney directed SA Wright to draft a document with all of the background information on the terrorism investigation and to task out a lead to the Dallas FBI office for the Muslim agent to conduct the meeting and record it in a covert manner.

SA Wright learned from colleagues in the FBI Washington Field Office that agents in their office had drafted a document and sent it to FBI Dallas, expressing concerns over the Dallas Muslim agent contacting the subjects of open active investigations and not disclosing the contacts to the case agents who were conducting the investigations.

SA Wright learned from another FBI agent in Tampa that the Dallas Muslim agent had also refused to record a meeting with the subject of another investigation. The Dallas Muslim agent prepared an official written report that contained only self-serving statements from the subject.

So, within its ranks, the FBI has coddled an agent who has repeatedly refused to do his duty on specious "religious" grounds that are contrary to the SAs' Oath of Office. The Muslim agent's refusal to do his duty and wear a wire bears directly on the investigation of Osama bin Laden's al Qaeda bombing attacks on the U. S. embassies in East Africa. The Muslim agent has repeatedly obstructed active terrorism investigations and contacted subjects of investigation without notifying case agents. Has the agent been reprimanded, reassigned or fired? No. The Muslim agent incredibly serves as a legal attaché in a U.S. embassy in the Middle East.

After the September 11th attacks, SA Wright came forward and offered to share his expertise and knowledge of terrorist operations in the United States. Through his legal counsel, David Schippers in Chicago and Judicial Watch in Washington, DC, SA Wright offered to provide information and assistance to members of Congress. When the FBI leadership learned that congressmen might be made aware of the FBI's poor track record on aggressively pursuing terrorism investigations, they responded by ordering SA Wright not to leave the "operational area" of the Chicago Division, and forbidding him from communicating with Congress without written permission from FBI headquarters.

FBI Critics Come Forward

SA Wright is not alone in his critical evaluation of the FBI. Soon after the September 11th attacks, the FBI came under sharp criticism from a number of very senior and experienced chiefs of police for its failure to communicate effectively with local law enforcement.

Dan Oates, the current Ann Arbor, Michigan Chief of Police, was the New York City Deputy Police Chief in charge of the Intelligence Division, a job he held from 1997 to 2000. He is a 21-year police veteran and an attorney. Oates believes the FBI failed utterly in sharing intelligence and counterterrorism information with local police forces across the country. Oates is joined by Edward Norris, the Baltimore Police Commissioner and a former New York City Police Deputy Commissioner of Operations. Norris points to the fact that local police vastly outnumber federal agents. By their sheer numbers, they should be considered a help to the FBI, not an adversary.[5]

On May 8, 2002, FBI Director Robert Mueller faced tough questioning concerning an electronic communication – "EC" in bureau parlance – from an FBI agent in Phoenix, Arizona who detected a pattern of Middle Eastern males attending flight training courses. A confidential source who was close to the Phoenix agent has told Judicial Watch that he warned the Phoenix agent of suspicious Islamist activity at Phoenix flight schools as far back as 1996. The Phoenix agent wrote the report in July 2001, a full two months before the attacks, in which he drew attention to the fact that a number of Arab men with possible ties to terrorist organizations had attended flight schools. He urged the bureau to conduct a nationwide review.[6] Director Mueller unapologetically conceded that the FBI could have "done more." By the end of May 2002, Mueller conceded that the FBI may have had all of the necessary pieces of information available to at least disrupt the September 11th attacks had the FBI acted on the all of the available leads. An important piece of the puzzle was the Phoenix memo.

The Phoenix agent wrote:

> Phoenix believes that the FBI should
> accumulate a listing of civil aviation
> universities/colleges around the country.
> FBI field offices with these types of schools
> in their area should establish appropriate
> liaison. FBI HQ should discuss this matter
> with other elements of the U.S. intelligence
> community and task the community for any
> information that supports Phoenix's
> suspicions.

The memo cited "an unusual number of Arab students" taking flight lessons in Arizona and raised "the suspicion that they had been sent there in a coordinated plot by Osama bin Laden in order to learn the U.S. civil aviation procedures."

The Phoenix agent also recommended that the FBI ask the State Department to provide visa data on flight school students from Middle Eastern countries so the bureau could track them more easily. FBI officials said there was reluctance at the time to mount such a major review because of a concern that the bureau would be criticized for ethnic profiling of foreigners.[7]

This instance confirms, again, the FBI's resistance to admit failure, and that no one at FBIHQ reviewed or attempted to link all the reports filed by the FBI field offices regarding terrorist activities in the United States. The Phoenix "EC" is further confirmation that the field office reports are merely filed and maintained at FBIHQ for future retrieval in the event that an act of terrorism occurs. SA Wright's experiences in Chicago and those of the agent in Phoenix are a one-for-one match.

So, who saw the "EC"? Where does the buck stop? National Security Advisor Rice has stated, "Neither the president nor I have recollection of ever hearing about the Phoenix memo in the time prior to Sept. 11. We've asked FBI, CIA, our own people to go back and see whether or not it's possible that it somehow came to him. I personally became aware of it just recently."

Director Mueller stated, "I am not certain as to the highest-level individual who received it. I do not believe at this juncture that it went so high as the director of the FBI [referring to himself in the third person]. But

36

I am not certain how high it went in the hierarchy."

In August 2001, another FBI agent speculated in notes, made when investigators sought to explain why Zacharias Moussaoui was enrolled in a Minnesota flight school, that Mr. Moussaoui might be planning to fly a plane into the World Trade Center. Mr. Moussaoui, a French citizen, who was soon arrested on immigration charges, was believed by the United States government to be the intended 20th hijacker on September 11th. Moussaoui has been indicted in federal court on six conspiracy charges: 1) to commit an act of terrorism, 2) to pirate and 3) destroy aircraft, 4) to use weapons of mass destruction, 5) to destroy property and 6) to murder Americans. Authorities plan to seek the death penalty, although Moussaoui is not accused of killing anyone himself.

Another Arizona flight school reported hijacker Hani Hanjour to the FAA repeatedly for his failure to attain proficiency in English – a requirement for a commercial pilot's license. An FAA inspector who visited the flight school and checked Hanjour's license failed to inform the FBI or the INS, nor did he rescind his license. Hanjour attended flight schools with two other Pentagon hijackers.

As a remedy to these missed clues, the FBI announced the creation of a new division, the "Office of Intelligence," on May 15, 2002. The purpose of the office is to assemble and evaluate information related to terrorist threats and to disseminate this information within the bureau or to other federal agencies. The new office's name and mission begs questions as to the purpose and function of the FBI's existing "Counterterrorism Division." The American public deserves to know if the new Office of Intelligence is simply the renamed Counterterrorism Division. Playing bureaucratic musical chairs will not save lives.

Despite evidence of relative technical sophistication on the part of terrorists in other attacks, both interdicted and effected (e.g., World Trade Center bomber Ramzi Yousef's use of cell phones and laptops), FBI Director Mueller claims that, "We have not yet uncovered a single piece of information, either here or in the treasure-trove of information that has turned up in Afghanistan and elsewhere, that mentioned any aspect of the September 11th plot," Mueller said. "As best as we can determine, the actual hijackers had no computers, no laptops, no storage media of any kind."

Director Mueller's remarks are both simplistic and self-serving. Not being able to find information, computers or storage media does not mean they do not exist. The interim result of an on-going investigation should not be used as an excuse or a "trend" to justify additional investigative shortcomings. On the contrary, the now obvious void in the FBI's intelligence "holdings" concerning technical and information systems support within al Qaeda terrorist cells should propel the issue to the top of the investigative queue. How did the terrorists communicate, plan, coordinate, address financial and logistical requirements, conduct reconnaissance, evaluate and select their targets, train and rehearse, without the FBI knowing about it?

FBI SA and Chief Counsel of the Minneapolis Field Office Coleen Rowley came forward on May 21, 2002, with a memorandum addressed to FBI Director Mueller that criticizes Mueller and upper echelons of the FBI for obstructing the investigation of Zacharias Moussaoui, failing to share information and deliberately misleading the public about who knew what and when. She criticizes the bureau's culture for thwarting bold, aggressive decision making and rewarding naysaying careerists. "Although the last thing the FBI or the country needs now is a witch hunt," she writes, the bureau must "come clean."[8]

Rowley's memorandum corroborates the experiences of SA Robert Wright and identifies four major problem areas within the FBI:

- Information within the FBI is not disseminated, and actions of field offices are not coordinated on related cases.

- Careerism and risk aversion dominate FBI culture.

- Supervisory and headquarters bureaucrats resist initiative and new, aggressive investigative techniques.

- There are personnel shortages, both in numbers and experience, as well as technical and/or linguistic expertise.

The FBI's integrity has been called into question in a very serious and pervasive manner. The foundation stone of the "world's premier law enforcement agency" is cracked. A large segment of the American public that was still willing to accept the word of the FBI Director without question and at face value now can no longer do so. Any hopes Director Mueller had of shaking off the remnants of the ethically challenged era of Clinton, Reno and Freeh are lost completely. Mueller has created his own whole new set of doubts, spin and double-talk for the American public, Congress and the media to pick over.

What strikes the concerned citizen and the analyst is the schizoid way the bureaucrats approached the problem, "we'll do everything we can but the inevitable is going to happen anyway," which betrays, first, the bureaucrats' inner but unspoken conviction that their agency is not equipped to deal with the threat, together with a fatalistic sense that the enemy is stronger, and second an attempt to save their skins in case an attack did happen.

To be charitable, the FBI's investigative progress has been "slow." Zacharias Moussaoui remains the only person indicted in the United States who has been linked to the events of September 11th. The American Muslim community's response to the Justice Department's detention of some immigrant Muslims has been very troubling. The Muslim community decries "racial profiling" when the demographic facts of the attackers reveal that they were all Muslim, Middle Eastern males between the ages of 18 and 40. No Muslim leader has come forward to spearhead a Muslim community effort to turn-over persons who are connected to terrorist organizations. There has been no public relations effort to encourage Muslims with information concerning persons affiliated with radical, militant Islamist groups to come forward. Reported leads have been few and far between. Perhaps most ominous, some law enforcement officials believe that members of an al Qaeda terrorist cell in North America are still at-large. In the aftermath of September 11th, North American al Qaeda cells are thought to have gone underground. Detained Muslims in America have provided no relevant information on its members.[9]

The Department of Justice and the FBI took almost a month to assemble and release a "most wanted" poster of al Qaeda members associated with Osama bin Laden and the September 11th hijackers. Yet, on the day of the attacks, a detailed profile of the terrorist network including: organizational structure, financial support, affiliations, tactics and capabilities, as well as personal profiles and photos was available from Internet bookseller Amazon.com for $17.50. Professor Yonah Alexander and Mr. Michael S. Swetnam of the Potomac Institute for Policy Studies had published "Usama bin Laden's al-Qaida [sic]: Profile of a Terrorist Network" on February 28, 2001. Again, the FBI's ability to react in a timely and meaningful way to publicly available information appears to have been mired in delays and inefficiencies.

America is faced with an FBI that is a shadow of its former self. The attacks of September 11th have revealed an FBI infected by negligence, sloth, corruption and an unwillingness to honestly come to grips with its failings in a way that will truly correct its shortcomings and lead to both a better law enforcement agency and a safer America.

* Judicial Watch has learned from a well-placed, reliable, confidential source that Director Freeh, while still FBI director, engaged in an employment interview for an unspecified position with the Saudi royal household or its government, at the residence of Saudi Prince (and Ambassador to the United States) Bandar Bin Sultan Bin Abdul Aziz Al Saud, in Northern Virginia. This helps explain FBI disinterest in pursuing Saudi terrorist connections.

[1] Stephen F. Hayes, "Why Does Tenet Have Tenure?; Clinton's CIA Chief Is Alive and Well As A Bushie,' *The Weekly Standard*, October 29, 2001.

[2] Rebecca Carr, "FBI On Terror Hunt Before 9/11 Attacks," *Cox News Service*, February 26, 2002.

[3] There are two types of investigations that the FBI pursues: intelligence investigations and criminal investigations. The purpose of an intelligence investigation is to gather information for information's sake. The purpose of a criminal investigation is to gather information so as to facilitate the prosecution of the subjects under the laws of the United States and, as a result, halt and prevent criminal activity.

[4] Complaint For Declaratory And Injunctive Relief in the Matter of *Robert G. Wright, Jr. v. Federal Bureau of Investigation, et al.*, Case #02-CV-915 (GK), U.S. District Court For The District of Columbia.

[5] Maryanne George, "Words From Police Chief In Spotlight; He Blames FBI For Intelligence Failures," *Detroit Free Press*, December 4, 2001.

[6] David Johnston, "FBI Says Pre-Sept. 11 Note Got Little Notice, "*New York Times*, May 9, 2002.

[7] James Risen, "FBI Told of Worry Over Flight Lessons Before Sept. 11," *New York Times*, May 4, 2002.

[8] Romesh Ratnesar and Michael Weisskkopf, "How the FBI Blw the Case," *Time*, May 28, 2002.

[9] Vincent M. Canistraro, "The War On Terror Enters Phase 2," *New York Times*, May 2, 2002.

Conducting the Intelligence *Post-Mortem*

While many Americans are looking forward to some light being shed on the September 11th attacks, the joint Congressional review for the September 11th inquiry promises to be a complete whitewash. Early problems in getting the panel staffed and operating were the first indicators. The first staff director named to lead the inquiry was former CIA Inspector General Britt Snider. Mr. Snider is a longtime, close associate of the DCI, George J. Tenet. They first worked together more than a decade ago on the staff of the Senate Select Committee on Intelligence, and Mr. Snider, a lawyer, was later a special counsel to DCI Tenet before taking over as the CIA's inspector general.

Mr. Snider was clearly too close to Tenet for the inquiry to maintain any semblance of objectivity. "'I don't know what the appointment of Snider means,' said a former senior CIA operations official. 'Will the investigation be a whitewash? The agency is being investigated by one of its own. You tell me.'"[1]

Mr. Snider did not last very long as the director of the Congressional panel. He resigned from the panel on April 26, 2002, and his action was announced on April 30, two months after he had started the job. By May 8, 2002 the *New York Times* was reporting that Snider resigned his post after admitting he had hired a former CIA officer for a position on the panel staff who was the subject of a counterintelligence investigation for failing a polygraph examination. In this case, the main problem for Mr. Snider appears to have been his failure to inform the joint committee's leadership of the investigation.

Mr. Snider was replaced by former Pentagon inspector general Eleanor Hill, who will operate at a distinct disadvantage because she was not on the job while the staff was assembling and analyzing the documentation from the intelligence agencies that will be critical to any conclusions the committee will reach.[2] Ms. Hill had oversight responsibilities for a highly questionable Defense Department Inspector General investigation of serious, documented, allegations of fraud, waste, abuse and corruption at the George C. Marshall European Center for Security Studies in Garmisch-Partenkirchen, Germany. The center is a multinational security and defense "think tank," designed to familiarize former Warsaw Pact military officers with the West. For the past five years, a number of field grade officers – lieutenant colonels and colonels – have filed "whistleblower" reports of fraud, abuse and corruption concerning the senior leadership of the center. Some officers faced career-ending retaliation for their honest reporting, and sought redress through Ms. Hill's former office, without satisfaction. Judicial Watch is pursuing an investigation of the Marshall Center.

Additional grave questions concerning the composition of the joint Congressional staff threaten the credibility and effectiveness of the inquiry. The intelligence panel's staff director charged with examining the role of the FBI in the September 11th attacks allegedly obstructed a Justice Department probe of the Bureau in 2000. Thomas A. Kelley, now retired from the FBI, was the Bureau's deputy general counsel. Kelley was the FBI's point of contact for special counsel John C. Danforth's inquiry into the 1993 Waco debacle in which 75 Branch Davidians – mostly women and children – died in a fire that broke-out during a raid by Federal agents, operating under the instructions of then-Attorney General Janet Reno. *Washington Post* reporters Richard Leiby and Dana Priest obtained a December 2000, internal FBI memorandum that stated Kelley, "continued to thwart and obstruct" the Waco investigation to the point that Danforth was forced to send a team to search FBI headquarters for documents Kelley refused to turn over. "This non-cooperative spirit was at the specific direction of [deputy general counsel] Kelley,"[3] The memo says Kelley should have been investigated for alleged "unprofessional conduct, poor judgment, conflict of interest, hostile work environment and retaliation/reprisal" related to his role in the Waco investigation.

Besides the highly questionable leadership and composition of the staff, the joint committee's efforts could be a waste of tax payer dollars due to the pre-disposition of the committee to hold closed or "executive" sessions. The closed door sessions allow the same "clubby" group of intelligence bureaucrats and their Capitol Hill counterparts to appear and testify outside of public or press scrutiny. Historically, executive sessions result in mild admonishments and promises for expanded appropriations for the intelligence services. Television news coverage for such sessions is normally sparse due to the lack of "testimonial" images. Prepared statements by the parties normally contain sound bites designed to instill confidence in future operations. Of course, some Senators and Congressman will take the opportunity to politicize the hearings, choosing to attack opponents rather than address the substance of the hearings, or the lack of real accountability. The joint Congressional review will be the Kabuki theatre of accountability. Some key facts will come out. Criticisms will be made. But specific individual and institutional accountability will fall by the wayside.

A Possible Answer: A Blue Ribbon Commission

Many editorials and analysts have suggested that a "blue ribbon commission" should conduct an independent inquiry into September 11th. They were joined on May 21, 2002, by Senate Majority Leader Tom Daschle who cited a "troubling trend that is now underway [with] regard to the administration's unwillingness to share information within the bureaus and the agencies of this White House and the administration itself, as well as with Congress, regarding the attacks of September 11th."

Daschle's call for an independent "Blue Ribbon Commission" followed a series of seemingly contradictory remarks by House Minority Leader Dick Gephardt. Gephardt had made what many considered to be rather accusatory comments concerning President Bush's foreknowledge of terror attacks on September 11th, and then reversed himself three days later, when polling data revealed the American public's support for President Bush remained firm, despite media speculation that a cover-up was underway in The White House. The Democrats' bald-faced attack on President Bush, with language that implied the president's deliberate, willful disregard of reports with specific terrorist activity and targets, backfired badly. Gephardt and others seeking raw political advantage saw the need to do some serious recalibrating of their message. Thus, Gephardt "re-framed" his criticism of the Bush-Cheney administration on May 19, 2002, saying, "I never, ever, thought that anybody, including the president, did anything up to September 11th other than their best."

On the Sunday, May 26, 2002, edition of NBC's "Meet The Press," Daschle told host Tim Russert that Vice President Cheney had asked Daschle not to investigate the events of September 11th, during a conversation on January 24, 2002, and that President Bush had made the same request of him during a conversation of January 28, 2002. Assuming Senator Daschle did not mis-speak or mis-remember (a uniquely Washingtonian affliction), the requests were either an extremely naïve political move or an overly optimistic view of the Majority Leader's ambition and motives by the Bush-Cheney administration. Perhaps they chose to ignore history as they basked in the glow of January's 90 percent approval ratings? Between 1942 and 1945, there were nine congressional investigations into what went wrong at Pearl Harbor, how could the Bush-Cheney administration hope to get a "pass" on September 11th? The notion that the Bush-Cheney administration should, in some way, be exempt from examination is constitutionally irresponsible and politically ridiculous.

While Daschle and Gephardt's motives are mostly selfish attempts to fling mud on their political opponent in the next general election, there is merit to the idea of a "Blue Ribbon Commission." It provides another way for the American public to arrive at something even remotely resembling the truth.

A credible investigation requires the exclusion of politicians and ideological "icons," of any stripe, from participation in any capacity.[4] Their presence actually distracts from the enormous scope of the job and the detailed analysis that will be required. Rather than a brutally frank discussion of the facts, politicians will attempt to reach consensus and water down any report so as not to offend anyone but the easiest, most obvious targets.

The commission should be staffed with persons having an in-depth knowledge of intelligence and intelligence operations. And its superiors should not be the usual suspects of past political hacks who feather their own nests, like former Senator John Danforth, who whitewashed his "investigation" of Waco in time to further his failed candidacy to be George W. Bush's 2000 vice-presidential running mate.

Knowledge of technical and human intelligence requirements, tasking, reporting, analysis and coordination is critical. Passing familiarity and/or vicarious experiences with the intelligence community are not enough for the task at hand. The staff must know not just the "textbook" organization and process, but the "real deal" about the day-to-day work and culture of the intelligence community. Fiercely independent intelligence "pros" are required for any serious, credible investigation. They also must begin their task with a proper sense of the public's anger, frustration and skepticism about other investigative commissions. Any public perception of cover-up, "cooking the books," or scapegoating will doom the commission to public rejection, or at best, skepticism about its work and its findings. The United States cannot afford another Warren Commission.

The volume of material and number of agencies to be reviewed and analyzed is enormous. The review must also be done without compromising important intelligence information. A balance between open, accountable government and a concern about providing terrorists with a list of our vulnerabilities and intelligence gaps must be struck.

To date, Congress has been at odds over the purpose and scope of its inquiry. Some want to see heads roll, while others say its purpose is to uncover and correct organizational and funding deficiencies within the agencies so we do not experience another surprise attack. The net result is that neither goal will be accomplished.

The Commission must be truly independent – a very frightening concept for all government parties concerned, and a difficult task to achieve in American political life. Once chartered, the Commission must be given a free hand to investigate where it wills – with subpoena authority and the ability to both grant immunity and hold witnesses in contempt. Transparency and openness should be its guiding concepts. The Commission's hearings and activities should be broadcast daily on C-SPAN TV and the Internet. In the spirit of full disclosure, the Commission's reports and documents should be posted on a Commission Internet site on a daily basis, with the appropriate redactions of national security information.

The only way to break the careerist, "risk averse" mentality of the government bureaucrats, who are in large part responsible for devolving our intelligence and law enforcement agencies into the pathetic caricatures of themselves that they have become, is to "smoke them out" with a high degree of pressure. Legal compulsion and a healthy respect for the Commission's ability to expose even the grimmest secrets of each government agency will prove to be the only way to legitimately "clean house." As long as "certain" people, programs and activities are free from accountability, U.S. intelligence and law enforcement efforts will continue to be an uncoordinated series of half-measures, missed opportunities and bureaucratic cover-ups.

Critics of the Blue Ribbon Commission model maintain that any questioning of the intelligence, security or law enforcement organs of the U.S. government during this constitutionally undeclared "war" is akin to treason. They rebuff calls for government accountability with catch-phrase invocations of "national security concerns," or "protecting our troops in the field." President Bush, in a response to reporters' questions concerning Congressional inquiries, stated:

> In terms of the gossip and the finger-pointing, the level-three staffers trying to protect – you know, trying to protect their hide, I don't think that's of concern. That's just typical Washington, D.C. But I am – what I am concerned about is tying up valuable assets and time – and possibly jeopardizing sources of intelligence.[5]

The "level-three staffers" who President Bush rejects as not being

45

"of concern" are precisely the people who make the decisions and run the operations of the U.S. government on a day-to-day basis. Surely, President Bush should realize that, despite what their aides assure them, he and his cabinet secretaries do not have a direct and daily influence on the operational decisions and activities of CIA case officers, FBI counterterrorism task forces, or INS officers at airports and border crossings. President Bush, obviously, is a strong opponent of any Blue Ribbon Commission. That's unfortunate, because it may be the only way to effect real change in an inefficient, bureaucratic, federal "colossus" that routinely punishes innovation and integrity while coddling and encouraging the dishonest, timid, maintainers of the *status quo*.

For its part, Judicial Watch will continue its efforts to pry the truth from the government, through Freedom of Information Act (FOIA) requests, lawsuits, the representation of whistleblowers and other proven techniques.

---

[1] Richard Sale, "CIA To Go Under Congressional Hammer," *United Press International*, March 12, 2002.

[2] Dana Priest and Juliet Eilperin, "Disputes Stall Panel Probing Sept. 11 Lapses: Joint Committee Puts Off Session as Lawmakers Debate Its Goals and Schedule," *Washington Post*, June 14, 2002.

[3] Richard Leiby and Dana Priest, "Head of Sept. 11 Probe Allegedly Obstructed Danforth's Waco Inquiry: Former FBI Counsel Held Onto Papers," *Washington Post*, June 22, 2002.

[4] Daniel A. Rezneck, "What did we know . . . and when did we know it . . . and could we have stopped it?," *Legal Times*, December 3, 2001.

[5] *Washington Post* Staff Writers, "Bush Cites CIA-FBI Breakdown: House-Senate Panel Starts Probing 9/11 Intelligence Failure," *Washington Post*, Wednesday, June 5, 2002; Page A01.

FATAL NEGLECT: The U.S. Government's Continuing Failure to Protect American Citizens from Terrorists

<u>Part Two: In the Air and On the Borders</u>

Airport Insecurity

On September 11, 2001, nineteen men with evil intentions boarded four airplanes in the United States. Some of the nineteen may have been carrying razor knives known as box cutters. Each of these men presumably passed through at least one airport security checkpoint.

In October 1996, Congress passed and the President signed into law a Federal Aviation Reauthorization Act that mandated:

- Upgrading of bomb detection scanners;

- Background and fingerprint checks for workers with access to secure airport areas;

- An increase in the number of FBI agents assigned to counterterrorism; and

- An increase in the inspection of mail and international cargo.[1]

In December 1996, a Presidential panel of twenty-three members from industry, government and public interest groups issued their recommendations for improving airline safety. The panel concluded that terrorists throughout the world who have a grudge against some U.S. interest would attack U.S. airports and airplanes. They recommended:

- The government should pick up the cost of airport security;

- Airport security workers should be required to be certified by the FAA;

- All baggage should be matched to a passenger;

- The bags of a profiled traveler matching the criteria of a terrorist should receive extra scrutiny;

- Only cargo containers that have been blast-tested should be used;

- The U.S. Postal Service should be required to check all mail cargo for explosive devices; and

- Intelligence agencies should be used to help identify terrorists.[2]

After September 11th, the government created the Transportation Security Administration (TSA) to replace the FAA as the government agency responsible for insuring safety at our nation's airports as well as other transportation systems. The TSA quickly put security directors in place at a number of major airports. Then, in the spring of 2002, it took over the management of the existing private sector security screeners as a temporary measure until the TSA could hire its own employees who met the qualifications set out by Congress. Thus, the simple recommendation that the airport security screeners be "certified" by the FAA went unfulfilled for six years.

Background checks and fingerprinting of workers with access to secure areas of airports and even passenger security screeners were not taken seriously either, until after September 11th. In fact, a recent nationwide operation has rounded up more than 450 workers at just 15 airports who lied on their employment applications, did not have the legal permission to work in the United States, had outstanding arrest warrants, or were convicted felons.[3]

Likewise, checked baggage was not matched to a corresponding passenger on board a domestic flight until after September 11th, and the baggage of passengers transferring from one flight to another connecting flight was exempted from this matching provision.

The explosive device that blew up Pan Am 103 over Lockerbie, Scotland in 1988 was believed to have originated in Helsinki and was transferred in checked luggage at Frankfurt, Germany. In this case, the unwitting passenger was on the plane so the luggage match to actual passengers did not discover a discrepancy. However, under the post-September 11th rules put in place in the United States, a passenger could have failed to board the connecting flight and the explosive would have been loaded with the other luggage.

The airlines were provided by our intelligence agencies with passenger "watch lists," but the upkeep and timeliness of those lists was more than lax. At least two of the 19 men who boarded the four airplanes on September 11th with the intent of hijacking them were known to have some connection to terrorists and the FBI was actively looking for them in the days leading up to September 11th. However, their names did not appear on a watch list for the airlines.

The 1996 recommendation for terrorist profiling of passengers to determine if they warrant additional scrutiny seems to have come from a different age. FBI Director Mueller, testifying before the Senate Judiciary

Committee in June 2002, all but said that his agency is afraid to profile passengers because it is not politically correct to take a second security look at someone because he falls into a certain category of people. Yet the inescapable truth is that the 19 men involved in the September 11th hijackings were all Middle Eastern men between the ages of 18 and 35. They fit the typical profile of a terrorist likely to hijack an airplane. This profile is not based on discrimination, hysteria or racism. It is based on fact.

- In June 1985, two Palestinian men, later joined by a third, hijacked Trans World Airlines (TWA) Flight 847. Some of the passengers and the crew were held hostage for 17 days. One passenger, a U.S. Navy diver, Robert Stetham, was executed by the hijackers and his body was thrown to the runway during a forced stop in Beirut, Lebanon.

- In 1986, five Palestinians from Syria and Lebanon commandeered a Pan Am aircraft in Karachi, Pakistan. They indiscriminately shot and killed 21 passengers and wounded 200. The hijackers intended to blow up the airplane over Israel.

- Pan Am Flight 103 was blown out of the sky over Lockerbie, Scotland in 1988. Libyan agents were later convicted of rigging a bomb in an electronic device placed in the luggage of an unwitting passenger on that flight.

- In 1994, a Philippine Airline Flight to Tokyo, Japan suffered an in-flight explosion. One passenger was killed. Authorities believe Ramzi Youssef the mastermind behind the 1993 bombing of the World Trade Center in New York left a liquid bomb on the plane when he disembarked the plane at an earlier stop.

- In 1995, Philippine police following up on a suspicious apartment fire arrested a man known as Said Ahmed. An accomplice got away. The fire gave away Ahmed's plan to kill Pope John Paul II. Further interrogation revealed a plot to make liquid bombs that could be disguised as shaving cream, aerosols or other liquids and smuggled onto airplanes. Additional interrogation and investigation determined the man's real name was Abdul Hakim Murad and the accomplice who escaped was Ramzi Youssef. Murad disclosed a plot to simultaneously blow up several airplanes over the Pacific Ocean en-route to the

United States. Murad, a US licensed pilot, also disclosed a plot to hijack airplanes and crash them into CIA headquarters in Langley, Virginia, U.S. monuments or landmark buildings like the World Trade Center or the Sears Tower in Chicago. Youssef and Murad are currently cooling their heels in a U.S. prison.

Despite hijackers being mostly Middle Eastern men between the ages of 18 to 35, since September 11th, time and again airport security screeners seem to make a point of aggressively searching the elderly, young women and children.

The airlines have instituted a second random security check at the boarding gate. Anecdotal reports say invariably the random search will skip over a Middle Eastern male ages 18 to 35 and subject people as far from the profile as possible to the random search. One can only conclude the airlines deliberately conduct the search in this manner to avoid lawsuits.

The history of airplane hijackings is quite clear; giving extra scrutiny to Middle Eastern men between the ages of 18 and 35 is just common sense, not discrimination. The perceived insult and injury to innocent Middle Eastern men ages 18 to 35 allegedly caused by profiling will be far less than the injury to innocent passengers, flight crew and people in or near the target site of a hijacked airplane.

The 1996 legislative requirement to upgrade bomb detection equipment is still unmet. Post September 11th, Congress required that all 400+ major airports in the United States have bomb detection x-ray machines in operation by the end of 2002. The chances of meeting that six year old mandate and the recent time deadline for improved bomb detection equipment to be installed and operating are somewhere between slim and none.

The existing x-ray bomb detection machines, which cost approximately $1 million each, are manufactured by two companies. One company produces machines that meet the specifications of the government and their product is relatively reliable. The machine made by the other manufacturer has a history of malfunctioning and long time periods when the equipment is out of service waiting for repairs.

In reaction to the September 11th hijackings, Congress specifically mandated that the purchase of x-ray bomb detection machines be split between both manufacturers. The manufacturer of the machines which had a history of malfunctioning now asserts that the problem was primarily software related and the problems have been corrected.

Interestingly, Senate Majority Leader Tom Daschle's wife, Linda Hall Daschle, is one of Washington's most powerful lobbyists on behalf of corporate interests, counting American Airlines, Northwest Airlines and Schering-Plough among her high profile corporate clients. In other words, both the Daschle family budget and campaign budget depend heavily on the success of big business – particularly the airline industry.

Consider the following:

- Linda Daschle's client, American Airlines, has lobbied for years to water down safety and security regulations that might have helped foil the World Trade Center attacks. Further, with the support of both Tom and Linda Daschle, the company received a whopping $583 million taxpayer bailout in the wake of September 11th.

- As reported on CBS *60 Minutes*, Tom Daschle was charged with inappropriately intervening to reduce safety inspections of an air-charter company owned by a family friend after one of the planes crashed in 1994, killing four. While at the FAA, Linda Daschle acted to exempt the friend's airline from intensified safety inspections.

- Linda Daschle's client, Boeing, is attempting to strike a sweetheart deal to lease 100 aircraft to the U.S. military. According to the Congressional Budget Office, the lease plan will cost taxpayers $37 billion, while outright buying the planes would only cost $25 billion. Tom Daschle will be responsible for scheduling a vote on the bill.

- The FAA is forced to buy baggage scanners from one of Linda Daschle's clients, L-3 International, according to the 2000 transportation budget, despite the fact that the Department of Transportation's Inspector General from the Transportation Department found the equipment to be substandard, some even leaking radiation. The inspector general told Congress that the FAA's requirement to buy L-3's machines is one reason airports will not be able to meet the new mandate to screen all luggage for bombs for many years, placing Americans seriously at further risk.

The air transport industry donated more than $100,000 to Daschle's campaign in the last election cycle. Linda Daschle's client, Northwest

Airlines, is the second largest contributor to the Senator's campaign in 1998.

- Linda Daschle was recently cited in an FAA report for failing to enforce a "zero tolerance" policy she announced in 1996 while Deputy Director of the FAA against violent airline passengers a pledge that some say could have prevented the September 11th terrorist hijackings.

- Judicial Watch has filed Freedom of Information Act (FOIA) requests with the FAA to uncover Linda Daschle's role in the selection of the faulty L-3 bomb detecting equipment prior to September 11th and to uncover Senator Daschle's role as well. Judicial Watch is now in court to try to force the release of these documents. Once obtained, Judicial Watch will consider legal action against the Daschles.

Beyond the fact that the two bomb detection companies combined cannot manufacture the quantity of machines necessary to meet Congress' mandated installation and operational date, there is another problem – space. Many commercial airport terminals do not have the physical space available to install such large machines. These airports will have to reconfigure their existing space or build additional space. Some other airports will have to reinforce their floors to safely accommodate the weight of the x-ray machines. Of course, the issue of who will pay for the construction is being debated, as are all costs that the government has not agreed to pay.[4]

When all those hurdles are finally overcome, and the x-ray bomb detection machines are installed and working properly at all airports, there is still at least one more problem.

Bogdan Dzakovic, a career employee of the FAA and a senior member of the FAA's Red Team which conducted unannounced airport security checks, is convinced that the machines are not fool proof. Prior to September 11th, Mr. Dzakovic and other members of the Red Team were frequently able to get simulated bombs past the bomb detection units.

We probably will not know how well the machines will work in the future. Mr. Dzakovic and the Red Team members were prohibited by the FAA from conducting random security checks after September 11th. As late as the spring of 2002, the Red Team was still grounded and assigned to pushing paper. Perhaps the FAA's philosophy is: "No inspections, no problems." Either way, the machines would never have stopped the September 11th hijackers.

The issue of compensation for the passenger security screeners was noticeably absent in the 1996 recommendations. Prior to September 11th, airports and airlines paid the cost of passenger screening personnel. Airports receive the funds for their share of the cost primarily from fees assessed against airlines for the use of the airport. Both the airlines and the airports have an incentive to minimize the cost of passenger security screening. The actual passenger screening work is contracted out by the airlines. Contracts are typically awarded to the lowest bidder. Because the bulk of the cost of providing security screeners is their personnel payroll, private security companies try to pay as little as possible in order to enhance their profits. The average hourly pay of a passenger security screener has been $6 per hour. The minimum wage at the same time was $5.15 per hour. The low wages, and probably some of the working conditions (like aggravation and a lack of adequate training) created a huge turnover among airport passenger security screeners.

Between 1998 and 2001, the General Accounting Office (GAO), the investigative arm of Congress, issued no less than five reports critical of airport security. In each of the five reports the GAO cited the low wages paid to screeners, inadequate training of screeners and the rapid turnover of screeners as a significant threat to security. Two of the four airplanes hijacked on September 11th originated from Boston's Logan Airport that has a passenger security screener turnover rate of 200 percent. Another airplane was hijacked out Dulles Airport just outside Washington, DC. The turnover rate at Dulles prior to September 11th was 90 percent.

A man arriving at the Chicago O'Hare Airport to board a domestic flight attempted to pass through the airport security checkpoint. The security check discovered that the passenger was carrying two knives, in clear violation of security regulations. The knives were confiscated and with no further delay the passenger was allowed to proceed to his departure gate. By chance, in a random second security check at the departure gate the personnel discovered this passenger still had in his possession a stun gun, a can of mace and seven more knives.

This incident did not occur prior to September 11th. It happened five months later, and it was not an isolated one. Following the September 11th hijackings there have been numerous breaches of security, mainly because the same low-paid screeners who are dissatisfied with their job are performing critical security checks on passengers who are typically in a hurry and whom the airlines do not want to aggravate.

On May 31, 2002, in a speech delivered to Japanese airline officials in Tokyo, Donald Carty, the Chief Executive Officer of American Airlines, the largest airline in the United States, spoke about the real concerns of aviation industry: "It will be a hollow victory indeed if the system we end up with is so onerous and so difficult that air travel, while obviously more secure, becomes more trouble for the average person than it is worth."[5] (It should be noted here that American Airlines reportedly lost about $535 million in the first five months of 2002.)

The issue of airport and airline safety has repeatedly popped up over the last 30 years leading up to September 11th. Thirty-one years to the day before September 11th, President Richard Nixon announced the creation of the Sky Marshal Program in response to a rash of hijackings in the later part of the 1960's and the first nine months of 1970. The Program would train armed law enforcement officers and have them ride on random flights posing as passengers. At the height of the Sky Marshal Program – still extant on September 11th – there were approximately 2000 marshals, certainly not nearly enough marshals to cover all domestic and overseas flights. They were only assigned to flights that appeared to have a high risk for hijacking.

However, by September 11th the Sky Marshal Program had been neglected for so long that there were only 32 sky marshals left in the system.

During the Gulf War in 1991, heightened security measures were instituted at all U.S. airports. One of the security measures was a prohibition against curbside baggage check-in. However, because of the inconvenience it caused travelers, the FAA eliminated the measure just two months and twelve days after putting it into effect.

An inflated bureaucracy responding more to aviation industry's interest in maximizing profits over the flying public's interest, the FAA, the agency responsible for insuring airport and airline safety and security, has failed the American citizens. It has acted spottily and opportunistically, without maintaining a constant high level of vigilance and alertness, as Western European airports do.

The September 11th attacks did not happen in a vacuum. For decades the international climate has been one of continuing threats of terrorism and hijacking, and the United States was often the target. For instance, in preparation for the 1988 Summer Olympics in South Korea, the United States convened an eight-nation summit out of concern that North Korean or international terrorists might stage attacks on airplanes. Likewise, three days after the Philippine police interrogated Abdul Hakim Murad in 1995, the

FAA itself issued a security alert for all U.S. airlines flying over the Pacific to ban hand-carried liquids, aerosols, and shaving cream. In May of 1995, the U.S. required Philippine authorities to hold all cargo for 48 hours prior to loading it on a U.S. airline plane. And in 1995, immediately following the conviction of Sheik Omar Abdel Rahman and nine other terrorists for the 1993 bombing of the World Trade Center, President Clinton ordered heightened security at American airports.

In October 1996, just three months after TWA Flight 800 exploded shortly after takeoff from New York's JFK airport killing 230 passengers and crew, Congress passed the Federal Aviation Reauthorization Act, mandating improved security.

In December 1996, the Aviation Security Advisory Committee (created shortly after the 1988 downing of Pan Am Flight 103) finally made its recommendations for aviation safety.

The FAA had responsibility over airline and airport security. Any one of these threats should have caused heightened security and kept the security at its highest level. There has been no let up in the terrorist threats. The spotty, sloppy and lax security at our nation's airports rests squarely on the FAA.

After September 11th, airline pilots, many of them former military pilots, asked for permission to have a gun in the cockpit as a final defense against hijackers. The Transportation Security Administration has refused the pilots' request, supposedly fearing (in addition to the anti-gun lobby) that a lack of proficiency with a handgun could result in mishaps and possibly endanger or wound one or more passengers.

The TSA's position is odd, since the handgun is a last resort before terrorists take control of the airplane. And if terrorists gain control of another airplane, an F-16 fighter jet is likely to blow the airplane and everyone on board out of the sky. The risk of harm to passengers from several bullets is a lot less than the risk of harm from an air-to-air missile. In fact, Congress passed a law after September 11th granting the TSA the authority to approve arming pilots subject to approval by the individual airlines. Prior to that provision of law being passed in the fall of 2001, pilots actually had a right, under certain circumstances, to possess a firearm in the cockpit. In the 1960's, the FAA, who had responsibility for all airline safety, adopted a rule allowing pilots to carry a firearm as long as the pilots' airline participated in an FAA approved training program.

This rule remained on the books right through September 11th, 2001. The need for Congress to enact legislative authority for the newly formed

TSA to decide the issue of guns in the cockpit arose when the FAA proposed a rule in July 2001, two months before the hijackers commandeered the cockpit of four airplanes, which would have repealed the 1960's FAA rule allowing guns in the cockpit. The repeal of the FAA rule allowing pilots to be armed took effect in November 2001.

The same FAA that proposed repealing the rule that permitted pilots to be armed less than 60 days before September 11[th,] issued several alerts to U.S. airlines warning of possible threats to airline safety in the months leading up to September 11th. The extent of dissemination of those alerts beyond airport and airlines offices is unclear.

The policy regarding dissemination of security threat warnings has been a matter of official concern and embarrassment since 1988. In December 1988, the U.S. Embassy in Helsinki received a phone call warning that an explosive device would be placed on a Pan Am flight from Frankfurt, Germany to the United States.

Aviation officials took the threat seriously and issued an alert to airlines and U.S. embassies. However, the alert carried a caveat: "The information in this bulletin is solely for the use of U.S. carriers and airport security personnel and may not be further disseminated without specific approval..."[6]

In spite of this specific alert and the rather extraordinary searches of passengers, luggage and airplanes, Pan Am Flight 103 from Frankfurt, Germany to the United States blew up over Lockerbie, Scotland after a stop in England on December 21, 1988. None of the passengers had knowledge of the FAA alert. If they had had knowledge of it they might have chosen not to take the chance of flying at that time or chosen to fly a different airline.

In reviewing the policy about the dissemination of threat warnings after the Pan Am Flight 103 disaster, President Reagan said that issuing a public warning based on an anonymous phone call "would literally have closed down air traffic in the world." A public policy calculation was made in light of safety considerations and the threat was deemed to be too vague. It is not dissimilar to the calculus made by Mr. Carty, American Airlines CEO, in his Tokyo speech in May of 2002.

Three months to the day after the September 11th hijackings, the FAA issued an alert warning airlines that terrorists might attempt to hide weapons in their shoes. Just 11 days after the warning was issued the crew and passengers on a flight from Paris to Miami subdued a scruffy looking man trying to light a fuse sticking out of his sneaker in which a bomb was hidden. The sneaker bomber, Richard Reid, was arrested and the FAA issued another order instructing that airport security checks include random inspection of footwear.

Richard Reid had actually been denied permission to board a similar flight two days earlier. Profiling characteristics – a man between ages 18 to 35, traveling without luggage on a ticket purchased within days of the flight for cash – brought Mr. Reid to the attention of French security officials. Yet, he managed to slip through security two days later.

The September 11th hijackers could not have been detected by x-ray bomb detection machines. They could not have been detected based on the possession of box cutters either, because box cutters were not prohibited from being carried on U.S. airliners on September 11th. There is no reason to believe that better training, certification, pay or working conditions for airport security screeners would have foiled the September 11th hijackers. The hijackers studied our commercial airline industry security measures carefully and exploited its weaknesses.

Curbside baggage check-in had no impact on the hijacker's ability to carry out their mission. Matching luggage to passengers actually on the airplane would have had no impact. Cargo inspections likewise had no bearing on the mission of the hijackers. Thorough background and fingerprint checks on airport personnel with access to secure areas might have had an impact if the hijackers relied on someone with access to the secure areas to supply them with weapons.

What could have made a difference on September 11th, and saved some or all of those lives, is better intelligence, profiling of passengers, arming of pilots and notification to passengers of a heighten security risk so the passengers could decide whether or not to subject themselves to that risk.

Intelligence gathering and dissemination has improved somewhat since September 11th, but the profiling of passengers is still held hostage to political correctness. Pilots are still denied the right to have a handgun in the cockpit, and public notice of safety threats is tempered by concern over interrupting the business of airlines and ultimately their profits.

In his speech in Tokyo, American Airlines CEO Donald Carty said that aviation is now so secure that terrorists will seek targets other than airlines. The facts do not support his belief. The best protection the flying public has against terrorists is its own vigilance, like the passengers who subdued sneaker bomber Richard Reid and the heroes of the September 11th hijacked airplane who accosted their hijackers and forced the plane to crash in a field instead of hitting a prime target like The White House.

In the final analysis, given the incompetence of the FAA and the political correctness of U.S. politicians and government officials, the ordinary Americans who constitute our "flying public" may be our best and only line of security.

---

[1] Federal Aviation Reauthorization Act of 1996, (P.L. 104-264), http://cas.faa.gov/readingroom/reports/ti2/ti2.html.

[2] James W. Brosnan, "Safety In The Skies A Matter Of Cold Numbers," *The Commercial Appeal* (Memphis), December 23, 1996.

[3] Jonathan D. Salant, "Terrorism 'Zero Tolerance' Policy Leads To Hundreds Of Airport Worker Arrests," *The Associated Press*, April 24, 2002.

[4] Matthew L. Wald, "Traces Of Terror: Airport Safety; Baggage Bomb Detector Is Unreliable, Experts Say," *New York Times*, June 9, 2002.

[5] Tom Kelly, "Falling Confidence In Terrorism War," *Press Association*, May 31, 2002.

[6] Doyle McManus, "U.S. Policy: Don't Publicize Anonymous Bomb Threats," *Los Angeles Times*, December 23, 1988.

U.S. Immigration and Naturalization Service:
Complete Disarray at Our Borders

Six months after Mohamed Atta and Marwan Al-Shehhi crashed hijacked airplanes into the World Trade Center, the Immigration and Naturalization Service sent out a "routine" notice informing a Florida flight school that the two men had been approved for student visas to study there.[1]

The embarrassing disclosure prompted the agency to finally acknowledge that its system is flawed and that severe problems have plagued it for years. "This incident also highlights the need to replace a student information collections system that INS has long stated was antiquated, inaccurate, untimely and of little utility to INS, schools or students," read a statement issued by the agency after the media made the mishap public.

The gaffe pushed the government to conduct a long overdue "thorough investigation," which discovered what many already knew.

In May 2002, a months-long Justice Department inquiry concluded that "a widespread failure by many individuals" within the INS was responsible for the mishandled paperwork pertaining to the hijackers. The 188-page report, which is posted on the Justice Department's web site (www.usdoj.gov), found that well before September 11th, the agency was lax in scrutinizing foreigners entering the United States to become students, and that the agency's foreign student program historically has been dysfunctional.[2]

Consider also that both Atta and Al-Shehhi had overstayed their initial visas. Yet, despite having no valid visas, both men left the country and were allowed to return on flights through Miami and New York only months before they hijacked the airliners.[3]

It was the September 11th failures that prompted Justice Department Inspector General Glenn A. Fine, who conducted the most recent inquiry to say, "The INS's current paper-based tracking system is inefficient, inaccurate and unreliable." [4]

This was hardly a new discovery. In fact, Congress has long criticized the INS for sloppy management, inept record keeping, and for being unable to control the borders or keep track of foreigners in the United States, legally or illegally.

In other words, the INS, perhaps the government agency best suited to have prevented September 11th, has a documented history of being incompetent and negligent.

This was already known after the 1993 World Trade Center bombings. Motivated by that event, Congress passed sweeping changes in immigration laws three years later. They included two key anti-terrorism measures that could have helped prevent the biggest act of terrorism against Americans eight years later in the same building.[5] The first key measure is an automated system meant to record when a foreigner enters and leaves the county. The second is a student visa database to track all foreign students in the country.

However, after intense political pressure by various interest groups, neither measure was ever fully implemented according to law, despite warnings that the nation was at risk without them.[6] Canadian officials, as well as business interests, lobbied strongly against the automated system, arguing that such a system would slow border traffic so much that it would be economically crippling.

Most of the nation's colleges as well as education groups – in particular the National Association of Foreign Student Advisers (NAFSA) – objected to the student visa database. Thousands of college administrators and NAFSA officials objected to singling out foreign students for anti-terrorism measures and sent thousands of letters to members of Congress expressing their objections.[7] The pressure was enough to delay both measures.

Evidently the 1993 World Trade Center (WTC) bombing was not severe enough to cause the implementation of measures that lawmakers had created to protect American citizens from terrorists, despite evidence that tremendous negligence on the part of the INS was responsible for the bombers entering the country.

When Sheik Omar Abdel Rahman was arrested for masterminding the 1993 WTC bombing, authorities made a chilling discovery. The blind Egyptian cleric, with a history of radical activities, had many times slipped through loopholes and lapses in immigration policy to plot terrorism on American soil.

Now serving a life sentence for his role in the 1993 WTC bombing, Rahman was on a State Department list of undesirables when he entered the country legally in 1990. He was nevertheless granted a green card, which allowed him to live in the United States permanently and easily plot to blow up several New York landmarks.

His accomplice, the Palestinian man convicted of driving the bomb-laden van into the WTC, entered the country with a student visa. After he dropped out of school, the INS never bothered to establish his whereabouts.[8]

No action was taken to prevent a similar or more devastating attack in the future. The 1993 act of terrorism obviously was not enough to rock the INS into shape, nor did it drive Congress to enforce its own measures in the future. In 1997, a year after Congress passed the two laws forecasted to help curb terrorism, nothing had changed. The worst part is that the Justice Department knew and did nothing to correct the problem, making this one of the government's most notable failures to protect its citizens.

A 1997 report by the Justice Department's Office of the Inspector General found that the INS could not identify people overstaying their visas or even provide accurate numbers of overstays. The report also pointed out that the 1996 laws Congress had passed called for the INS to add 300 staffers to investigate visa overstays, but that those positions were never funded.

The September 11th WTC plane attacks, much like the 1993 bombing, proved that high-ranking government officials have known for years about widespread problems with the INS's inability to track immigrants, its severe loopholes in enforcement and, in particular, the agency's inability to track foreigners who overstayed their visas. Of 19 hijackers identified in the September 11th attacks, 13 had entered the United States legally. Most arrived with tourist, business or student visas, and some remained here unnoticed even after their documents expired. One suspect who entered on a student visa never showed up at the English school he was supposed to attend in California.[9]

No one in the government checked up on their status because, as we already mentioned, the INS has no way of tracking foreign students or visitors after they enter the United States and no way of checking when and if they leave. The agency estimates that 3 to 4 million people who have overstayed their visas are in the country, but clearly immigration officials do not really know the actual figure.

On the other hand, the Census Bureau estimates that the number of illegal immigrants in the United States has more than doubled during the 1990's.[10] The 2000 census reveals that roughly 8.7 million undocumented immigrants live in America and about 115,000 of them are from Middle Eastern countries. While the majority of Middle Eastern immigrants are not terrorists, it is disturbing to know that tens of thousands of people from that region – and millions more from other parts of the world – can settle in this country illegally. Obviously, terrorists who wish to enter the United States will meet few obstacles.

Attorney General John Ashcroft stated the obvious days after terrorist-hijacked planes slammed into the WTC and the Pentagon, saying the events "underscored in the most painful way for Americans that we need better control over individuals coming to our shores from other nations."[11]

In a desperate effort to correct the monumental errors of past administrations, the INS announced shortly after September 11th that it would add more than 300,000 people who evaded deportation orders to the FBI's National Criminal Database in order to allow local law enforcement to identify them in traffic stops and other routine police work.

Immediately after September 11th, about 1,200 foreigners, mostly of Middle Eastern background and with immigration violations such as expired visas, were jailed.

The Justice Department has also targeted for deportation thousands of men known to be from countries where Osama bin Laden's al Qaeda network operates. The men, thought to be in the country illegally, have ignored orders to leave, according to Justice Department officials.

Why did it take a catastrophe, in which thousands of innocent people were brutally killed, for our government to finally act?

More importantly, has the government taken the necessary actions to correct this deep-rooted problem within an agency notorious for its failures?

Apparently not. According to yet another Justice Department Office of Inspector General Report conducted in January 2002, even after September 11th, immigration inspectors at some international airports still failed to consistently check passport numbers of foreign nationals against terrorist watch lists, posing a continuing national security threat.[12]

The report also revealed that INS inspectors have not stuck to a 1999 promise to quickly record the numbers of stolen or lost passports from visa-waiver countries, and that an INS database, which records lost or stolen passports was grossly inadequate.

Another example of continued INS failure took place in San Diego months after the September 11th attacks. Authorities in that Southern California border city discovered that 10 illegal immigrants were working at a Navy submarine base in nearby Point Loma, with access to sensitive U.S. military information and equipment. INS officials said the men used counterfeit green cards to gain employment with a company that has 150 workers at the base.[13] How did this happen? If the country is supposedly on high alert, how could these illegal immigrants penetrate a naval base with access to sensitive military information?

Yet another example of INS negligence took place after September 11th. In April 2002, the agency handed a valid five-year visa back to an Egyptian architect who had been deported months earlier. One Aly Sabra Galal Abdelella was carrying a box cutter in his briefcase when he tried to enter the United States through Miami International Airport with that visa. INS agents discovered the "mishap" during a computer check in Miami that showed his deportation order from earlier in the year.[14] The agency offered an interesting explanation via a Washington spokesman: While it appeared Abdelella's visa was never canceled as it should have been, the cancellation stamp *may* have been erased.

The embarrassing news caused finger-pointing between the State Department and INS, since both agencies were involved on some level. "Visas are issued by the State Department, but the INS controls what goes on in our country with visitors," a State Department spokesman said following the incident. "If they deport the guy, it was their responsibility to cancel the visa."

It sounds simple. But nothing is that easy in the intricate world of the INS. Remember the so called computer network meant to track foreign students that Congress ordered six years ago? Well, INS officials have reluctantly admitted that it is still in the testing stage and will not be running for "some time."

The clearest – and most maddening – announcement by high-ranking INS officials was that, even when the system gets going, there will not be enough enforcement agents to check on all of the visa violators flagged by the system. This, despite the fact that the culprits involved in the deadliest attack on America we have ever seen, came here with student visas.

It is obvious and undeniable that the INS has a monumental task. Besides curbing illegal immigration, the agency is in charge of regulating the admission of visitors to the United States by issuing visas, granting residence, and naturalizing American residents born abroad. It also has the task of examining and granting or rejecting applications for refugee status, an enormously complicated enterprise that requires a lot of manpower and analytical acumen.[15]

In 2000 (the latest available data), the Border Patrol processed about 550 million border crossings. Of those, 330 million who crossed were non-Americans. It was a $4.8 billion operation that apparently is still below what is needed.

There are also serious security and immigration issues concerning foreign students studying in the United States. Foreign students represent a lucrative business for this country's universities and trade schools, creating immense pressure to grant foreigners student visas, as was the case with many of the September 11th terrorists. In many cases the former foreign students become much-needed professionals in communities which would not be able to function without them. This is the case, for example, with physicians who take jobs in rural areas or inner-city hospitals where American-born physicians do not always choose to go.

The nation has 550,000 foreign students, according to INS figures, and tracking them is virtually impossible under the existing system.

However, the INS restructuring plan announced by the attorney general months after September 11th does not appear to specifically address this issue. Under reform, the agency will be split into two new bureaus, one for immigration services and another for law enforcement. Yet, considering its storied history, it will take more than a split to improve the INS. The Justice Department's latest available report for the fiscal year 2000 helps explain the problem.[16] The INS apparently has an insufficient system to monitor alien overstays, which leads to the agency's failure to identify many deportable criminal aliens, including aggravated felons. The report is also critical of INS management, stating that the agency needs to take steps to clarify lines of communication, establish roles and responsibilities, and create organizational policies and guidelines.

While in such disarray, Americans cannot expect the INS to protect them against deadly terrorists. In fact, this error-prone agency, with a detailed record of poor management and outright negligence, contributed directly to the deaths of thousands of Americans by allowing the September 11th terrorists enter the country, remain here illegally, and commit horrific acts.

Bang 'em In

"Bang 'em in" is the slang phrase used by INS managers, supervisors and employees to describe the rushed processing of foreigners through immigration inspection points at U.S. ports of entry. The pressure to process foreigners seeking admission to the United States rapidly through our ports is enormous, and is driven principally by overtime costs that are billed to "transportation carriers" (the airlines and cruise lines) as user fees. The overtime costs are paid by the airlines, whose activities require the work of the INS immigration inspectors for their passengers to lawfully enter the country. These costs are politically sensitive, since the airline and travel industry pressures the INS and lobbies Congress to minimize the costs that are passed along to private industry.

INS Districts that successfully hold down overtime costs reward their senior managers and inspection supervisors with bonuses and incentive pay. Since it is "incentivized," overtime costs are cited repeatedly by INS management as the driving consideration for immigration inspection, operational, and staffing decisions.

In a number of lengthy interviews, South Florida immigration inspectors explained how the pressure to process foreigners rapidly emanated from the INS District Director level all the way down to the supervisory personnel at airports and seaports.

Veteran INS immigration inspectors in South Florida have revealed a pattern and practice by INS managers and supervisors of hurrying and harassing inspectors who identify suspicious foreigners for evaluation and questioning in "secondary" (a second processing area where INS inspectors have an opportunity to closely examine the documents of persons seeking entry to the country and can question the traveler in detail).

Immigration inspectors who identified travelers for further examination in "secondary" – a sometimes time-consuming process of document verification, interviews and record checks – were told "not to worry about it" and "bang 'em in." Inspectors who requested additional time to investigate and question suspicious foreigners seeking entry to the United States were routinely denied permission to conduct their investigations and told to go home. Immigration inspectors seeking to conduct a complete and thorough review of foreigners' identification and travel documents jeopardize the supervisors' cash awards by "dragging out" the immigration process and potentially increasing overtime costs. The last resort of INS immigration inspectors faced with supervisory pressure to "bang 'em in" is to draft an Intelligence Report. The report is a way to document the suspicious circumstances and/or documentation of a foreigner entering the United States, in the hope that it will result in future enforcement activity or further analysis should the subject of the report resurface to the INS.

Even after September 11th, INS management failed to grasp the counterterrorism "front line" status of the INS immigration inspectors, telling them that identifying and apprehending terrorists was the job of the CIA and the FBI. Field level immigration inspectors who attempted to cooperate and coordinate with U.S. Customs officers are often viewed as "communicating with the enemy." Bureaucratic rivalry and petty competitions still mar the operational and managerial relations between INS and Customs. Despite the vulnerabilities exposed by September 11th, problems are sloughed-off between agencies and finger-pointing sessions characterize "inter-agency working groups."

The volume of passengers seeking entry to the United States and the volume of international air traffic alone is so staggering that, under the best conditions, the INS is stretched too thin. For example, South Florida INS standing operating procedures call for U.S. citizens to simply be waived through immigration points, even when there are circumstances that appear questionable to the trained eye of an INS immigration inspector. U.S. citizens reentering the country are still only required to provide either a birth certificate and driver's license, or – amazingly – a verbal declaration and a driver's license.

The sieve-like security of INS facilities, such as its Port Everglades, FL operation, is particularly disturbing. Pleasure boats, private yachts, and cruising vessels entering Port Everglades are only required to check-in by radio. Those vessels that comply with the virtually unenforced procedure provide their U.S. Customs clearance number and then answer two questions (over the radio): 1) How many U.S. citizens are aboard the vessel and, 2) How many others are aboard the vessel? The "others" are *requested* to visit the Port Everglades INS office, but there is no follow-up or cross-check with Customs to ensure that each vessel complies and that each person entering the United States is documented. On a positive note, Miami Seaport requires *every* vessel to physically report in for inspection. While Miami's procedures may seem somewhat more reassuring, it only highlights the inconsistencies and weaknesses of our defenses against those who would attack us. Worse yet, it is manifest proof of the failure of the INS to "get it" after the horrific attacks of September 11th and of the federal government's absolute inability to manage and coordinate anything resembling a coherent defensive strategy for our borders and ports.

INS managers in South Florida have attempted to inoculate themselves from responsibility should terrorists again exploit the Districts' procedural weaknesses, leadership failures, and professional negligence. The Miami District Office leadership has spent countless man-hours writing memos, issuing warnings, and threatening field-level inspectors, officers, and agents with a new "Zero Tolerance" policy that is sure to reinforce the sort of risk-averse, hostile work environment that actually exacerbates security vulnerabilities and extinguishes any spark of *esprit de corps*. The leadership's self-protective mentality results in INS workers watching their backs instead of watching the foreign travelers. Let us use the example of an INS inspector who has serious reservations concerning a foreigner and wishes to place him in "secondary" for additional questioning. The inspector knows that he faces the scrutiny of a supervisory inspector, ever-mindful of overtime costs with the goal of "banging 'em in." There are numerous instances of supervisory inspectors ordering a line inspector to let the suspicious foreigner into the country. The immigration inspectors are placed in an unenviable position. If they follow their conscience and sense of duty, their supervisory inspector will identify them for disciplinary action for insubordination. If they allow the suspicious foreigner entry to the United States, they betray their oath and duty and subject themselves to the provisions of the INS "Zero Tolerance" policy. A few brave line inspectors have told supervisory inspectors to use their own visa stamp to allow entry – marking the suspect foreigner's immigration form (an "I-94") with the supervisors' INS identification number. While the line inspector has forced the supervisor to accept responsibility for ordering the entry of the suspicious foreigner, these sorts of confrontations have a corrosive effect on the effectiveness of the INS and are self-defeating in the long term.

Persons holding Canadian passports and travel documents pose a unique problem for INS enforcement actions. While the vast majority of our neighbors to the north are law-abiding and share much in common with Americans, that unique friendship and bond has, ironically, been used against the United States by terrorists. They seek to exploit the vulnerabilities of our immigration policies with Canada and our long, essentially unguarded border.

South Florida INS inspectors point to the case of a Middle Eastern man with a Canadian passport, who claimed to have come to Canada as a refugee. When he arrived in South Florida, he possessed identification documents and passports in the names of other persons. He also had a number of signed, blank checks. Fortunately, in this case, supervisory immigration inspectors grasped the seriousness of the Canadian's situation and allowed the man to be interviewed at length. He provided that he was a chemical engineer and a former army officer in a Middle Eastern country. In addition to the other documents, the man possessed a military identification card, but the photograph on the military discharge papers he carried did not match the photo on the ID card. He claimed that the documents he was carrying were to "help a friend," but he would not elaborate. Another Middle Eastern male was traveling with the Canadian. He too presented Canadian travel documents that appeared to be in proper order and was allowed entry to the United States. A third man traveling with the Canadians, who was from the same Middle Eastern country (but in possession of a U.S. passport) was allowed reentry, without questioning, despite that fact that he was carrying over $7000 dollars in cash. The Canadian with the multiple identification documents was returned to Canada within 24 hours. The second Canadian was returned to Canada by the Border Patrol within 30 days of his arrival in the United States, after he was arrested for his involvement in the operation of an "escort service" and for his association with a business with suspected ties to money laundering for HAMAS. Unfortunately, each of the Middle Eastern-born Canadians could have reentered the United States quite easily the very next day by simply driving over the border. The whereabouts and activities of the American member of this trio are unknown.

The South Florida INS employees interviewed during the course of our research related additional disturbing stories of senior INS supervisors and managers merely "going through the motions" of defending our borders – more concerned with "banging 'em in" than being the vanguard of our domestic security. Mere days before the attacks of September 11th, two Middle Eastern males arrived in Miami via a major European airline "hub." The older of the pair was reportedly an Imam and dressed in traditional, Middle Eastern, Islamist garb, while his younger assistant dressed in Western clothes. A third man, who appeared to be German, but carried a French passport with Iranian and Iraqi entry/exit stamps, and who claimed to be a "pharmaceutical salesman," seemed to be traveling with the Middle Eastern pair. The Imam's name "alerted" in the INS computer system as a possible terrorist, according to U.S. Customs service information. There was some confusion with the Imam's identity and travel documents over the spelling of his name and his date of birth. These factors lead to a slowdown in the pair's processing that came to the attention of the supervisory immigration inspector. The "line" immigration inspector had marked the Imam's Customs Declaration Form with a code for additional Customs Service scrutiny, based on the Customs' computer notice concerning possible terrorist connections. The line inspector also wanted to make copies of all three men's documentation for further investigation. The supervisory immigration inspector rejected the concerns and plans of the line inspector, changed the notation on the Imam's Customs Declaration form, forbade the copying of documents, and ordered all three men entered into the United States. The line inspector frantically attempted to make an entry in the computer to alert the Customs Inspectors of the approaching Imam and his assistant, as well as the European "pharmaceutical salesman" – to no avail. The supervisory immigration inspector then ordered the line inspector back to work, commenting sarcastically that the inspector "read too many spy novels."

The Imam and his assistant listed Coral Springs, Florida, as their residence while in the United States. Coral Springs was the home town of Mohammad Atta – the September 11th ringleader.

Interestingly, the Imam's assistant and the European pharmaceutical salesman left the United States two weeks later, shortly after September 11th, –on the same flight – American Airlines flight 56 to London. The Imam left the United States approximately two weeks later.

The Tip of the Iceberg

These anecdotes of managerial recklessness and dereliction of duty point to a larger and continuing pattern and practice by the INS. They are a fraction of the total story of the continuing vulnerability the country faces and of the U.S. government's utter failure to correct the glaring flaws in our defenses. The Bush-Cheney administration is aware of these immediate threats to American security, but its response, if any, is strangled in the bureaucratic maze and layers of inefficiency, complacency, neglect, and recklessness at the Department of Justice. In the meanwhile, we all continue to be at risk.

---

[1] David Johnston, "6 Months Late, INS Notifies Flight School of Hijackers' Visas," *New York Times*, March 13, 2002.

[2] Glenn A. Fine, "Inspector General's Report, May, 20 2002," United States Department of Justice, Washington, DC.

[3] David Stout, "Inquiry Finds Widespread Failure at INS in Handling of Hijackers' Student Visas," *New York Times,* May 20, 2002.

[4] U.S. Department of Justice Inspector General Glenn A. Fine, quoted in May 20, 2002, Department of Justice, Inspector General's Report.

[5] 1996 Congressional Transcripts; *Immigration Changes Include Key Anti-Terrorism Measures*, United States Congress.

[6] Sandra Peddie and Eden Laikin, "Easy Entry Stirs Calls for Tighter Visa Controls," *New York Newsday*, October 15, 2001.

[7] Association of International Educators, 1996-97 Strategic Plan Report; Leadership and Public Policy.

[8] Inspector General Report, U.S. Department of Justice, September 1997.

[9] Patrick J. McDonnell and Russell Carollo, "An Easy Entry for Enemies," *Los Angeles Times,* October 1, 2001.

[10] United States Census, 2000 National Figures, Category: Undocumented Foreigners.

[11] U.S. Department of Justice, *Message from the Attorney General; John Ashcroft,* September 13, 2001.

[12] Alfonso Chardy, "Security Gaps Found in Airport Screenings," *Miami Herald,* January 30, 2002.

[13] *KGTV Channel 10,* San Diego, Daily Transcripts, "Illegal Immigrants Worked at Navy Base," January 20, 2002.

[14] Jay Weaver, "Man Came to U.S. After Deportation," *Miami Herald,* April 16, 2002.

[15] Immigration and Naturalization Service, "Handbook and Duties," United States Department of Justice, Washington, DC.

[16] U.S. Department of Justice Fiscal Year 2000 Performance Report and Fiscal Year 2002 Performance Plan for the Immigration and Naturalization Service, http://www.usdoj.gov.

FATAL NEGLECT: The U.S. Government's Continuing Failure
to Protect American Citizens from Terrorists

Part Three: Unraveling the Foreign Terror Connections

Iraq's State Sponsorship of Osama bin Laden and the al Qaeda Terror Network

The attacks of September 11th were well planned, sophisticated terrorist operations that took years to develop. The size and scope of the attack, as well as the personnel, finance, logistics and communication considerations, point to state sponsorship, or at the very least, state "facilitation" of the terrorists. Osama bin Laden's personal fortune provides him and his al Qaeda organization considerably more freedom of action than other terror cells, but there are certain resources, capabilities and facilities terrorists seek or require that are only available to a nation state. An examination of the September 11th attacks requires a detailed examination of Iraq's ties to bin Laden and the al Qaeda terror network.

Osama bin Laden represents and articulates a thoroughly developed Islamist theology and philosophy with a broad appeal that goes beyond a simple hatred of Israel. He expounds and defends a religious obligation of Muslims to attack U.S. military and civilian targets; demands the immediate expulsion of U.S. Forces from Saudi Arabia; calls for the creation of a "Muslim" nuclear weapon; criticizes harshly "moderate" Muslim states such as Egypt and Jordan for not instituting "truly" Islamic law; and he also calls for the end of all sanctions against Iraq. Osama bin Laden sees an opportunity for holy war, literally, across half of the globe.[1]

The Middle Eastern terror groups of the 1970's and 1980's relied on the patronage of a number of states – principally the Soviet Union and its Warsaw Pact satellites – for financial backing, intelligence, weapons, explosives, training and logistics. Often these resources made their way to the terror groups through states acting as regional surrogates for the Communists. The infamous terrorist organization that captured headlines throughout the 1970's and 1980's, the "Abu Nidal Organization," was established in Baghdad by a Palestinian named Sabri al-Banna, whose *nom de guerre* was Abu Nidal. Iraqi intelligence, who at the time were trained by the Soviets, trained members of the organization.[2]

Osama bin Laden and the al Qaeda terror network are a twenty-first-century variant on the Islamist model that has dominated the last sixty years. Bin Laden's personal fortune finances much of the organization's terrorism. Bin Laden wields influence, power and notoriety unlike other terror group leaders, but there are still circumstances and occasions when his interests and those of the al Qaeda network are best served through a sovereign state, or through the official apparatus of a state. Two prime

75

examples are the advantages of official diplomatic status and a national intelligence organization. While recent news coverage has highlighted bin Laden's hijacking of the Taliban's medieval administration of Afghanistan, that country provided bin Laden simply with a haven, but not a political venue. It is Saddam Hussein's Iraq that has been bin Laden's active political, military and intelligence sponsor for just over three years.

Osama bin Laden had dealings with Iraqi Intelligence as early as 1993 in Somalia. During that period, various militant Islamic groups, to include bin Laden and Iraqi intelligence and military operatives, were in Somalia to organize, train and mobilize radical factions within the Somali populace.[3] In June 1994, while in Khartoum, bin Laden met with Faruq al-Hijazi, then the director of the Iraqi Intelligence Department. However, at that time, Iraqi concern over bin Laden's militant Islamist zeal restrained their dealings with bin Laden and limited their willingness to provide practical support and cooperation.[4] Within approximately three years, Iraqi hesitance and concerns regarding bin Laden evaporated. Pragmatic considerations, driven by the deepening political and social crises in Iraq resulting from UN sanctions as well as growing Shiite revivalism in southern Iraq and Kurdish nationalism in northern Iraq, led Saddam Hussein to reassess cooperation with bin Laden. Bin Laden's charities and Islamist social services programs eased the shortfalls in food, medicine and basic necessities resulting from the UN sanctions. Arab "Afghans," Muslim Brotherhood groups and other like-minded fundamentalist Islamists who came to Iraq in support of these new initiatives provided an ideology and structure that met Saddam Hussein's domestic political needs and either diffused or suppressed nationalist or splinter movements. The Iraqi leader could claim credit for averting the suffering of the Iraqi people and insuring political instability at the "cost" of allowing bin Laden a foothold in Iraq through social and religious means.[5]

On February 22, 1998, bin Laden announced the formation of the "World Islamic Front for Jihad Against the Jews and the Crusaders," merging Egypt's Jihad Group, the Islamic Group, the Ansar Movement of Pakistan and the Bangladeshi Jihad Movement under one umbrella.[6]

Bin Laden reportedly visited Baghdad for consultations in March 1998. Giovanni De Stefano, an international lawyer visiting Baghdad on business, had a chance encounter with bin Laden in the lobby of the five star Al-Rashid Hotel during which the two men introduced themselves and engaged in polite conversation. De Stefano did not, at the time, recognize bin Laden's name. Five months after the chance encounter, bin Laden's suicide bombers attacked the American embassies in Nairobi and Dar-es-Salaam.[7]

Between April 25 and May 1, 1998, two of bin Laden's senior military commanders, Muhammad Abu-Islam and Abdallah Qassim, visited Baghdad for discussions with Saddam Hussein's son, Qusay Hussein, the "czar" of all Iraqi intelligence matters.[8] Qusay Hussein's participation in the meetings highlights the importance of the talks in both symbolic and practical terms. Iraqi commitments for training, intelligence, clandestine Saudi border crossings, as well as weapons and explosives support to al Qaeda were a direct result of the meetings.[9]

An outcome of the April meetings was Iraq's commitment to train a network of bin Laden's operatives within Saudi Arabia. By mid-June 1998, bin Laden's operatives were at the al-Nasiriyah training camp, receiving a four-week course of instruction from the Iraqi intelligence and military on reconnaissance and targeting American facilities and installations for terrorist attacks. Another group was organized and trained for smuggling weapons and explosives into Saudi Arabia – and used their return to the kingdom as the first (successful) operation. A third group of bin Laden's Saudi operatives received a month of sophisticated guerrilla operations training later in the summer of 1998.[10]

Bin Laden quickly sought to strengthen and reinforce Iraqi support. In mid-July 1998, bin Laden sent Dr. Ayman al-Zawahiri, the Egyptian co-founder of al Qaeda to Iraq, to meet with senior Iraqi officials, including Iraqi vice president Taha Yassin Ramadan, to discuss and plan a joint strategy for an anti-U.S. jihad. Baghdad pledged their full support and cooperation, on the condition that bin Laden not incite the Iraqi Muslim Brotherhood against Saddam Hussein's reign. Zawahiri was taken to tour a potential site for bin Laden's new headquarters near al-Fallujah, and to observe training at terrorist camps run by Iraqi intelligence, to include the training conducted at al-Nasiriyah to bin Laden's Saudi operatives. Zawahiri assumed responsibility for the al-Nasiriyah training camp in the name of Osama bin Laden, as part of Iraq's recognition of bin Laden as the "local authority" in the jihad against the United States.[11]

Both Saddam Hussein's and Osama bin Laden's objectives are served through their alliance. They mutually loathe both the House of al-Saud (the royal family of Saudi Arabia) and the United States. Bin Laden accomplishes, as a non-state actor, what Hussein cannot and vice versa. The existence of an Iraqi-sponsored al Qaeda capability or "wing," poised to strike at Riyadh or regionally against U.S. interests, complicates and narrows counterterrorism options for the United States and its allies.

By mid-November 1998, Saddam Hussein came to the conclusion, (with the advice and prompting of his son and intelligence chief, Qusay), that a campaign of terrorist attacks against the United States, under the "deniable" banner of Osama bin Laden, was the most effective means of deflecting U.S. attempts to topple the Hussein regime. Meetings between Iraqi intelligence operatives and bin Laden in Afghanistan followed shortly. Both parties agreed to joint efforts in a detailed, coordinated plan for a protracted war against the United States. Iraq pledged further assistance with a chemical weapons expert, while bin Laden agreed to hunt down Iraqi opposition leaders who cooperated with the West against Saddam Hussein.[12] Following through on his part of the agreement, bin Laden reportedly dispatched 400 "Afghan" Arabs to Iraq to fight Kurds.[13]

In December 1998, the Clinton-Gore administration engaged in a bombing campaign against Iraq that was viewed by many, particularly Islamist leaders, as a political distraction or "Wag the Dog" side-show to diminish or deflect attention from President Clinton's scandals and domestic political trouble. The launching of anti-American Islamist terrorism in retaliation for the bombing campaign was certain. Iraqi trade minister Muhammad Mahdi Salah stated that he expected "terrorist activities" against the United States to increase as a result of the bombing of Iraq.[14]

The Arabic daily newspaper, *Al-Quds al-Arabi*, first raised the issue of cooperation between Saddam Hussein's Iraq and Osama bin Laden's al Qaeda in a late December 1998 editorial that predicted, "President Saddam Hussein, whose country was subjected to a four-day air strike, will look for support in taking revenge on the United States and Britain by cooperating with Saudi oppositionist Osama bin Laden, whom the United States considers to be the most wanted person in the world." The editorial noted that this type of cooperation was very likely considering that "bin Laden was planning moving to Iraq before the recent strike."[15]

Following the December air strikes, Saddam Hussein dispatched Faruq al-Hijazi to Kandahar, Afghanistan in order to meet with bin Laden. Hijazi was the former deputy chief of Iraqi intelligence and had first met bin Laden in 1994.[16] Hijazi offered expanded cooperation and assistance to bin Laden, as well as a re-extension of the offer of shelter and hospitality in Iraq for al Qaeda. Bin Laden agreed in principle to give Iraq assistance in a revenge campaign against the United States, but suggested further study and coordination before committing to a specific course of action or agreeing to a particular terrorist strike. To demonstrate Baghdad's commitment to al Qaeda, Hijazi presented bin Laden with a pack of blank, genuine Yemeni passports, supplied to Iraqi intelligence from their Yemeni contacts.[17] Hijazi's visit was followed by a contingent of Iraqi military intelligence officials who provided additional training and preparation to the al Qaeda terrorists in Afghanistan. These Iraqi officials included members of Unit 999 of Iraqi intelligence, who conducted advanced sabotage and infiltration training for seasoned, veteran, al Qaeda fighters. By January 1999, al Qaeda terrorists were being trained by Iraqi intelligence and military officers at camps on the outskirts of Baghdad.[18]

Following the Hijazi meetings, Qusay Hussein dispatched representatives to follow up with bin Laden and obtain his firm commitment to exact revenge against America. Baghdad offered an open-ended commitment to joint operations against the United States and its "moderate" Arab allies in exchange for an absolute guarantee that bin Laden, al Qaeda and their fundamentalist Islamists would not overthrow Saddam Hussein's regime in Iraq.[19] Israeli sources claim that for the past two years Iraqi intelligence officers have been shuttling back and forth between Baghdad and Afghanistan. According to the same sources, one of the intelligence officers, Salah Suleiman, was captured last October by the Pakistanis near the border with Afghanistan.[20]

In January 1999, Iraq began reorganizing and mobilizing intelligence front operations throughout Europe in support of al Qaeda.[21] Iraq's intelligence service has operated a network of outwardly legitimate businesses across Western Europe, using them as bases for espionage, terrorism and weapons procurement. Hans Josef Horchem, former chief of West Germany's *Bundesamt für Verfassungsschutz* (domestic intelligence service) stated that most of the Iraqi intelligence front companies in Germany were import-export firms and used-car dealerships. In the fall of 1990, at least three firms were operating in Hamburg and the German state of Hesse, with roughly seven additional Iraqi front operations in the rest of Europe.[22]

In the spring of 1999, Iraq's Unit 999 increased the intensity of its operations, moving funds and people around Europe and activating previously dormant intelligence contacts and operatives. Together with intelligence officers assigned under diplomatic cover, these operations activated agents who began scouting safe houses, vehicles, letter drops, communications, arms caches and other logistical requirements. Concurrent with this activation of Iraqi's European intelligence assets appeared the previously unheard of "Armed Islamic Front," who, it turned out, were made up of bin Laden's "Afghans" and "Bosniaks," that would now conduct terror strikes against both bin Laden's and Hussein's enemies.[23]

According to Czech intelligence sources, Mohammad Atta, the September 11, 2001 hijacking ringleader, met in June 2000 with Ahmed

Khalil Ibrahim Samir al-Ani, a consul and second secretary at the Iraqi embassy in Prague.[24] At 43, al-Ani is one of Iraqi's most highly decorated intelligence officers: a special forces veteran and senior leader of Iraq's "M-8," unit – the country's "special operations branch."[25] There are additional reports of a second meeting with another hijacker – Khalid Almihdar. Czech Interior Minister Stanislav Gross has also confirmed that Atta met with al-Ani in early April 2001 in Prague.[26] Atta also reportedly met with Iraqi ambassador to Turkey and former Iraqi deputy intelligence director Farouk al-Hijazi in Prague sometime in early April 2001.[27] Al-Ani had been expelled from the Czech Republic earlier in 2001 for espionage activities. The significance of this Iraqi connection to bin Laden and al Qaeda was so important that Czech Foreign Minister Jan Kavan flew to Washington, DC to deliver the intelligence files on the meetings to Secretary of State Colin Powell.

Additional intelligence surrounding the Iraqi – Al Qaeda connection continues to mount. The CIA reportedly believes Iraq provided falsified genuine passports for the 19 hijackers of the September 11th attacks.[28] Further, senior U.S. intelligence sources say that in the spring of this year, Marwan al-Shehri and Ziad Jarrah, two of Atta's closest associates and members of al Qaeda's "German cell," met with known Iraqi intelligence agents outside the United States.[29] Czech intelligence sources reported that al-Ani had been under surveillance because he had been observed apparently "casing" the Radio Free Europe/Radio Liberty headquarters in Prague. Czech authorities believed the site had been selected for attack by terrorists.[30] The intelligence sources further report that Atta and al-Ani embraced upon meeting at Prague's Ruzyne airport, and that Atta may have visited the Czech capitol on four occasions.[31] Iraqi opposition leaders in Prague reported that al-Ani visited Iraqi dissidents in Prague and attempted to persuade them to return to Iraq, on one occasion allegedly threatening an Iraqi student.[32]

Recent discoveries of anthrax in letters sent via the U.S. Postal Service raise additional significant questions concerning the possible involvement or sponsorship of Iraq, as the Iraqi government has experience with biological and chemical weapons, including the chemical bombing of Kurds in northern Iraq that killed over 5000 people in 1998. Only the United States, Russia and Iraq could have produced a chemical additive enabling the anthrax spores to become airborne.[33] UN inspectors have repeatedly documented evidence of anthrax experiments on the part of the Iraqi government after the 1991 Persian Gulf War. UN inspectors have also identified and documented Iraqi government stockpiles of sarin and VX gas.[34]

The German newspaper *Bild*, citing Israeli intelligence sources, says that Atta was handed a vacuum flask of anthrax by his Iraq contact – al-Ani. Atta flew from Prague to Newark, NJ. The letters laced with anthrax that were sent to news media and politicians were posted from New Jersey.[35] While the FBI has suggested that the anthrax may have come from a domestic malcontent, the FBI has been unable to actually identify a suspect, other than publicly naming a "person of interest," Steven J. Hatfill, a scientist who worked from 1997 to 1999 at the Army's infectious diseases lab at Fort Detrick, Md., where anthrax is made and studied. Hatfill has complained of an FBI "whispering campaign," aimed at convicting Hatfill in the media, similar to the treatment received by Richard Jewell who was wrongly identified by the FBI as the Atlanta Olympics bomber. The FBI's anthrax investigation has effectively reached a dead-end.

Italian security sources have reported that Iraq made use of its Rome embassy to foster and cultivate Saddam Hussein's partnership with al Qaeda. Habib Faris Abdullah al-Mamouri, a general in the Iraqi secret service, and from 1982 to 1990, a member of the "Special Operations Branch" (M-8) charged with developing links with Islamist militants in Pakistan, Afghanistan and the Gulf states, was stationed in Rome as an "instructor" for Iraqi diplomats. Al-Mamouri reportedly met with Mohammed Atta in Rome, Hamburg and Prague. Al-Mamouri has not been seen in Rome since July, shortly after he last met Atta.[36] Recent Iraqi defectors provide additional details of Saddam Hussein's support of international terrorism through the 1990's. The PBS documentary program "Frontline" has interviewed former Iraqi intelligence and army officers with first-hand accounts of highly secret installations run by an international terrorist known to Iraqi staffers only as "the Ghost." "The Ghost"[37] is reportedly Abdel Hussein, the chief trainer at a camp outside Baghdad called Salmon Pak, and responsible for conducting assassinations outside Iraq to support Saddam Hussein's regime.[38] The facility contained a Boeing 707 jet fuselage used to practice hijacking scenarios. UN inspectors independently confirmed the existence of the terrorist training camps.[39] The Iraqi defector known as "Saddam's Bomb-maker," Dr. Khidhir Hamza, who served as Iraq's Director of Nuclear Weaponization analyzes Iraqi's sponsorship of bin Laden as follows:

> What I think is there is somehow a change
> in the level of the type of operation bin
> Laden has been carrying [out]. What we are
> looking at initially is more or less just
> attempts to blow some buildings, just

normal use of explosives for a terrorist. What we have in the September 11 operation, [is a] tightly controlled, very sophisticated operation; the type an Iraqi intelligence agency, well versed in the technology [could pull off]. ... So my thinking is a guy sitting in a cave in Afghanistan is not the guy who will do an operation of this caliber. It has to have in combination with it a guy with the sophistication and know-how on how to carry out these things. ... Iraq [also] has a history of training terrorists, harboring them, and taking good care of them, by the way. A terrorist is well cared for with Saddam. So he has a good reputation in that type of community, if you like.[40]

Several leading authorities on Saddam Hussein and bin Laden's al Qaeda network concur on the likelihood of Iraq's state sponsorship and coordination of the September 11th terror attacks. The former head of Israel's Mossad secret service, Rafi Eitan, and former CIA Director, R. James Woolsey, share the view that Saddam Hussein and bin Laden conspired in the attacks.[41] Their views are shared by Laurie Mylroie, an academic and Iraqi affairs expert with the American Enterprise Institute. Mylroie cites the role of Iraqi operatives in the 1993 bombing of the World Trade Center to support her claim that the September 11th attacks are a matter of unfinished business from the perspective of Saddam Hussein, who still considers himself at war with the United States.[42]

Conflicting Reports Raise Troubling Questions

On May 1, 2002, the *New York Times* reported, "Federal authorities have concluded that there is no evidence that Mohamed Atta, the suspected ringleader of the September 11 attacks, met with an Iraqi intelligence officer before the hijackings. . . Federal law-enforcement officials have said for months that their investigation, including a search of immigration records in the Czech Republic and the United States, had found no evidence."[43] The original report concerning the U.S. government's failure to uncover INS records documenting Atta's Prague trip was reported in *Newsweek* magazine and sourced to an "anonymous official" who referenced a speech by FBI Director Robert Mueller in San Francisco, CA in late April 2002. The anonymous Bush-Cheney administration official did not explain why an international terrorist, who was traveling to a foreign capitol to meet with an Iraqi intelligence officer, would necessarily do so using his true name. Despite the position of some unnamed U.S. government officials concerning Atta's travels, the Czech government stands by its original intelligence sources and reporting. The *Prague Post* quoted Czech Interior Minister Stanislav Gross commenting, "Right now I do not have the slightest information that anything is wrong with the details I obtained from BIS [Czech Intelligence Service] counterintelligence. I trust the BIS more than journalists." The *Prague Post* pursued the story with Czech government spokesman Libor Roucek, who told the paper, "What's been said, we stick to it."

The question now is whether the reader trusts the Czech Intelligence Service or the record keeping "efficiencies" of the INS.

Veteran columnist William Safire has his own take on the U.S. government's latest efforts to disconnect Atta from his Czech-reported April meeting with al-Ani in Prague. Writing in the May 9, 2002 edition of the *New York Times*, Mr. Safire proposes that a "misdirection play" is being orchestrated by the CIA in order to cover-up a missed signal from Prague about September 11th, and organizational weaknesses in covering Iraq. Mr. Safire wrote:

> If the report proves accurate, a connection would exist between Al Qaeda's murder of 3,000 Americans and Iraq's Saddam. That would clearly be a *casus belli*, calling for our immediate military response, separate from the need to stop a demonstrated mass killer from acquiring nuclear and germ weapons. Accordingly, high C.I.A. and Justice officials — worried about exposure of the agency's inability to conduct covert operations — desperately want Atta's Saddam connection to be disbelieved.
>
> They are telling favored journalists: Shoot this troublesome story down. In March, a *Washington Post* columnist obliged with: "hard intelligence to support the Baghdad-

bin Laden connection is somewhere between 'slim' and 'none.' " In April, *Newsweek* headlined: "A spy story tying Saddam to 9-11 is looking very flimsy," and its Michael Isikoff wrote: "the much touted 'Prague connection' appears to be an intriguing, but embarrassing, mistake."

Everybody jumped aboard the C.I.A. bandwagon. The *Washington Post's* Walter Pincus followed up with a "senior administration official's finding that eliminates a once-suggested link between the terrorist attacks and the government of President Saddam Hussein." *Time* magazine this week labels the Czech report about Atta "discredited."

The C.I.A.-Justice misdirection is masterly; even White House staff members have bought the Tenet-Chertoff line about "serious doubts." The *New York Times* reported all too accurately that "a senior Bush-Cheney administration official appeared to close the matter, saying F.B.I. and C.I.A. analysts had firmly concluded that no meeting had occurred."

Notice how this parade of pooh-poohing never has an official's name attached to it. Rarely do you see such skillful manipulation by anonymous sources whose policy agenda is never revealed to readers. [44]

Our Czech allies continue to be troublesome for the CIA and the curious disinformation campaign Mr. Safire believes the agency is running. As of June 4, 2002, Czech UN Ambassador Hyneck Kmonicek, stood by the Czech government's account that al Ani and Atta met in Prague last year. "Atta and al Ani met. The meeting took place as confirmed by the interior minister last fall."[45]

So, whom do <u>you</u> trust – the Czech Intelligence Service or the INS?

[1] Peter L. Bergen, "Holy War, Inc.," The Free Press, New York, 2001, page 37.

[2] Laurie Mylroie, "Study of Revenge," American Enterprise Institute Press, Washington, DC, 2001, page 18-19.

[3] Youssef Bodansky, "Bin Laden; The Man Who Declared War on America," Prima Publishing, Roseville, CA, 2001, page 323

[4] Bodansky, page 323.

[5] Bodansky, page 323.

[6] Berger, page 95

[7] Tom Walker, "Hotel Clue Points To An Iraqi Connection," *Sunday Times* (London), September 30, 2001.

[8] Bodansky, page 324.

[9] Bodansky, page 325.

[10] Bodansky, page 324.

[11] Bodansky, page 324-325

[12] Bodansky, page 346-347.

[13] Daniel McGrory, "Hijacker 'Given Flask by Iraqi Agent'," *The Times* (London), October 27, 2001.

[14] Bodansky, page 360.

[15] Bodansky, page 360-361.

[16] Justine Smith, "Investigation Into Saddam's Fingerprints On The Terror Attacks: The Link," *The Mirror*, October 8, 2001.

[17] Bin Laden's family is Yemeni. His father moved to Saudi Arabia to pursuebusiness opportunities with his construction firm.

[18] Bodansky, page 361.

[19] Bodansky, page 362.

[20]http://www.janes.com/security/international_security/news/fr/fr010919_1_n.shtml.

[21] Bodansky, page 381.

[22] Ferdinand Protzman, "German Terror Expert Says Iraqis Have Front Companies Across Europe," *New York Times*, October 30, 1990.

[23] Bodansky, page 381.

[24] Richard Beeston, "Iraq Accuses U.S. of Trying to Settle Old Scores," *The Times* (London), October 10, 2001.

[25] David Rose, "Focus Special: The Terrorism Crisis: The Iraqi Connection,". *The Observer*, November 11, 2001

[26] Patrick E. Tyler with John Tagliabue, "Czechs Confirm Iraqi Agent Met With Terror Ringleader," *The New York Times*, October 27, 2001.

[27] Evan Thomas, "The Manhunt: Cracking The Terror Code," *Newsweek*, October 15, 2001 .

[28] Smith, *ibid*.

[29] Rose, *ibid*.

[30] Tyler, *ibid*.

[31] McGrory, *ibid*.

[32] *Newsweek*, Periscope: "Hard Questions About an Iraqi Connection," October 21, 2001.

[33] Peter Finn, "Czech's Confirm Key Hijacker's 'Contact' With Iraqi Agent in Prague; Atta Communicated With Diplomat Who Was Later Expelled," *The Washington Post*, October 27, 2001.

[34] Glen Schloss, "Suspicion Falls on Saddam," *South China Morning Post*, October 12, 2001.

[35] McGrory, *ibid*.

[36] McGrory, *ibid*.

[37] http://www.pbs.org/wgbh/pages/frontline/shows/gunning/interviews/general.html; and
http://www.pbs.org/wgbh/pages/frontline/shows/gunning/interviews/khodada.html

[38] Chris Hedges, "Defectors Citing Iraqi Training For Terrorism," *The New York Times*, November 8, 2001.

[39] Tyler, *ibid*.

[40] http://www.pbs.org/wgbh/pages/frontline/shows/gunning/interviews/hamza.html

[41] Dennis Eisenberg, "Saddam Links to Attacks," *The Herald Sun*, September 23, 2001.

[42] Mylroie, *ibid*.

[43] *New York Times,* "U.S. Drops Last Link of Iraq to 9/11," May 1, 2002.

[44] William Safire, "Mr. Atta Goes To Prague," *New York Times*, May 9, 2002.

[45] Edith M. Lederer, "Czech Ambassador Defends Meeting," *Associated Press*, June 4, 2002.

Fidel Castro: The "Forgotten" Terrorist

Ninety miles across the Florida Straits from Miami resides Fidel Castro, the brutal Communist dictator and sponsor of worldwide terror, who poses a direct and continuing threat to U.S. security. With strong ties to violent radical extremists, a decades-long support of terrorist groups throughout the world and an open, vitriolic hatred of the United States, it is reasonable to conclude that Fidel Castro may have played a role in the September 11th World Trade Center attacks. Castro has for years supported and harbored terrorists belonging to the most lethal Middle Eastern, South American and European groups, earning Cuba a spot on the U.S. State Department's list of terrorist-sponsoring nations.[1]

About a month before the September 11th attacks, three Afghani nationals and suspected al Qaeda members were caught trying to deposit $2 million in a Cayman Islands bank. They had entered the British colony on a commercial flight from nearby Cuba. The three men used false Pakistani passports. British authorities, who arrested the men, believe that they were handling drug proceeds laundered in Havana.[2]

Americans should consider Castro a lethal force equipped to cause enormous damage, rather than dismiss him as an erratic old man in combat fatigues, whose power disappeared along with the support his country received from the collapsed Soviet Union.

Supporting the notion that Castro is in fact a tremendous danger to U.S. security is the recent announcement by Undersecretary of State for Arms Control, John Bolton, that Cuba is a developer of weapons of mass destruction. At a Heritage Foundation address in May 2002, Bolton stressed that Cuba's threat to our security has often been underplayed. He revealed that Cuba not only has offensive biological warfare capability, but has also provided dual-use biotechnology to other rogue nations such as Iraq and Syria. "For four decades Cuba has maintained a well-developed and sophisticated biomedical industry, supported until 1990 by the Soviet Union," Bolton said. "This industry is one of the most advanced in Latin America and leads in the production of pharmaceuticals and vaccines that are sold worldwide."[3]

Such an admission by a government official was a great vindication for Miami's Cuban exiles, who for decades have documented the dictator's atrocious human rights violations, but have only seen a diminishing interest and even neglect, especially during the Clinton-Gore administration.

Castro has repeatedly denounced the U.S. war on terrorism, blaming the September 11th attacks on "the terrorist policies of the United States." Philosophically, the 75-year-old dictator belongs to the "old school" of communist revolutionaries, like Lenin, Stalin, Mao and Pol Pot, who viewed terror as a legitimate tactic to achieve revolutionary objectives. The reason for the embracing of terrorism is self-evident; none of these leaders established their regimes through legitimate means. They are a distinct set, the deadly dinosaurs of communism, who had no stomach for the finer arts of subversion, cultural changes, sensitivity training and so on. They seized power by the force of guns, and it is the language of weapons they understand best.[4] That is also the explanation why Castro still wears military fatigues and why Saddam Hussein celebrates whatever he thinks is worth celebrating by shooting his AK-47 in the air.

During a 2001 tour of Iran, Syria, and Libya, Castro was quoted by many of the world's media outlets as saying: "Iran and Cuba, in cooperation with each other, can bring America to its knees. The U.S. regime is very weak and we are witnessing this weakness from close up."[5]

Havana earned its place on the State Department's list of terrorist-sponsoring states for long providing a safe haven for terrorists. Castro is known to be harboring terrorists from Colombia, Spain, and the Middle East, as well as fugitives from the United States. Among them, the murderer of a New Mexico state police trooper who recently gloated about how safe he feels from extradition. "I am convinced the Cuban government considers me a political figure," Michael Finney recently told Agence France Presse from his Havana home earlier this year.[6] Indeed, to Castro, Finney is a propaganda tool on par with those who defected to the Soviet Union in earlier days. Finney hijacked a jet to Cuba from the United States in 1971 and lives quietly in Havana working as a translator, out of the reach of U.S. justice.

The FBI's list of fugitives living in Cuba features 74 violent-crime offenders, including convicted multiple murderer Ishmael Ali and Black Liberation Army member Joanne Chesimard, who murdered a New Jersey state trooper.[7] Castro has proudly admitted through the years that these violent criminals live on his island and are welcome to do so as long as they are evading American justice.

Besides providing a safe haven for violent U.S. criminals, Castro also trains, harbors, and financially supports numerous terrorist groups throughout the world, including the Puerto Rican Macheteros; Colombia's radical Revolutionary Armed Forces and National Liberation Army; the Palestine Liberation Organization; and the Irish Republican Army, which has its Latin American headquarters in Havana.[8]

Cuba has also provided advanced weapons and demolition training to Peru's Tupac Amaru Revolutionary Movement, which in 1984 attacked the U.S. embassy in Lima and, a year later, bombed the Texaco offices and attacked the residence of the U.S. ambassador.

More recently, a Basque terrorist organization, which seeks a separate homeland in Spain's Basque region, established its headquarters in Havana. Founded by militants and leftist students from the University of Madrid, guerillas of the Basque separatist movement ETA ("Euskadi ta Askatasuna," which means "Basque Fatherland and Liberty" in the Basque language) commit violent terrorist acts and have close relations with the IRA.[9]

A study conducted by the University of Miami's Institution for Cuban and Cuban-American Studies documents with detail Castro's strong ties to these terrorist groups and his hatred for the United States. It chronicles Castro's beginnings in terrorism as a young student who actively participated in the 1948 revolt in Bogota, Colombia, that left 5,000 dead and a third of Bogota in ashes. Since then, Castro has been driven by two objectives, according to the study: A commitment to violence and a virulent anti-Americanism.[10]

His true reign of terror began with his takeover of Cuba in 1959, with his summary executions and massive incarcerations. His visceral hatred for the United States led him to ask Nikita Khruschev, the then-Secretary General of the U.S.S.R., to launch a nuclear attack against this country in October 1962. During the Vietnam War, Castro gladly sent henchmen to Hanoi to viciously torture U.S. prisoners of war. This was documented by several historians, including Stuart Rochester and Frederick Kiley in their book *Honor Bound*.[11] Castro's hatred for the U.S. has manifested itself throughout his dictatorship, while nine successive U.S. presidents have come and gone.

Jaime Suchlicki, director of the University of Miami's Cuban Studies program, writes in a detailed report published by the school that in the 1960's Castro and his brother Raul believed that the same political and economic conditions that produced the Cuban revolution existed throughout Latin America and that anti-American revolutions would occur all over the continent.[12]

Cuban agents and diplomats were everywhere in the 1960's making contacts with communist sympathizers and revolutionary, terrorist and guerrilla groups throughout Central and South America, distributing propaganda and financial aid. Many Latin Americans were brought to Cuba for training and then returned to their countries, just as many Cuban youngsters went to the Soviet Union and Eastern European countries to study professions and Marxism-Leninism.

At a 1966 Havana conference attended by revolutionary leaders from throughout the world, Castro promoted his violent, anti-American line and insisted that "bullets not ballots" was the way to achieve power.[13]

For decades, Castro has used his armed forces to help guerillas and leftist groups achieve power in Latin America and Africa and that support, given in the name of the "people," has caused immense suffering and a chronic addiction to violence.[14] In Nicaragua, Cuban military personnel, weapons and intelligence supported and helped bring to power the Sandinistas. El Salvador's bloody civil war was largely aided by Cuba. In Africa, wherever possible, Castro was pursuing the same strategies. Thus in Angola, a former Portuguese colony, Castro helped bring the Movement for the Liberation of Angola into power, and he trained and supplied the South-West African Peoples Organization and the African National Congress.

Similarly, Cuban military and intelligence personnel have long aided Middle Eastern groups and regimes in their struggle against Israel. Cuban troops were sent to fight on the side of Arab States – particularly Syria – during the Yom Kippur war. It would not be an exaggeration to say that for two or three decades Cubans were the "universal soldiers," ready to give a helping, brotherly hand wherever there was the chance to overthrow what they called "reactionary" governments. Castro has cast himself in the role of mentor in the art of revolution, a "giant" in a dying breed whose profession was that of revolutionary.[15]

After the demise of the Soviet Union and its satellites, Castro's regime received a heavy blow, both politically and economically. Yet those who believed Castro would fall without his main crutch have been proven naïve. Castro's genius has been to create a corps of professionals, of "consultants" in different domains, whose expertise would be much needed in newly liberated countries or those regions still in the throes of a "struggle for national identity." Of course, along with engineering, those experts would export their knowledge of revolution. Thus, Castro sent military instructors and advisors into Palestinian bases, cooperated with Libya in the founding of the terrorist movement World Mathaba and established close military ties with Iraq, Libya, Southern Yemen, the Polisario Front for the Liberation of Western Sahara, the PLO, and others in the Middle East.[16] This intricate web of relationships during the past four decades with the world's most lethal terrorist groups proves that Castro is a dangerous force.

Domingo Amuchastegui, a former Cuban intelligence officer, now living in Miami, who was heavily involved in the country's Middle Eastern and African policy-making process, published a report in 1999 detailing Cuba's ties to Middle Eastern terrorist groups. The publication features exclusive inside information never before documented or confirmed by a Cuban government insider.[17]

Amuchastegui not only reveals Cuba's close connection with Middle Eastern terrorists, but also a tight-knit Cuban-Iranian relationship that includes sharing of doctors and pharmaceutical and biotechnology products. Amuchastegui also details Cuba's strong relationship with the PLO leaders, who have given Castro access to specialized military and intelligence training, both on Cuban and Palestinian soil.

He chronicles Cuba's deep-rooted relationship with radical Middle Eastern groups, dating back to Cuba's first contact with the Palestinian FATEH in 1965 and its strong support of the radical National Liberation Front in Southern Yemen a few years later. Cuba sent military instructors and advisors into Palestinian bases in Jordan to train Palestinian Fedayeen in 1968 and, in 1970, a high-level delegation from the FATEH-PLO visited Cuba.

Amuchastegui also documents the increase in Iranian-Cuban relations after several high-ranking delegations from Iran (including the vice president, the minister of foreign relations, and the minister of public health) visited Cuba in the late 1990's. In the last two years, the number of Cuban doctors, paramedics, and medical services hired by Teheran has increased, along with the purchase of Cuban pharmaceuticals and biotechnology products. "After a close relationship with Middle Eastern groups and countries for 40 years, Cuba enjoys today an exceptional position in the region, with embassies in almost all countries and with a wide variety of political connections within the ruling elites," Amuchastegui writes in his introduction.

In his analysis, the Middle East and North Africa have been extremely important to Castro's foreign policy since 1959. Today, Africa remains a region of special priority in Castro's redesign of foreign policy after the collapse of Cuba's alliance with the former Soviet Union.

All of the above raises the question: Would any of these countries or radical Islamist militant groups attempt to use Cuba as a springboard for terrorist actions against the United States? Amuchastegui believes it is quite possible. Castro has also proven that he is willing to commit terrorist acts with or without the collaboration of outside forces.

In 1996, Cuban Air Force MiGs shot down, in international waters, two small and unarmed civilian planes belonging to the Miami-based humanitarian group Brothers to the Rescue, killing three American citizens. Castro has publicly admitted ordering the shoot down and, in fact, bragged about doing so on American television. Then-President Bill Clinton did nothing to punish Castro for brutally murdering three of this country's citizens and so far, President George W. Bush has only acted by leaking the possibility of doing so to the media through an "unnamed official."

Another brutal Castro act of terrorism occurred in 1994, when he ordered Cuban fire boats to sink a tugboat full of freedom-seekers trying to escape the island prison in the middle of the night. Forty-one unarmed civilians – many of them women and children – were brutally drowned at sea by the Cuban state boats. As mothers hopelessly clenched their babies, they begged Cuban state security officers to have mercy. Instead, Castro's armed men continued to spray the tugboat with powerful hoses in order to destroy it. Then they rammed their fire boats into the ailing tugboat until it sank.[18] Cuban state security officers then drowned the floating survivors by circling around them in their speedboats and creating a powerful whirlpool that sucked the innocents into the chilly ocean water. The ABC television network broadcast a grueling segment on the incident and an Amnesty International report condemned the Cuban government for not carrying out a full and impartial investigation of the incident, and for intimidating and harassing those who attempted to do so.

These are just a few examples of vintage Castro terrorism. With continuous connections to terrorist groups and tremendous, lasting hatred for the United States, the world's last hard-line Communist requires vigilance despite the fact that Cuba is less of a conventional military threat to the United States since the collapse of the Soviet Union. Castro's entire career has been predicated upon Leon Trotsky's concept of "permanent revolution," a revolution that cannot rest until it has eliminated all its enemies (even when other communist countries were attempting changes in Soviet doctrine and were trying to build instead of pursuing the enemies of the "proletariat").

In October 2001, Judicial Watch filed a lawsuit on behalf of Jose Basulto and Brothers to the Rescue, as well as survivors of the tugboat incident described above, and other political prisoners of the communist Cuban regime in the Belgian Royal Court in Brussels, Belgium, naming Fidel Castro for committing "crimes against humanity." The case has been accepted by the Royal Court and been assigned to an investigative judge. Castro is personally responsible for the deaths of tens of thousands of Cubans who suffered as a result of his use of forced labor camps, physical and mental torture, political repression and imprisonment, and executions to maintain his dictatorial control over the Cuban people.

Even after September 11th, Castro continued to support terrorism openly. Only a few months after the attacks, when many world leaders publicly condemned any association with terrorist groups, the leader of the Irish Sinn Fein, Gerry Adams, spent time "schmoozing" with Castro in Havana.[19] Castro's explanation for this has been that he wants to nurture his longtime friendship with Adams and the Irish Republican Army.

In February 2002, the head of the State Department's Intelligence and Research branch, Carl Ford, testified before a Senate Intelligence Committee that Cuba is sheltering 20 Basque terrorists affiliated with the ETA. He told the committee that: "There are 20 ETA members in Cuba and they provide some degree of safe haven and support to the Colombian FARC and ELN groups." He was referring to the Marxist guerrillas of the Revolutionary Armed Forces of Colombia and the National Liberation Army. Ford also testified that an Irish nationalist arrested in Colombia last summer on charges of training the FARC guerrillas in terror tactics turned out to be a Havana resident who was acting as the Irish Republican Army's representative in Cuba.

With so much documentation and evidence, why has Cuba's true threat been "underplayed" for so many years, and why do many Americans view Castro, in his trademark olive fatigues and grimy beard, as a non-issue? More importantly, why did a 1998 official U.S. government report conclude that Cuba did not represent a significant military threat to the United States or the region?

The answer lies largely in the Clinton-Gore administration.

For years, the Defense Intelligence Agency's senior Cuba analyst, Ana Belen Montes, was a spy for Cuba. Montes not only helped draft the 1998 Cuba report, she also passed some of our most sensitive information about Cuba back to Havana. She compromised the identities of CIA agents, revealed U.S. military secrets and exposed the contents of classified files.[20]

The 44-year-old, of Puerto Rican heritage, also regularly briefed policymakers on matters involving Cuba and was well-known for advocating a softened Cuba policy. Apparently Montes succeeded, because at an April 26, 2001, House hearing, Secretary of State Colin Powell said Castro "has done good things for his people" and "he's no longer the threat he was."[21]

Montes was finally arrested in the fall of 2001, only days after the September 11th attacks, and pleaded guilty to espionage months later. The

FBI believes Montes had been a spy since at least the fall of 1996, transmitting classified information to Castro's Directorate of General Intelligence through Cuba's mission to the United Nations following the September 11th attacks. After Montes' arrest, Castro reportedly ordered a military alert in Cuba and called up the reserves, leading intelligence specialists to believe he may have had reasons to fear possible U.S. retaliation.

There is no telling how much damage Montes caused. Shortly after her arrest on September 21, 2001, the director of the Defense Intelligence Agency, Vice Admiral Tom Wilson, expressed concerns about Cuba's continuing threat to U.S. national security. "Cuba could initiate information warfare or computer-network attacks that could seriously disrupt our military," Wilson told reporters before entering a closed session of the Senate Select Committee on Intelligence.

Months later, in Congressional testimony, Carl Ford talked about Cuba's dangerous biowarfare program, which U.S. government officials have said violates Biological Weapons Convention rules. This includes the capability to produce agents such as anthrax and smallpox and other deadly substances with the potential to cause mass destruction. There have been conflicting reports, however, regarding Cuba's biological weapon capability. In June, Ford appeared to backpedal from previous pronouncements by saying Cuba's biological weapons research is an "effort" and not a full-fledged weapons "program." Ford made the comments, published in the *Miami Herald*, to the Senate Foreign Relations Subcommittee on June 5, 2002.

On the spy issue, however, there has been no backpedaling. While Montes is the highest-ranking American found guilty of spying for Castro, Cuba has had other agents operate in the United States. A military spy ring code-named "Wasp Network" operated in Miami for years. Four of its members were convicted after a lengthy federal trial. Late last year, "Wasp Network" ringleader Gerardo Hernandez received a sentence of life in prison, as did fellow spy Ramon Labanino. Two others, Fernando Gonzalez and Rene Gonzalez, were sentenced to 19 and 15 years, respectively.

The FBI has stated that this ring was directly involved in orchestrating the deliberate 1996 shoot down of the Brothers to the Rescue planes. The FBI has also charged Cuba's Directorate of General Intelligence with conducting espionage against U.S. military and civil aviation through a network of some 300 agents operating across the continent. The Federal Communications Commission (FCC) has joined the criticism, alleging that Cuba is capable of interfering with U.S. communications and air traffic control.

Decades-long denial and negligence on the part of the U.S. government is not the only thing to blame for this country's underestimation of Castro's real threat to the United States. The media has also played a huge role in shaping the way Americans see the Cuban leader. For instance, CNN, the only U.S.-based news organization with a full-time bureau in Cuba in 30 years, ignores stories about human rights or the island's dissidents in favor of soft features about ice cream, young ballerinas, Castro's birthday celebration and "cool digs" office. Other networks and local channels follow CNN's lead. For the week of June 2, 2002, the ABC affiliate in Washington, DC, Channel 7, scheduled a nostalgic visit by one of its reporters to her homeland, Cuba. The promotional advertisement made sure to tell the viewers that this visit was not about <u>politics</u>, but about <u>people</u>. The promotional showed images of cute children and eccentric, colorful, old women smoking cigars while working. A process of de-politicization of the Cuban issue seems to be making more and more headway.

After studying more than 200 CNN reports during the network's five years on the island, the Washington-based Media Research Center, a media watchdog group, concluded that CNN is "Castro's megaphone."[22] In the first few months of 2002 alone, CNN did more stories on human rights abuses by the United States against terrorist prisoners held at Guantanamo Bay than it did on Cuban dissidents in five years.

For instance, CNN gave the communist regime a major advantage, broadcasting sound bites from Castro's speeches and his spokesmen six times more frequently than non-communist groups such as Catholic Church leaders and peaceful dissidents. The network's stories also included six times as many sound bites from Cuban citizens who voiced agreement with Castro and supported his policies than from Cubans disagreeing with the government, leaving American audiences with the impression that Castro's communist government is overwhelmingly popular among the Cuban public.

During former President Jimmy Carter's landmark Cuba trip this year, all the big television networks provided pro-Castro coverage. CNN led the way with an anchorwoman saying she fretted about the "hard-line" views of President Bush and Cubans in Miami as she hoped Carter's visit might "moderate" Cuban-Americans.

Then she touted the successes of Cubans under Castro, praising their schools and admiring how every Cuban has a primary care physician who even makes house calls...and it's free! This echoed an argument used by many left-leaning politicians and academics for the past four decades. And it is the argument philosophers and political scientists have warned

95

against: People will try to convince others that the satisfaction of basic human needs and a semblance of equality are worth losing one's freedom.

At Fox News, the so-called conservative equivalent of CNN, reporting has hardly been better. During the Elian Gonzalez saga, one of its principle anchors, Shepard Smith, appeared to be a Castro apologist.

NBC went so far as to stress the weakness of recent U.S. government charges that Cuba has biological weapons, saying they were made by "hard-liners in the Bush-Cheney administration."

ABC practically sided with President Carter's assertions that the U.S. has no evidence of such weapons in Cuba, when a popular anchorman attributed the charges to "one of President Bush's political appointees to the State Department."

With a highly influential entity like the media painting such a rosy picture of Castro, it's no wonder many Americans are clueless about who this man really is – a big player in the global terror network.

---

[1] United States of America, State Department list of terrorist nations.

[2] Martin Arostegui, "Fidel May be Part of Terror Campaign," *Insight on the News Magazine*, December 3, 2001.

[3] John R. Bolton, *Beyond the Axis of Evil: Additional Threats from Weapons of Mass Destruction,* Heritage Foundation Lecture, May 6 2002, http://www.heritage.org/library/lecture/hl743.html.

[4] Esteban M. Beruvides, *Cuba: Anuario Historico*, 1959.

[5] *Agence France Presse*, "US Fugitive Says He Doesn't Expect Cuba To Send Him Home," April 3, 2002.

[6] *Agence France Presse*, "US Fugitive Doesn't Expect Cuba to Send Him Home," April 3, 2002.

[7] Federal Bureau of Investigation, list of "Wanted Fugitives," 2002.

[8] Orlando Gutierrez-Boronat, "Castro and the Terror Coalition," *Center for the Study of a National Option*, October 15, 2001.

[9] *CubaNet News*,"Fidel Castro: Comandante en Jefe de ETA," December 1999.

[10] Eugene Pons, *Castro and Terrorism, a Chronology*, School of International Studies, University of Miami, September 2001.

[11] Kiley, Frederick T. and Rochester, Stuart I., *Honor Bound, The History of American Prisoners of War in Southeast Asia, 1961-1973* (United States Naval Institute, Washington, DC, March, 1999).

[12] Cuba On-Line: An Online Database of Information, http://cuba.sis.miami.edu/, Coral Gables: Institute for Cuban and Cuban-American Studies, University of Miami, 2001.

[13] Tricontinental Conference Transcripts, University of Miami Library for Cuban Studies, http://www.cubacenter.org/media/news_articles/um_report.html.

[14] Georgia Anne Geyer, *Guerrilla Prince: The Untold Story of Fidel Castro*, Boston, Little Brown and Company, 1991.

[15] Domingo Amuchastegui, *Cuba in the Middle East: A Brief Chronology*, University of Miami, 1999.

[16] Agustin Blazquez, *Castro and International Terrorism, Covering Cuba Chronicles, Covering Cuba 2*, September 2001.

[17] Haim Shaked, *Cuba in the Middle East, a Brief Chronolgy*, Institute at the University of Miami, 1999.

[18] Jorge A. Garcia, *El Hundimiento Del Remolcador 13 De Marzo*, Endowment for Cuban-American Studies, Washington DC, 2002.

[19] Prensa Latina, "Leader of Irish Terrorist Group in Havana," *El Nuevo Herald*, December 16, 2001.

[20] Post Staff, "FBI Arrests Cuba Pentagon Spy," *Washington Post*, September 24, 2001.

[21] Carol Rosenberg, "Powell's Castro Comment Upsets Exiles Words Of Praise Came Amid Rebuke," *Miami Herald*, April 27, 2001.

[22] Rich Noyes, "Megaphone for a Dictator: CNN's Coverage of Castro's Cuba, 1997 – 2002," *Media Research Center*, May 9, 2002.

FATAL NEGLECT: The U.S. Government's Continuing Failure
to Protect American Citizens from Terrorists

Part Four: The War on Terror at Home

Department of Homeland Security:
Treating the Symptoms, Not the Disease

"Reorganization is a splendid method of producing the illusion of progress whilst creating confusion, inefficiency and demoralization."

Petronius Arbiter, 60 A.D.

"So creating a cabinet office doesn't solve the problem."[1]
[In responding to the question: "Why not create a Department of Homeland Security, as many lawmakers have suggested?"]

Ari Fleisher
White House Spokesman
March 19, 2002

"I'd probably recommend he veto it."[2]
[On how he would advise President Bush concerning legislation creating a congressionally authorized Office of Homeland Security]

Tom Ridge
Director, Office of
Homeland Security
May 30, 2002

On June 6, 2002, on the fifty-eighth anniversary of the Allied invasion of Normandy during World War II, President George W. Bush appeared before the evening prime-time television cameras to announce to the American public his proposal for the largest reorganization of the federal government since Harry S. Truman created the Department of Defense in 1947. President Bush stated: "Tonight, I propose a permanent Cabinet-level Department of Homeland Security to unite essential agencies that must work more closely together, among them, the Coast Guard, the Border Patrol, the Customs Service, Immigration officials, the Transportation Security Administration and the Federal Emergency Management Agency."[3]

The surprise announcement gave the Bush-Cheney administration's war-on-terror agenda a strong boost, taking the initiative from administration critics in the media and Congress who were uncovering a series of FBI and CIA blunders, and swinging the momentum of news reporting back in line with the administration's agenda. President Bush's proposal to reshape a large portion of the federal government dominated the news. Headline issues from just days before President Bush's announcement – such as FBI whistleblowers complaining of the Bureau's institutional obstructions of terrorism investigations – became footnote matters for staffers to hammer out in Congressional subcommittee meetings.

The magnitude of the government's reorganization is enormous and is far more complex that Truman's merging of the armed forces under one umbrella organization. Truman's armed services shared the mission of "identifying, closing with, and destroying the enemy on land, air and sea." None of the affected agencies shares the commonality of Truman's armed services. The creation of the DHS is the Bush-Cheney administration's attempt to merge a broad array of diverse government offices and functions, totaling over 170,000 employees, with an initial annual budget of $37.5 billion,[4] into one coherent, manageable organization. Current Office of Homeland Security Director Tom Ridge, who lacks any professional background or experience in counterterrorism or intelligence, appears to be slated for the new cabinet post, although there are reports indicating Mr. Ridge would like to move on. The conservative weekly *Federalist Digest* provides an interesting and important perspective on Mr. Ridge's background that may help illuminate some of the Bush-Cheney administration's post-September 11th policies:

> Tom Ridge is the "Norm Mineta" of Homeland Security, and if he is confirmed, that should give all American patriots pause. For the record, Tom Ridge has broken with the doctrine of his faith, in that he is a "pro-choice Catholic" (oxymoron), leading one to question how closely he will adhere to constitutional doctrine. Mr. Ridge has certainly broken with conservative doctrine. As a member of Congress while Ronald Reagan was in office, he voted for the so-called "nuclear freeze" and Pat Schroeder's plan to bar nuclear tests above one kiloton, to abolish the MX missile, to deny funding for the Nicaraguan Contras, and he led the charge against missile defense. He has also — ironically — failed to defend the Second Amendment — a key constitutional provision for Homeland Security — against legislative assault.

As HomSec advisor, Ridge has rejected
terrorist profiling. "To those Americans
who would lash out at your fellow citizens
simply because they worship differently or
dress differently or look differently than
you do, there is a word for such behavior:
TERRORISM," Ridge said when
appointed. He added, "We will continue to
secure liberty, as we secure this nation.
Liberty is the most precious gift we offer to
our citizens. (We reminded Mr. Ridge that
"liberty" is an unalienable, God-given right,
which the government is instituted to
protect, not something Washington
bureaucrats can dole out and restrict like
candy to children.)[5]

Debate over the Bush-Cheney administration initiative has already
shifted attention away from the month-long, steady drumbeat of failures and
miscommunications between the CIA, FBI, and other intelligence and
security agencies that occupied headlines throughout May 2002.

The concept for the proposed new department was conceived in
secret – now an operational hallmark of the Bush-Cheney administration.
For months, Congressional leaders, such as former vice-presidential
candidate Senator Joseph Lieberman of Connecticut, had proposed and
sought the creation of a new cabinet post for homeland security. The Bush-
Cheney administration had consistently rejected the notion, preferring that
Mr. Ridge act as the president's confidant and coordinator on all matters
pertaining to domestic security. Ridge faced criticism questioning his
relevance and effectiveness given that he had no real authority or organic
mechanism for making, acting on or enforcing policy or counterterrorism
action. His greatest official achievements consisted of successfully dodging
Senator Robert Byrd's attempts to have him testify on Capitol Hill about the
activities of his office, and for developing the nation's new color-coded
terrorism threat warning level. One week before the announcement of the
proposed creation of the new department, Ridge touted that he would
recommend the president veto any attempt by Congress to authorize the
creation of a homeland security cabinet post.

Meanwhile, White House Chief of Staff Andrew Card, Director of
the Office of Management and Budget Mitchell Daniels, White House
Counsel Alberto Gonzalez, and Ridge began meeting in late April, 2002, in

The White House basement bunker known as the Presidential Emergency Operations Center ("PEOC"). The secret PEOC meetings were highly compartmentalized and treated on a strict need-to-know basis. The group's formula for success required the continuation of strict secrecy protocols as plans were developed, since they feared that any leak concerning their activities and deliberations would result in a loss of initiative and open the floodgates for bureaucrats, pundits, and naysayers to critique and dissect their every move. The PEOC Group also desired an element of surprise in the announcement of the proposed new department. Secret development was not enough. Implementation of the plan required an abrupt and dramatic political and public relations move that would give the public and Capitol Hill a focus in one bold move. The sweeping scope of the plan was meant to stifle bureaucratic bickering and Congressional committee "turf wars." The group decided that a large, aggressive plan had a far better chance of surviving the authorization process than a series of smaller "fixes" which could be "nickeled and dimed" to an administrative death and would consequently make the administration's efforts to combat terrorism appear ineffectual.[6]

The PEOC Group undertook a research project: compiling, studying, and evaluating different proposals and resources that addressed how the government should respond to the threat of international terrorism on U.S. soil. The group studied Congressional bills, committee reports, open source publications and professional journals, think tank white papers, and reference material. Of the various organizational structure models considered, the PEOC Group even weighed the reassignment of the National Guard and large portions of the FBI to the new department.

While the group eventually decided not to take those actions, it seems clear that all segments of the federal government were "on the table" for possible reassignment or restructuring. What remains unclear, and is sure to be hotly debated as the authorization for the proposed department moves through Congress, are questions concerning lines of responsibility and accountability. For example, the corrupt and incompetent INS will be moved to the DHS, but not the State Department's consular division, which issues visas.[7] This failure to consolidate the visa entry requirements and enforcement functions into one responsible organization points to continuing problems and contradictions in the DHS proposal. If the creation of DHS is meant to consolidate and improve accountability in order to "harden" America from terrorist attack, there are major flaws in the plan that demand critical evaluation and reconsideration.

While few would criticize the Bush-Cheney administration's initiatives for taking positive action to improve the country's security posture, the DHS reorganization does not do enough to address the serious failures of the FBI and CIA leading up to September 11th. The proposed reorganizations are a long-term project, which will take months, if not years, to achieve. Nowhere in the plans for the DHS is there a charter for a new "National Counterterrorism Strike Force," or some other such agency, with executive law enforcement powers, heavy weapons, and all the hi-tech hardware, vehicles, aircraft and vessels required to take the terrorists head-on. The Bush-Cheney administration lost an opportunity to carve out a new, aggressive agency that would be custom designed to fight, and perhaps even interdict, acts of terrorism. Instead, the administration cobbled together a bureaucratic colossus with crossed purposes and incompatible functions, which will require even more time and energy to sort out and gain Congressional authorization before it can lift a finger to do anything about terrorism. In short, the creation of a new department could divert valuable time and resources from the urgent need to stop the next terrorist attacks.

The DHS will have four divisions:

- **Border and Transportation Security**, which would take over the INS from the Justice Department, the Coast Guard from the Transportation Department, the Customs Services from the Treasury Department, as well as the Animal and Plant Health Inspection Service from the Agriculture Department and the Federal Protective Service from the General Services Administration.

- **Emergency Preparedness and Response**, which would combine the independent Federal Emergency Management Agency, the chemical, biological, radiological, and nuclear response assets from the Health and Human Services Department; the domestic emergency support team from the Justice Department; the nuclear-incident response from the Energy Department; the Office of Domestic Preparedness from the Justice Department and the FBI's national domestic preparedness office.

- **Chemical, Biological, Radiological, and Nuclear Countermeasures**, which would oversee the work of the Lawrence Livermore National Laboratory in Livermore, California, the Health and Human Services Department's biodefense research program, and the Agriculture Department's Plum Island Animal Disease Center.

- **Information Analysis and Infrastructure Protection**, which would analyze intelligence from the FBI and CIA and absorb the Secret Service, the Critical Infrastructure Assurance Office at the Commerce Department, the Federal Computer Incident Response Center from GSA, the National Communications Systems Division at the Defense Department, and the National Infrastructure Protection Center at the FBI.[8]

Besides the enormous bureaucratic and political ripple effects of such a massive shift and consolidation of federal government operations, there will be a crucial shift in intelligence operations and policy. During his June 6, 2002, address to the nation, President Bush stated: "And this new department will review intelligence and law enforcement information from all agencies of government and produce a single daily picture of threats against our homeland. Analysts will be responsible for imagining the worst and planning to counter it."

The White House proposes that the intelligence duties of the new organization will focus on making the decisions and issuing the alerts to local police agencies and the general public. The proposed new department seems focused more on warnings and response than on being an intelligence clearinghouse or "fusion point."

The administration's plan has created only more confusion and bureaucratic layering concerning the intelligence functions of the FBI, CIA, and DHS (not to be confused with another "DHS," the Defense HUMINT Service – the Defense Department's human intelligence collection agency, that functions as both a CIA surrogate and competitor). Clearly, the new scheme reduces the DCI to the "Director of Foreign Intelligence." The FBI's recently created Office of Intelligence, headed by a CIA senior analyst, appears to be redundant when compared with the proposed DHS staff. One supposes that the new DHS Intelligence Chief would take on the role of "Director of Domestic Intelligence."

Another hotly debated point is organizational reporting and tasking authority. Will the DHS intelligence staff be able to task a CIA Clandestine Service case officer and his recruited agent, who is reporting information of interest to homeland security analysts? It is almost unimaginable for the CIA to disseminate raw intelligence to any outside organization. Raw intelligence refers to the reports filed directly from field offices before they have been analyzed and summarized by officials back at headquarters.

However, in testimony before Congress on June 27, 2002, both CIA Director Tenet and FBI Director Mueller promised to turn over all of their terrorism-related intelligence reports and even much raw intelligence data once the proposed department is running.[9] Mr. Tenet would withhold only information related to the identities of the CIA's sources, along with information on its most secret technical methods of collecting intelligence. Mr. Mueller pledged to share raw information used in grand jury investigations with the CIA, and said that he believed the Bureau would also be able to share that information with a new Homeland Security Department under the provisions of the new USA Patriot Act.

Congress is now the scene of fierce battles waged over questions of oversight and budgetary control of the new DHS. In fact, the principle stumbling block to quick passage of legislation authorizing the creation of the DHS will be the "turf battles" between members of Congress seeking control and authority over the new department – and that is a very good thing. The longer Congress and the American people have to examine and discuss the DHS, the better. Important questions remain that must be thought through, analyzed, and answered with an eye towards a variety of potentially dangerous "unintended consequences." Perhaps a sober examination of the organization, missions, and operations of the department will result in a revamping of the current proposal. Time cures many ills and in this case, the currently configured DHS is in need of a long, slow review. The PEOC Group took approximately one month to piece together the DHS, and there are few who have taken the time to thoroughly examine all of the implications, both organizationally and constitutionally, to the creation of the country's first domestic intelligence agency.

Another point of caution and careful consideration was the near universal reaction of acceptance and relief on the part of members of Congress and media pundits that the Bush-Cheney administration had "finally" proposed the creation of the DHS. Surely something must be "wrong" with the DHS when that sort of reaction is elicited from such a wide, ideologically diverse group. Only a tiny minority within Congress have even "dared" to question or voice concern over the reorganization of the government. Conservative Tennessee Congressman John J. Duncan Jr. is one of the brave few who harbors serious doubts about the new federal department, saying that he is seriously considering voting against the creation of the DHS. Duncan has a record for trying to limit the size of the federal government and is concerned that it too, like much of the federal government bureaucracy, will grow far beyond anything resembling the initial plans currently being drafted and debated. "Almost everyone in Congress wants to be seen as doing something big and lavish for homeland security, so they'll vote to create this new department. But I'm not sure it's going to make the dramatic difference that some people are hoping for," stated Duncan.[10]

Liberal California Congressman Henry A. Waxman is also troubled by the pace of DHS authorization, stating. "It leads me to believe that [lawmakers] care less about what's in the bill than that there's a bill within that time frame." Waxman is also one of the rare few on Capitol Hill who has been critical of the drive to create a cabinet level department specifically chartered for Homeland Security before the administration has even unveiled its homeland security strategy.[11]

While there appears to be no realistic hope in halting or restricting the authorization for the creation of the DHS, there is an opportunity to pause and reflect on the nature and scope of the enterprise. Unfortunately, the creation of the DHS must be viewed as a significant victory for al Qaeda. The terrorists' goals have been achieved. The acts of 19 suicide hijackers in four planes caused the largest reorganization of the U.S. government since World War II. The hijackers changed the way Americans live their lives. Their terror prompted the passage of the USA Patriot Act. Viewed from the hillsides of Pakistan or the sandy wastes of Saudi Arabia, the American government has been sent into convulsions. Certainly these are uncomfortable notions for most Americans to contemplate, but we ignore our opponents' perceptions at our peril.

The rush to endorse and enact the authorization of the DHS may say something even more disturbing about the changing national character of America's citizens. Public opinion poll after poll points to an increasing number of Americans willing to surrender their civil liberties and privacy in exchange for security. "Feeling safe" now trumps our God-given liberties as enshrined in the Constitution. A June 2002, Gallup Poll shows:

> Four in five Americans would give up some freedoms to gain security and four in ten worry terrorists will harm them or their family. About one-third of those polled favor making it easier for authorities to access private e-mail and telephone conversations. More than 70 percent are in favor of requiring U.S. citizens to carry identification cards with fingerprints, and 77 percent believe all Americans should have smallpox vaccinations.[12]

Benjamin Franklin said, "They that can give up essential liberty to obtain a little temporary safety deserve neither liberty nor safety." The DHS provides neither to a clearly "anxious" American public. Endorsement and enactment of the legislation authorizing the Bush-Cheney administration's proposed DHS is a hollow bureaucratic half-measure that generates make-work and newspaper headlines, accomplishing little in terms of the immediate threat posed to the United States. The Bush-Cheney administration has succeeded masterfully in a public relations campaign. It has failed, however, to bring swift, corrective action to the FBI or the CIA, and it has failed to create an agency tasked exclusively with combating terrorism. The Bush-Cheney administration has treated the symptoms, but ignored the far more threatening disease.

[1] White House Press Briefing by Ari Fleischer, March 19, 2002, http://www.whitehouse.gov/news/releases/2002/03/20020319-7.html#12.

[2] National Journal's *CongressDaily*, "Ridge: Bush Should Veto Cabinet-Level Security Position," May 30, 2002.

[3] White House Press Release, June 6, 2002, http://www.whitehouse.gov/news/releases/2002/06/20020606-8.html.

[4] Elizabeth Bumiller and David E. Sanger, "Bush, as Terror Inquiry Swirls, Seeks Cabinet Post on Security," *New York Times*, June 6, 2002.

[5] *Federalist* No. 02-23/24, 7 June 2002, http://www.federalist.com/pub/02-2324_Digest.html

[6] David Von Drehle and Mike Allen, "Bush Plan's Underground Architects in Silence and Stealth, Group Drafted Huge Security Overhaul," *Washington Post*, June 9, 2002.

[7] David Firestone, "Support for a New Agency but Concern About the Details," *New York Times*, June 12, 2002.

[8] Joseph Curl, "Bush Wants New Cabinet Post," *The Washington Times*, June 7, 2002.

[9] James Risen, "CIA and FBI Promise to Share Data with New Agency," *Washington Post*, June 27, 2002.

[10] David Firestone, "Conservatives Question Reorganizing Domestic Security," *New York Times*, July 1, 2002.

[11] Siobhan Gorman, "No Time to Sweat the Big Stuff?" *National Journal*, June 29. 2002.

[12] Jennifer L. Brown, "Poll: U.S. Security More Important," *Associated Press*, Tuesday, June 11, 2002.

Unholy Deeds:
Muslim Charities in the United States and Their Connection to Terrorist Organizations

Ever since the events of September 11th, we have become, overnight, a nation of linguists and religious scholars. Media talking heads miraculously developed an expertise in the subtleties of Arabic and in the various groups, sects and nuances of Islam. We are learning – all too deeply and tragically – the rich semantics of the concept of "jihad," and we are being told, by so-called "moderate," "rational" practitioners of Islam, that "jihad" is a spiritual struggle, an inner focus on attaining holiness, and not "holy war," as we might have believed on and after September 11th. We are refamiliarizing ourselves with "fatwa," and we are discovering, on mushrooming Islamic sites on the Internet, that Osama bin Laden belongs to a "puritanical" sect of Islam, "Wahhabism." They are the fanatics, the bad guys. The Wahhabis, on the other side, maintain that theirs is the true path to holiness. We found out that the sinister-sounding "al Qaeda" means nothing more than "base," "camp," or "headquarters." Some are discovering that not all Arabs are Muslim.

Even President Bush recently has been trying to define the terms of the conflict more narrowly. Our "enemies" are the "extremists," the "fanatics" of Islam, the "radical elements." Yet to the innocents who lost their lives and their families it matters little what side of Islam the killers were on. To President Bush, what matters is the politics of cultural interaction, and in not "offending" the sensibilities of a vast group of so-called law-abiding, peace-loving people.

The public has been subjected to a cultural, sociological and religious "crash course" confused by shifting meanings and relative interpretations. Things are not what they seem, and words mean more, or less, than what they apparently mean. If only these forays into language and culture happened strictly in lecture halls and not as a consequence of a violent and criminal loss of life.

On Christmas Day 1992, Steven Emerson, then a CNN reporter on assignment in Oklahoma City, walked by chance into a meeting of the Muslim Arab Youth Association at the city's convention center. As he recounts in his book *American Jihad: The Terrorists Living Among Us*[1], to his amazement, he heard speaker after speaker calling for "jihad" in America, for killing the "infidels" and destroying Western civilization.

111

Soon after the first bombing of the World Trade Center in 1993, Emerson embarked on a project for PBS that sought to connect the dots between the bombing and what he had witnessed in Oklahoma City. The project first materialized in a documentary on radical Islam and terrorism in the United States. What he discovered was that "international terrorist organizations of all sorts had set up shop here, in America."[2] Simultaneously, he learned how members of these organizations used religious, charitable and even academic institutions as a front for sponsoring terrorism, taking advantage of American educational institutions' quest for "multiculturalism" and "diversity."[3]

During his project, Emerson learned what the Bush-Cheney administration later was forced to finally confront and combat after September 11th: how another Islamic concept, "Zakah," has been used, deceptively, to collect money for terrorist organizations such as Hamas, Hezbollah and al-Qaeda.

Muslims are required by their faith to donate each year approximately 2.5 percent of their accumulated wealth to assist the needy and the poor. No central collection point is mandated for this obligatory giving – the "Zakah" – so individuals can make direct contributions to charities. However, the local mosque is typically the location where the money is collected and dispensed.

Numerous Islamic charitable organizations, some centered around mosques, operate throughout the United States under the Internal Revenue Service (IRS) regulations but with little further public or government oversight. Responding to political and cultural trends, the IRS had shown little interest in auditing Islamic charities before September 11th. Emerson goes to great lengths to emphasize that most Islamic charities run legitimate operations.

However, under seemingly benign, sentimental names such as "mercy," "relief," "development" – a shibboleth word in American culture – and the pretense of fundraising for orphaned children, some of these organizations have been known to divert the money they collect to terrorist groups. Nine days after the terrorist attacks, Judicial Watch asked the IRS and the Bush-Cheney administration to conduct audits of several Islamic charities suspected of laundering money to fund terrorist operations on American soil. Among them was the Holy Land Foundation for Relief and Development, based in Richardson, Texas, whose assets were finally frozen by the Bush-Cheney administration in December 2001.

The *Dallas Morning News* published a report at that time about a previously undisclosed FBI memorandum which showed an active investigation of these charities dating back to 1993, an eventful year of terrorism in the United States. In February 1993, the World Trade Center was bombed. Six people died and more than 1000 were injured. During the summer of that year, a terrorist plot to blow up a bridge, several tunnels and an FBI building in New York City was uncovered. The eight years that passed between those events, the FBI memorandum and the September 11th attacks show the Clinton-Gore and the Bush-Cheney administrations' inability, or unwillingness, to dive into the murky waters of ethnic and religious hatreds, and risk their political futures by offending or alienating other religious groups or cultures.

As previously detailed, an FBI agent in the Chicago FBI Field Office, Robert G. Wright, Jr., specialized in tracking the activities of U.S. charities suspected of funneling money to overseas terrorist organizations. Special Agent Wright spent years following the money trail, yet his investigation was shut down by his superiors long before September 11th. Months after the attacks and months after the first raid on U.S. charities suspected of funneling money to terrorists, the FBI still prohibits Special Agent Wright from talking publicly about his frustrated investigation.

Some of the facts, however, are coming to light. According to a 1993 FBI memo, federal agents eavesdropping on a meeting in Philadelphia between Holy Land officials and Hamas activists, learned that the two parties were there to "discuss increasing funds for the families of suicide bombers, prisoners and the wounded."[4]

The irony of terrorists raising money under the provisions of the U.S. tax code which require taxpayers to essentially subsidize the charitable contributions is not lost on most Americans. There are even more outlandish examples of U.S. taxpayer subsidies awarded to terrorist front groups posing as charitable organizations. The Holy Land Foundation for Relief and Development had applied for and received federal grant money through the U.S. Agency for International Development. Similarly, according to Judicial Watch, the Islamic African Relief Agency (IARA) received two U.S. State Department grants in 1998 worth $4.2 million dollars. IARA reportedly transferred money to Mercy International, another non-profit organization that purchased the vehicles used by bin Laden to bomb the U.S. embassies in Kenya and Tanzania in 1998.[5]

As Terry Eastland points out in his review of Emerson's book, "Raising money is not the only purpose served by establishing 'charitable' fronts."[6] What terrorist organizations crave most is a cultural shift, an acceptance by the host culture, a legitimacy that can help disguise the work of providing for terrorist activities. Taking advantage of contemporary America's institutionalized guilt about its former treatment of minorities, these fronts work from within, paradoxically, to annihilate that very same host culture that enables them to exist and prosper.

[1] Emerson, Steven; *"American Jihad: The Terrorists Living Among Us,"* The Free Press, NY; (February 2002).

[2] Quoted by Terry Eastland, "American Jihad: The Terrorists Living Among Us," *Commentary*, No.3, Vol. 113 (March 1, 2002): 77.

[3] Now dubbed the "American Cassandra" for his prophetic vision of the course "jihad" would take in the U.S., Emerson was vilified as a "bigot" and "racist," was banned from NPR; an Islamic group has apparently tried to kill him.

[4] Richard Williamson and Matthew Sinclair, "Islamic Charities under Spotlight's Red Glare," *The Non-Profit Times*, No. 1, Vol. 16 (January 1, 2002): 1.

[5] Judith Miller, "U.S. Contends Muslim Charity Is Tied To Hamas," *New York Times*, August 25, 2000.

[6] Eastland, 78.

FATAL NEGLECT: The U.S. Government's Continuing Failure to Protect American Citizens from Terrorists

Part Five: What the Future May Hold

Winds of War: Bioterrorism

The Nightmare Scenario:

He stood for a moment on the corner of Court and Tremont streets, observing the gaggles of people purposefully making their way to work. Several inches of snow had fallen the day before, but the streets and walkways had been quickly and continuously plowed, leaving behind a dirty residue of slush.

Much of the activity centered around the odd-shaped brick building in front of him on the plaza of City Hall. He sloshed across Court Street, briefcase in hand, blending in as businessman, with his long overcoat providing protection against the brisk December wind. Though Christmas was only 9 days away, it was still too early in the day for shoppers. At the entrance to the building, he stopped to exchange a dollar bill for a token. With a momentary glance at the flower vendor and the string of lights adorning a small fake Christmas tree, he joined the line of commuters passing through the turnstile and descending the stairs into the bowels of Boston's MBTA subway system.

At the bottom of stairs, he briefly surveyed the scene before him, though it was unnecessary. He had been here on the first level of the Government Center station twice before, at the exact same time of day. The other instances had been dry runs. This was for real.

At 8:00 in the morning, the platform for the Green Line trains was crowded with people. Here, separate tracks carried commuters in one direction to other stations in the heart of Boston, such as Park Street or Boylston, or in an opposite direction to North Station and ultimately Lechmere. On a lower level were trains for the Blue Line, but it was the "wall" on the Green Line level that originally caught his attention.

Situated much like the crossbar of the letter "A," the sides being formed by the intersecting subway lines, the wall was a ceiling-high barrier located at the far end of the station platform, and it effectively blocked the view of the tracks beyond. Yet, to his satisfaction, he had noted on a previous "dry run" that it was easy to walk around the wall to the other side. Decorated with small orange and red ceramic tiles, the wall was almost certainly not there to improve the appearance of the station, but instead had been erected for purpose of signifying the stopping point for the lead outgoing car. He had another purpose in mind.

This early in the morning, trains were either entering or leaving the station every few minutes. He timed the sequences until he was sure he had at least the 60 seconds he would need to do the job.

As he waited for the right moment, the train to Lechmere left the station, and shortly afterwards, the train to Park Station entered, drained the platform of people, and left also. With nobody near him, he stepped around the wall and into the semi-darkness beyond. Placing his briefcase down and reaching into the pocket of his coat, he quickly removed a flat glass container about 3 inches square and an inch high. He peeled the paper off the bottom, exposing a sticky tape surface underneath, and pressed the sealed container down on the rail closest to him, applying enough pressure for the box to stick to the rail, while being careful not to crack the glass. He had debated about wiping the rail first, but the box only needed to remain in place for a couple of minutes, and the rail would be clean enough anyway, due to constant use.

He then picked up his briefcase, stepped back around the wall, crossed the platform to the stairs, and left the station. The entire process had taken a little more than 30 seconds. No one had paid any attention to him.

At 8:21 am, the next train to Park Street entered the station, crushing the container between the wheels of the train and releasing the contents of the box to the atmosphere. Inside the container were 100 grams of a fine white powder, Variola major, the virus that causes smallpox. Millions of spores of the deadly and highly contagious agent were dispersed by the wheels and ushered into the platform area by the draft of the train. The particles, under 5 microns in diameter, were inhaled by people waiting on the platform, and by those entering and exiting the trains. Once lodged in the lungs, the microbes began to multiply, slowly overwhelming the immune systems of the unsuspecting commuters.

Highly contagious and virtually undetectable in early stages, the infection spread relentlessly through coughing, sneezing, talking, and direct contact, even touching of clothing. The particles of virus would continue to infect people in the station for at least a couple of days, stirred up by air currents and indiscriminately attacking holiday shoppers, as well as those making their way to and from work. This Christmas would be remembered as the time the United States suffered its most serious disaster ever.

An unlikely scenario?

Not at all. The described attack is certainly feasible, and could be accomplished today by a terrorist group with the ability to produce – or buy – the dried and powdered smallpox. And with one smallpox carrier typically infecting up to 20 other people, the consequences are also realistic.

The miracle is that it has not happened yet. Epidemiologists have found that *Variola major* "needs a population of about 200,000 people living within a 14-day travel time from one another" in order to keep its life cycle going.[1] Episodes would have died out naturally in the days when walking and horseback were the primary modes of transportation between villages, but Boston and just about every other city and town in the world today fit that requirement.

While handling *Variola major* requires extreme care because it is both virulent and contagious, with the proper laboratory containment, the agent can be grown by injecting the virus into chicken eggs, which provide the necessary proteins and nutrients. The eggs are sealed with paraffin and incubated in thermostatic ovens, which keep them stabilized. They are then freeze-dried and milled into particles with diameters measured in microns.[2]

Laboratories capable of growing and processing dried smallpox exist in the United States and Russia. They are also almost certain to be found in countries known to support terrorism, such as China, Iran, Iraq, Libya, North Korea, and Syria, as well as other nations such as India, Israel, and Pakistan.[3]

No weapon in the hands of a terrorist is potentially more devastating to the population of the United States than a bioweapon. According to Dr. Ken Alibek, President of Advanced Biosystems, Inc., deadly viruses and bacteria can be obtained from more than 1,500 microbe "banks" around the world.[*][4]

By allowing other countries, such as the Soviet Union and Iraq, to develop potent offensive weapons while U.S. biological arsenals were destroyed, and offensive development efforts were shelved, we have created seemingly insurmountable challenges and have left ourselves vulnerable to the efforts of a single determined individual carrying a glass container filled

---

[*] Dr. Karatjan Alibekov was formerly Deputy Chief of Biopreparat, which was responsible for the Soviet Union's bioweapons program. When he defected to the United States in 1992, he took the name of Ken Alibek, and ultimately became President of Advanced Biosystems, Inc., a subsidiary of Hadron, Inc. Dr. Alibek remains one of the world's foremost authorities on biological agents.

with a white powder.

In the words of retired Major General Philip K. Russell, M.D., former Commander of the U.S. Army Medical Research and Development Command, "If smallpox really got going, people should be most concerned about a lack of effective leadership on the part of their government." *5

Why biological weapons? The answer is easy. They are cheaper to produce than nuclear weapons and more lethal than chemicals. The advantage of a biological agent is that only a comparatively small quantity is required (e.g., 100 grams of *Variola major* powder might equate to hundreds of kilograms of a chemical agent for a particular target and still have a more devastating, long-term effect). It can be dispersed, preferably by aerosol, in a subway or any place where people collect; and the person doing the dispersing can be long gone before the effects of the attack become evident. There is also little risk of detection while the microbes are being released; and unless the terrorist group chooses to identify itself, determining where the attack came from can be difficult.

Another advantage is that the attack can occur in a location where people are likely to scatter geographically, thus spreading the disease to other cities and other countries. A subway meets the criterion as a prime target, but an international airport could have even more widespread effects.[6] Bioterrorism lends itself to hoaxes as well, which can tie up resources and cause the public to panic.

Historically, bioweapons have not been used on a large scale against people in warfare, mainly because of the difficulty controlling "who" becomes infected. Sunlight and wind, for instance, can play a role in the direction and potency of an attack. Other obstacles have been the somewhat sophisticated microbiology required to isolate and grow the microbes in sufficient quantities, and the engineering required to develop effective delivery systems. Biological agents must be either inhaled, consumed, or taken in through cuts on the skin. Of the potential dispersion methods, 1) dispersing an agent into the air, particularly in a confined area, such as a building or a subway, and 2) contaminating food are logical choices. In the

---

* In fairness, at the time he made the statement, Dr. Russell was referring to administrations prior to that of President George W. Bush. An expert on infectious diseases and author of more than 100 papers on the subject, he currently serves as a special advisor on vaccine development and production in the Office of Public Health Services, directed by Donald A. Henderson, M. D. Dr. Russell was named to the position by U.S. Department of Health and Human Services Secretary Tommy G. Thompson.

case of a building, the heating and air conditioning system may even help to disseminate the pathogen.

Today, the barriers limiting the use of bioweapons have been lowered. With the disappearance of vast numbers of scientists from the Soviet Union, the technology has, without question, become available to various terrorist groups and nations. Not only that, seed stocks can be produced from nature; and the organisms themselves can be obtained from companies that sell them, as well as by stealing them from legitimate, government-approved laboratories.

In the recent past, the most virulent viruses, bacteria, and toxins could still be purchased by almost anyone from the American Type Culture Collection (ATCC), currently located in Manassas, Virginia. One may have had to demonstrate a connection with a lab or medical facility, but how difficult would that have been for a scientist in Iraq or Iran? Without question, deadly pathogens from ATCC and other sources are in the hands of technicians throughout the world. And the equipment necessary to create bioweapon materials is widely available.

In building a weapon, terrorists have a wide number of choices in terms of agents and delivery systems. More than a dozen microorganisms offer potential for development into bioweapons. Not only that, pathogens can be combined into a single compound (Ebola with smallpox, for example), which would make the use of a vaccine impractical.

A smallpox vaccine, even if sufficient quantities were available (less than 10 percent of the United States could be vaccinated today), would be ineffective against the combination.

Include genetic engineering as a possibility, and it is easy to see why vaccines are far from a perfect solution for protecting the United States against a bioterrorist attack.* [See Appendix A for a discussion of the different types of viruses, bacteria, and toxins, including *Bacillus anthracis* (anthrax) and *Yersinia pestis* (plague), either of which could wipe out a

---

* The Soviet Union experimented with peptides, "strings of amino acids which perform various functions in our bodies, from regulating hormones and facilitating digestion to directing our immune systems." The Soviet Union was successful in synthesizing genes for a regulatory peptide which, in large quantities, could damage the myelin sheath that protects the transmission of electric signals from the brain and spinal cord to the rest of the body. The present status of this development is unknown, but such a deadly weapon would not be in violation of the Biological Weapons Convention, since it would be based on compounds occurring naturally in the human body.[7]

significant portion of the U.S. population.] Bioweapons can even be used against livestock and crops grown in fields; and they can be devised not to kill, but instead to incapacitate – for example, to neutralize front-line troops from resisting a conventional ground attack.

After the September 11th attacks against the World Trade Center in New York City and the Pentagon in Arlington, Virginia, and the subsequent anthrax attack mailings, our shield of invincibility as a nation has dissolved.

Can we expect another bioterrorism attack on the United States anytime soon? According to Bill Patrick, renowned bioweapons expert, it's only a matter of time.[*] "Whoever is doing this [mailing of anthrax] is probably loading up in the lab, making material for the next attack. Only, I think another means of dispersal will be used. The mail is not all that effective."[8]

A killer combination of corruption and incompetence on the part of the U.S. government has allowed this country to become vulnerable to a bioterror attack. Among other glaring errors, U.S. officials:

- Permitted lethal pathogens to be sold for decades – by mail – to known terrorist countries;

- Ignored the continued development of bioweapons by the Soviet Union, Iraq, and other countries, and permitting stockpiles to exist;

- Shut down labs in the United States devoted to developing biologicals as offensive weapons, thereby causing our scientists to "fall behind" in terms of technology;

- Failed to develop a line of defense at the health-care level (doctors, nurses, and hospitals) for diagnosing and responding to disease outbreaks caused by biological agents;

---

[*] William C. Patrick III was formerly Chief of the Product Development Division of the Agent Development and Engineering Directorate for the U.S. Army Biological Warfare laboratories at Fort Detrick, Maryland. After his retirement in 1969, he formed his own company, BioThreats Assessments, and has been a consultant to the FBI, Defense Intelligence Agency, and CIA, as well as private organizations, on biological weapons. He is considered to be one of the nation's top authorities on the use of anthrax and other agents in bioterrorism.

- Refused to fund the production of sufficient quantities of vaccines for the most likely agents to be used as weapons, such an anthrax and smallpox;* and

- Until recently, were unwilling accept bioweapons as a legitimate threat to the United States.

The *Five-Year Interagency Counterterrorism and Technology Crime Plan*, prepared by the Department of Justice in 1999, found that "By far, our greatest deficiency in regard to WMD [Weapons of Mass Destruction] lies in our limited capability to detect, prevent, and respond to the use of biological agents."[9] Unfortunately, even after the anthrax attacks of October 2001, such a statement is as true today as it was then.

The clock is ticking.

U.S. Foreign Policy: See No Evil

The potential for the "nightmare" bioterrorism scenario described at the beginning of this section were sown more than 30 years and seven presidents ago...

The Soviet Union

In 1969, President Richard M. Nixon made a startling announcement: "all existing biological weapons stockpiles in the United States would be destroyed."[10] Nixon, badly in need of a public relations victory during Vietnam, publicly cited humanitarian reasons for his new policy. Privately, however, Nixon had been convinced by his Defense Secretary William Laird and the Joint Chiefs of Staff that biological weapons did not provide the same level of military effectiveness as did the United States' nuclear power.[11]

"We'll never use the damn germs, so what good is biological warfare as a deterrent," Nixon rhetorically asked speechwriter William

---

* While genetic engineering and mixed compounds are a possibility, the degree of laboratory sophistication required to produce such agents suggests that a biological terrorist attack is most likely to involve either anthrax or smallpox, for which the pathogens are available and can be grown. For this reason, the United States needs to have sufficient quantities of vaccine on hand to combat both diseases. Having said that, as mentioned, vaccines are probably not a long-term solution as a biodefense system.

Safire. "If somebody uses germs on us, we'll nuke 'em."[12]

What Nixon and his military strategists failed to realize is that with the loss of the offensive biological warfare capabilities came the loss of technical expertise as to how these weapons work, expertise vital to the capability of developing an adequate defense.

Compounding the lack of foresight with respect to the value of biological weapons, U.S. intelligence badly underestimated the Soviet Union's (now Russia's) bioweapons (BW) program and its willingness to continue its development despite numerous promises to the contrary.

Following World War II, the United States pursued the development of offensive biological weapons with vigor, investing more than $726 million in a program the equal of two other competing superpowers, the Soviet Union and Great Britain.[13] However, in 1969, when both the United States and Great Britain voluntarily agreed to BW disarmament, that left the Soviet Union as the lone star in the biological arms race. And it had no intention of giving up that status.

Nixon and his advisors believed otherwise. They felt they could apply international pressure to the Soviets to force them to comply with an international treaty banning the development, use and stockpiling of offensive biological weapons. Eventually, the Nixon Administration succeeded, but it was only a short-term public relations victory at best. The United States was desperate to secure an agreement and the Soviets knew it. In a shrewd bit of political maneuvering, they refused to sign any treaty that involved enforcement procedures. U.S. officials ultimately decided "it was better to have a treaty with no verification, than to have no treaty at all."[14]

As a result, the Biological and Toxin Weapons Convention (BWC)*

---

* Signed by 143 nations in 1972, including the United States and the Soviet Union, the Biological and Toxin Weapons Convention (its full name) went into effect in March 1975. The agreement prohibited research and development using deadly agents, except for defensive purposes. However, it had no teeth, no provisions for inspection, and was based on a pledge by the each country to honor the provisions of the accord. President Richard Nixon had unilaterally ended the U.S. offensive bioweapons program in November 1969, but with the 1972 Convention, administration officials hoped that the Soviet Union would shut down its offensive program as well. *It did not.* As we learned with the defection of Vladimir Pasechnik, former director of the Institute of Ultra-Pure Biopreparations, to the United Kingdon (UK) in 1989 and Ken Alibek to the United States in 1992, the Soviet Union not only continued such research, but produced tons of the world's most lethal pathogens, developed the delivery systems, and aimed their missiles at U.S. cities.[15]

was developed and signed by all three superpowers in 1972 without any procedures for ensuring its enforcement. It would take three additional years to earn ratification. For the Soviets, "the cheating began before the ink was dry."[16] One year after signing the BWC agreement, the Soviet Union created Biopreparat, a compendium of forty research and production facilities designed to cure existing diseases, and to build new ones.[17]

Over the next three decades, the Soviets would build the most successful biological weapons program on earth. In addition to producing mass quantities of thousands of dangerous agents such as anthrax and smallpox, the United States would ultimately learn that the Soviets were genetically engineering "super diseases," such as *Yersinia pestis*, or plague, that could not be cured with antiobiotics. Perhaps more importantly to U.S. national security, the Soviets had also found a way to weaponize these diseases and deliver them to American soil by loading the microbe of choice onto intercontinental ballistic missiles, "and they had taken the political decision to use them in the event of an all-out war."[18]

Throughout this period, a killer combination of naiveté, incompetence and timidity kept the United States from stopping the steamrolling Soviet BW program. Among the foreign policy mistakes committed during this period:

- "For the first fifteen years of the Soviet's massive BW program, the CIA had uncovered virtually no clear evidence of its existence.[19]

- Despite evidence from U.S. satellite intelligence that the Soviets were cheating on the BWC, the State Department and White House ignored the evidence because, according to former Defense Secretary Laird, "They didn't want to accuse the USSR of treaty violations because they feared they would lose their other programs," such as SALT 1 and SALT 2, "by making such accusations."* [20]

- In 1975, Soviet defector Arkady Shevchenko, a senior Soviet official with the United Nations, told U.S. officials the Soviets were deliberately violating the BWC because it had no enforcement procedures. The United States took no action.[21]

---

* SALT = Strategic Arms Limitation Talks. The initial round of talks began in November 1969.

- "The worst accident in the history of biological weapons production"[22] occurred on April 2, 1979, when several pounds of anthrax were accidentally released through an air duct at a military facility in Sverdlovsk, killing 200 to 300 people. The Soviets were caught in a lie and cover-up, but the United States failed to take meaningful action. Congress passed a resolution calling on President Jimmy Carter to take a hard line against the Soviets, but Carter instead sided with then Deputy Secretary of State Warren Christopher, who believed that a confrontation might "embarrass the Soviets."[23]

- In the late 1980's, the United States compiled satellite evidence proving the Soviets were test-launching missiles with refrigeration units attached, a clear indication that biological weapons were involved, yet President George H. Bush's administration refused to confront them because, according to a former CIA official, "some senior CIA analysts still did not believe the Soviets had a BW programme."[24]

- The Reagan Administration "officially complained" six times to the Soviet government about its offensive BW program, but took no effective action to stop it.[25]

- Due to the era of good feeling following the meltdown of the Cold War, President George H. Bush's administration kept the BW issue in the "pending tray."[26]

- As previously indicated, defector Vlademir Pasechnik, a leading Soviet biochemist, told British and American officials in 1989 that the Soviets had violated the BWC, despite their protestations, and continued to do so right through Gorbachev's reign. Pasechnik also confirmed the Soviets were engineering microbes, against which the West would be defenseless, and that the "United States was a so-called deep target."[27]

- Ultimately, Margaret Thatcher persuaded President George H. Bush to take a more forceful stance against the Soviet Union, demanding that the Soviets allow inspections of their Biopreparat facility. Gorbachev agreed; however, during their tour, Western inspectors "were met with denials, evasions, and large rooms that had been stripped of equipment and cleaned up."[28] They did, however, manage to uncover enough evidence to verify Pasechnik's contention that the Soviets were still involved in the production of offensive biological weapons.

This inspection of the Soviet Union's civilian facility, Biopreparat, would be the last inspection allowed for American and British officials. With the exception of information contained in scattered intelligence reports that hinted at a significant Russian BW program, the extent to which Russia continues its pursuit of offensive BW power has remained a well-kept secret, especially with regard to military installations.

Though former Russian leader Boris Yeltsin, following Gorbachev's lead, pledged to destroy Russia's BW program, the same Ministry of Defense and Biopreparat officials who developed the program during the Cold War were left in power years after Boris Yeltsin assumed leadership.[29]

"Today, when I read the recent work of my former colleagues in scientific publications, it is hard for me to imagine that their efforts have no relation to biological weapons," says Ken Alibek, the Russian defector who once ran the mighty Soviet biowarfare program. [30]

The Soviet/Russian BW problem is significant to U.S. security for three reasons. First, it has become increasingly clear that Russia is still willing to violate international law and to lie to U.S. officials, which calls into question its trustworthiness as an international partner. Second, while relations with Russia are currently cordial, a future conflict with the Russians (or its allies) would leave the United States open to a biological attack, as the Russian government has already expressed a willingness to use the weapons under wartime conditions. While according to Dr. Alibek, Russia is less of a concern than other countries today, he also indicted that, in his opinion, bioweapons would be used "as a last resort."[31] Third, after the break-up of the Soviet Union, more than 10,000 scientists who had been involved in the Soviet BW program were without jobs and began to market their services to other countries. Many have disappeared.

"One can guess that they've ended up in Iraq, Syria, Libya, China, Iran, perhaps Israel, perhaps India ? But no one really knows, probably not even the Russian government," says Alibek.[32]

In addition to the proliferation of Soviet BW technical expertise, the United States has also discovered that the former Soviet Union's research facilities are "poorly guarded and susceptible to corruption and theft." [33] At the top of the list of microbes causing anxiety is smallpox, which can allegedly only be found in two places, Atlanta, Georgia and Koltsovo, Russia. Very likely, however, the pathogen is in the hands of a number of other countries.

127

To help stop the leakage of BW expertise to rogue nations, the U.S. government structured a program to develop non-military jobs for Russian weapons scientists in the United States to prevent them from acquiring military jobs elsewhere. However, according to the General Accounting Office (GAO), the program has been largely ineffective. In fact, Russian scientists have received only 37 percent of the $63.5 million spent during the programs first four years. Furthermore, the GAO analysis also revealed that program funds were being distributed to Russian scientists *still working on military projects for Moscow*.[34] They have also asked for assistance from the Russian government to increase lab security. Unclear is whether or not such measures have proven effective.

Of course such programs would not even be necessary if the United States had made a serious attempt to disarm the Soviets at any point during the last three decades. As it stands, U.S. policy allowed Russia to gain a significant advantage in biological warfare while enabling a flood of Soviet scientists to hone their crafts before taking them to other nations, such as Iraq.

Iraq

In the early 1990's, while Vladimir Pasechnik was educating his American and British intelligence officials about the scope of the Soviet Union's offensive biological weapons program, the conflict in the Middle East was already underway. Of course, one of the significant goals of the United States "Operation Desert Storm" was the wholesale destruction of Iraqi President Saddam Hussein's capacity for producing and delivering weapons of mass destruction, including biological weapons. For Hussein's attitude extended beyond the Soviet "willingness" to use biological weapons during wartime.

According to Richard Butler, the former chairman of the United Nations Special Commission (UNSCOM) in charge of dismantling Hussein's weapons of mass destruction, Hussein was "addicted" to biological warfare and "holds a deep belief that somehow these weapons will make him the leader of the world."[35]

To help achieve his dream of unlimited power, Hussein assembled what the Pentagon called, "the largest and most advanced biological warfare program in the Middle East"[36] and demonstrated a willingness to use it.

"What did they have?" asked Butler during a PBS interview. "Everything. Anthrax, plague, *Botulinum*, gangrene and camelpox," to name a few."[37]

According to Mangold and Goldberg, further assessments of the Iraqi Gulf War inventory of germs prepared for use yielded the following findings: [38]

- 157 bombs (100 filled with *Botulinum* toxin, 50 with anthrax, seven with *Aflatoxin*).

- 25 Scud/Al Hussein missile warheads (16 filled with *Botulinum* toxin, five with anthrax, four with *Aflatoxin*).

- Several 122 mm rockets filled with anthrax, *Botulinum* toxin and *Aflatoxin*.

- Spray tanks and drop tanks ready for fitting to fighters or remotely piloted vehicles (drones) capable of spraying 2,000 litres of anthrax over a target.

- Four 155 mm artillery shells used in trials for ricin dissemination.

- An unknown and unspecified quantity of primitive delivery systems for the dissemination of freeze-dried plague bacteria; and possibly smallpox.

Recognizing the significant threat posed by Hussein's biological arsenal, the U.S. military severely damaged Hussein's production capacity by blasting suspected BW facilities during the Gulf War. And when the Iraqis agreed to a cease-fire, chief among the demands made of Hussein was unfettered access to production facilities and permission for inspectors to locate and destroy any documentation, hardware and software related to Weapons of Mass Destruction.[39]

However, what was supposed to be a short-term postwar inspection process dragged on for more than seven years. During that time, the Iraqis lied about the program, delayed inspections and violated their agreements, just as the Soviets had for the prior 20 years. To date, the United Nations and the United States do not have any idea how sophisticated Hussein's BW capabilities are because he has refused to allow any inspectors into his facilities since 1997.

"The degree of resistance that the Iraqis showed to our investigation of their biological weapons program exceeded all other deceptions and resistances," said UNSCOM's Butler.[40]

129

While the Iraqi's were interfering with the inspection process, they were getting assistance from three members of the UN Security Council - Russia, China and France. Russia, in particular, had a vested interest in weakening the sanctions on Iraq, as the two countries had developed into close trading partners. Additionally, Iraq owed the Soviets more than $7 billion for weapons it had acquired during the Cold War.[41] Many times during confrontations between UNSCOM and Iraq, the Russians would argue for more lenient criteria by which the Iraqis were to be judged, especially with respect to the oil embargo, the easing of which could provide cash for Iraq to pay Russia for its BW program.

At the same time, however, Russian "assistance" to the Iraqi cause was not limited to mere lobbying.

According to a February 1998 *Washington Post* story, UNSCOM inspectors found "highly unsettling evidence of a 1995 agreement by the Russian government to sell Iraq sophisticated fermentation equipment that could be used to develop biological weapons."[42] Furthermore, the article revealed, "U.S. intelligence agencies have privately warned UN officials that Russian intelligence operatives are spying on the commission and its personnel in New York and overseas," and that "the Russian spy agency, which was formerly headed by Foreign Minister Primakov, may have passed some of the information it collects directly to Iraq."[43]

This evidence indicated to U.S. officials that despite protestations of innocence and promises to the United States, the Russians not only continued to bolster their already fearsome BW program, but that they were also aiding the Iraqis well into the Yeltsin regime. At the center of this covert and subversive effort was Yevgeny Primakov. Intelligence reports obtained by the UN indicated that the Russian foreign minister was "on the take," receiving personal payoffs from Iraq in exchange for his assistance.[44]

As far as the Iraqis are concerned, the Russian official earned his keep.

Seven years after the Gulf War, the U.S. government acknowledged the failure of UNSCOM and its own failed military and foreign policy, when it admitted, "On the basis of the last seven years' experience, the world's experts conclude that enough production components and data remain hidden and enough expertise has been retained or developed to enable Iraq to resume development and production of WMD."[45]

"[Hussein's] stance on weapons of mass destruction and the failure of the community of nations to deal with him means that he holds a lit match, and with each passing day he brings it closer to the fuse," writes

Butler in his book, *The Greatest Threat*.[46]

Alibek agrees. "Iraq is by far the biggest threat. Hussein knows that the United States wants to eliminate him and is liable to do anything."[47]

Other Rogue Nations

Though Iraq is the most high profile beneficiary of Soviet "generosity" with respect to biological weapons, there are others. In 1980, the Soviet Union was the only government to have been named by the United States as violating the BWC. By 1995, 17 countries were believed to have launched BW programs.[48] Many of these nations owe the genesis of their biological weapons technology to the Soviets and Russians.

"For many years, the Soviet Union organized courses in genetic engineering and molecular biology for scientists from Eastern Europe, Cuba, Libya, India, Iran and Iraq among others," explained Alibek in his book, *Biohazard*. "Many of them now head biotechnology programs in their own countries."[49]

One such country, Cuba, has emerged as a particularly virulent threat to U.S. national security. Thanks to the support of the Soviets, Cuba developed what has been described as the most advanced biomedical industry in Latin America. Defectors and analysts in the past have suggested that suspicious activities were being undertaken by these facilities, a contention that has recently proven prophetic.

Though a Clinton-Gore administration report in 1998 concluded that Cuba was not a significant military threat to the United States, President George W. Bush's administration has accumulated evidence that, in fact, Cuba has at least a limited offensive biological warfare program and is allegedly attempting to transfer this technology to other enemies of the United States.[50] According to John Bolton, Undersecretary of State for Arms Control, Cuban dictator "Fidel Castro visited Iraq, Syria and Libya last year, all of which, like Cuba, are on the State Department list of state sponsors of terrorism."[51]

While the extent to which Castro has built an offensive BW program is unclear, his laboratories do have the means, courtesy of the Soviets, to genetically alter viruses. During a tour of a Soviet BW laboratory in 1981, Castro learned the Soviets had discovered a way to genetically alter *E. Coli* bacteria to produce interferon. It was believed, at the time, that interferon was a key to curing cancer.

Soviet Premier Brezhnev, impressed by Castro's enthusiasm, offered the Cuban dictator assistance in developing his own program, arranging for the transfer of germs, equipment and expertise to Cuba. "Within a few years, Cuba had one of the most sophisticated genetic engineering labs in the world."[52] Now, that technical expertise renders Cuba one of the most dangerous state sponsors of terrorism in the world.

So, this being the case, why did the Clinton-Gore administration overlook the Cuban threat? According to Bolton, one of the authors of the 1998 report exonerating Cuba, Ana Belen Montes, a senior analyst for the Defense Intelligence Agency, was a spy for Cuba. "Montes not only had a hand in drafting the 1998 Cuba report but also passed some of our most sensitive information about Cuba back to Havana."[53]

Following a May 2002, visit to Cuba, President Carter said that he did not believe Cuba was involved in bioweapons research. Alibek's response was terse. "A person who has no experience with bioweapons can not possibly determine whether or not Cuba has a hidden program… and President Carter certainly could not have found that out in two days." He added, "General Kalinin [head of Biopreparat and Alibek's boss at the time] told me after he visited Cuba that he was convinced Cuba had a biological weapons research program."[54]

Among the other nations causing U.S. officials concern:

- **Iran**: A July 2000 report by the U.S. Arms Control and Disarmament Agency, concluded, "The Iranian BW program has been embedded within Iran's extensive biotechnology and pharmaceutical industries so as to obscure its activities."[55] The Pentagon warned in 1997, "While only small quantities of usable agent may exist now, within 10 years Iran's military may be able to deliver biological agents effectively."[56]

- **North Korea**: The CIA in March 1995 noted that, although a party to the BTWC, North Korea has "an active BW program in the early research and development stage."[57]

- **Syria**: The U.S. Arms Control and Disarmament Agency said in July 1998 that, "it is highly probable that Syria is developing an offensive biological warfare capability." The Pentagon suggested in a 1997 report, "Syria is pursuing the development of biological weapons. Syria probably has an adequate biotechnical infrastructure to support a small biological warfare program."[58]

- **Libya**: The U.S. Arms Control and Disarmament Agency reported in July 1998 that "Evidence indicates that Libya has the expertise to produce small quantities of equipment for its BW program, and that the Libyan Government is seeking to move its research program into a program of weaponized BW agents."[59]

- **China**: China is commonly considered to have an active biological warfare program, including dedicated research and development funded and supported by the government for this purpose. "China possesses an advanced biotechnology infrastructure as well as the requisite munitions production capabilities necessary to develop, produce and weaponize biological agents."[60]

Though some have argued that terrorist groups lack the technical and material means to produce weapons of mass destruction, evidence in a 1999 Egyptian trial of 107 suspected terrorists offered a different and more disturbing reality. Testimony revealed that bin Laden already had dangerous biological agents in his arsenal. Furthermore, Islamic Jihad military commander, Ahmad Salamah Mabruk, told a reporter that bin Laden had purchased BW agents from countries in Eastern Europe for as little as $3,865, "shipping included," and had drawn up a list of 100 U.S. and Israeli targets.[61]

Overall, the procurement of dangerous microbes has become dangerously easy. In fact, if President Bush is interested in finding out which states have provided terrorists with biological weapons, he might want to start with the United States. Hussein obtained most of his original strains of biological agents between 1985 and 1989 by mail order through the American Type Culture Collection. ATTC is a non-profit agency that supplied "the most virulent organisms to microbiologists throughout the world without ever checking on who, why, or where the germs would end up."[62] Hussein ordered 36 different strains of deadly pathogens under the auspices of the University of Baghdad and then diverted them to the biowarfare effort.[63]

Furthermore, in the early 1990's, lab specimens of anthrax spores, Ebola virus and other pathogens went missing from the Army's biological warfare research facility located in Fort Detrick, Maryland. An internal Army inquiry also uncovered evidence that someone entered the lab late at night to conduct unauthorized research, apparently involving anthrax. Two former scientists who left the lab told *The Hartford Courant* that "controls at Fort Detrick were so lax it wouldn't have been hard for someone with security clearance for its handful of labs to smuggle out biological specimens."[64]

Summary

U.S. foreign policy with respect to biological warfare has been compromised by extreme naiveté, incompetence and corruption. The United States allowed the Soviets to gain considerable knowledge with respect to biological warfare and repeatedly violate the BWC without the United States taking action. As a result, after the break-up of the Soviet Union, more than 10,000 scientists were available to take their expertise in biological warfare to countries hostile to the United States, including Iraq and Cuba. The United States also assisted countries such as Iraq in developing biological weapons by allowing the export of dangerous microbes from a non-profit storehouse in Maryland and, through lax lab security, allowed specimens of dangerous biological agents to be stolen from its biological warfare research facility for still unknown ends. Finally, the Clinton-Gore administration permitted a Cuban spy to help formulate a more lenient foreign policy with respect to Cuba, even as Castro was spreading BW expertise to enemies of the United States.

Postscript

On May 24, 2002, President George W. Bush and Russian President Vladimir V. Putin each agreed to "remove from deployment" two-thirds of the long-range nuclear weapons stockpiled in their respective countries. With respect to biological weapons, they issued a joint statement confirming their "strong commitment to the 1972 Convention on the Prohibition of the Development, Production and Stockpiling of Bacteriological and Toxin Weapons and on Their Destruction."[65] Despite their kind words towards one another, however, actions taken by both countries in the last year suggest that a new era of mistrust and secrecy has begun. The United States has never been able to secure an agreement allowing inspection of Russian biological weapons production facilities. At the same time, in November 2001, the United States (noting that the protocol was unenforceable) prevented the passage of a BWC protocol that would have incorporated provisions for inspection of BW facilities in any BWC member nation.

The Nightmare Scenario (Continued)

December 24

Joe Carter slowly lifted his head off the pillow and stared blurry eyed at the digital clock next to his bed, blinking a couple of times to make sure his eyes were telling the truth. It read 9:30 a.m. He was late.

As he rose from the bed, Joe shot a quick glance at the green-stained plastic Nyquil cup next to his bed, and vowed never to use the stuff again. True, it had helped him sleep through the night, but it had also made him sleep through his alarm and miss an 8:30 a.m. staff meeting.

Making his way to the bathroom, Joe became acutely aware that the knot in his lower back that had kept him awake two nights prior was still there; and, worse, it had migrated up his spine to the top of his skull. The fever, too, that had caused the late-night dash to the drug store for the aforementioned "so you can sleep" medicine, had hit a high point.

For the last couple of days, Joe had felt as though he were coming down with the flu like everyone else, but he didn't have time for doctors and hospitals and germ-filled waiting rooms. Today was the day before Christmas. Not only did he have to put the finishing touches on a couple of progress reports at work, he had hoped to be able to knock off early and run by the mall before meeting his fiancée for dinner.

Opening the mirror-faced medicine cabinet, Joe fumbled through the meds, cracked open an old Tylenol bottle and tossed a couple of pills into his mouth. Closing the door, he swallowed, and then took a deep breath while eyeing himself carefully in the mirror. As expected, his face was flush and the circles under his eyes were a slightly darker shade of blue than the day before. But what was that thing near his upper lip?

Joe snatched his glasses from the shelf above the sink and moved in for a closer look. It appeared to be a small, pink bump encircled by a red rash. Taking his index finger, Joe gave it a poke and winced as the pain shot through his cheek.

Of all the days to come down with a freakish blister on his face, he thought. Mulling over his options, Joe decided to make a couple of calls, first to work, and then to his fiancée. It looked as if he would have to make that dreaded trip to the clinic . . . and the sooner the better. Maybe he could still salvage some of his Christmas Eve.

December 31

    A robust crowd of after-Christmas shoppers stood slack-jawed in front of a bank of televisions at Sears in the Burlington Mall. The words, "smallpox outbreak in Boston" scrolled across the bottom of the screen as a clearly shaken Health and Human Services Secretary continued his press conference...

    "We have received word in the last 24 hours that there have been seven documented cases of smallpox in three separate hospitals in Boston, Massachusetts. There are also two other suspected cases, one in Raleigh, North Carolina and another in Portland, Oregon. Given the recent spike in warnings issued by terrorist groups, we are investigating this case as a possible act of terrorism, though we do not have any evidence yet to prove this is the case. You should know that your government is taking this situation very seriously and is doing everything it can to keep the situation from deteriorating. As a precaution, however, we are asking American citizens in these three cities to restrict their travel and to limit public gatherings to only those that are completely necessary, as this disease is extremely contagious. We will now take a few questions."

    <u>Mr. Secretary, is it true that at least two of the patients who sought medical attention for their symptoms were misdiagnosed and sent home with prescriptions for flu medicine leading to more potential infections?</u>

    "I have no information on the initial diagnoses of any of the seven patients. However, clearly there is a learning curve here with respect to the medical profession that needs to be addressed. A majority of doctors and nurses have never seen a case of smallpox because there hasn't been a single documented case anywhere in the world in the last 24 years. The Department of Health and Human Services and the Centers for Disease Control have established a 24-hour hotline and are presently distributing information kits to medical facilities around the country to ameliorate the problem."

    <u>Mr. Secretary, I understand that there is a very limited supply of smallpox vaccine available. Would you please comment on vaccine stocks and how you plan to distribute them?</u>

    "The Centers for Disease Control currently has 15 million doses of smallpox vaccine available, more than enough to handle those affected in Boston and the other two cities mentioned. These doses will be allocated to those infected, their contacts and essential personnel, including hospital staff. I should mention, however, that individuals born before 1972 have already been vaccinated and most likely need not concern themselves with

vaccine stocks. Next question."

Mr. Secretary, you mentioned the terrorist warnings. Was there any specific information in those warnings that might indicate where these infections took place?

"That is probably a better question for the Attorney General...Mr. Attorney General?"

"The Secretary is referring to the warnings issued on December 15th that specifically referenced attacks on shopping malls, but that failed to specify any geographical region. I do want to stress, however, that we have not as yet located the source of the infections, nor do we have any information as to whether or not this is an act of terrorism. We would like to therefore refrain from drawing any premature conclusions."

Whether or not the Attorney General was ready to draw conclusions, the 45 or so people in Sears were fully prepared to do so. They pushed and shoved their way into the parking lot adjacent to the mall, scrambling for their cell phones and digging for the numbers of their physicians. After all, they too had a headache and felt a little feverish, and they had been in several shopping malls in the last two weeks. The roads were unusually heavy with traffic.

January 5

"As the cases of smallpox continue to climb, 700 cases in five states at last count, cities across America are being torn apart at the seams. Hospitals are overtaxed, vaccine stocks are dwindling and public unrest is growing at an alarming rate as food shortages are being reported in most major cities. Riots in Boston, Los Angeles and New York have caused the deaths of more than 1,250 people, many of which are of Arab descent. Though the Administration has discouraged interstate travel, the streets are littered with thousands of cars fleeing those cities most affected. The American people have avoided public transportation ever since it was discovered that this devastating outbreak originated in Boston's subway system on approximately December 16. Three U.S. drug companies have been contracted to produce a new vaccine, however, the first deliveries will not be available for five more weeks. All of America is wondering, will this crisis ever end? This is Martin Wolf for the Cable News Channel."

January 12

As the National Security Council gathered, the scene was grim. The United States was at war in the Middle East, while at the same time fighting for its life at home. The economy had plunged into recession, and the streets of most major cities were in chaos. The National Guard had been called in to restore order. Food shortages, a depleted stock of vaccines, overwhelmed hospitals and violence continued throughout America with no end to the crisis in sight. At the same time, power struggles between agencies and between different levels of government added to the chaos. The HHS Secretary was asked to submit an updated report to the President.

"Mr. President, I have been asked to provide you with an update and with those figures you requested for 'worst case scenario' projections. To date, a total of 4,800 smallpox cases have been documented in eight states. An additional 5,200 are expected within the next 12 days, bringing the total number of second-generation cases to 10,000. Of those, approximately 3,300 are expected to die. Though the administration of the new vaccine and containment procedures can limit further proliferation, worst case scenario statistics are as follows: a third generation of cases would lead to 100,000 new cases of smallpox and 33,000 deaths, and a fourth generation of cases could conceivably comprise as many as 1,000,000 new cases and 330,000 deaths."

"Mr. President, I should also tell you we have received another series of warnings, similar to those issued on December 15th."

January 13

He was not supposed to be on that platform at 8:30 a.m. on December 16th. This was all Joe Carter could think about as he lay in Massachusetts General Hospital wheezing his last breaths. The small pink bump he had discovered on his face the day before Christmas had grown to the size of a walnut and spread across his entire body. The pain was intolerable, even with the medication. And the smell was distinct – that of rotting flesh.

That day Joe was supposed to be across town at his office, safely nestled in his cubicle working. Instead he was forced to make the trek to Government Center for a meeting, taking the place of a colleague sick with the flu. His co-worker friend had recovered a day or two later. Joe would never recover. He would never marry and have children. He would never grow old with his wife and watch his kids start families of their own.

This was what Joe Carter was thinking as he closed his eyes and prayed for death.

For those who think this nightmare scenario unlikely, in July 2001, the federal government conducted a study called "Dark Winter" that unfolded in much the same way, yielding even worse results. The initial smallpox infections in that study were 3,000, ultimately leading to 3,000,000 infections and 1,000,000 deaths.[66]

"The enemy is invisible, the enemy is insidious and spreading everywhere, and you don't know how to contain it, you don't have the tools," said Senator Sam Nunn, who played the President during the exercise. "I would like to tell you that the people sitting around the table were just amateurs, but these are the real players and these are the people who have the knowledge. I can say without hesitation, this country is not prepared."[67]

Furthermore, a January 2001, Centers for Disease Control and Prevention study confirmed that the public health infrastructure "is not adequate to detect and respond to a bioterrorist event."[68] And a study by the GAO in 1999 found "major gaps in the nation's system for protecting itself against biological attacks. Inspectors found shortages of vaccines and medicines, stockrooms filled with expired drugs, and lax security measures where crucial drugs were stored."[69]

However, in discussing the massive deficiencies of the public health system, one need not stay in the theoretical realm. The nation's vulnerability to bioterrorism is evident by two actual bioterror events, one preceding and one following on the heels of the September 11th attacks. The first occurred during the days when the country was still naïve about terrorism and little thought was given to what might have happened had a serious biological attack occurred by a capable enemy, such as Iraq or Libya. The second incident happened after the United States awakened to the possibilities, and it received continuing, in-depth, media coverage and commentary.

Salmonella Poisoning in the Northwest

In mid-September 1984, the Wasco-Sherman Public Health Department began to receive complaints from residents of a town in Oregon called The Dalles. People were becoming ill after eating at various restaurants in the town. The source of the illness was soon diagnosed as *Salmonella typhimurium*, a bacteria which can be resistant to a range of antibiotics. This particular strain is treatable, but is serious enough to cause severe diarrhea, chills, fever, and vomiting in victims.

The bacteria was ultimately attributed to a religious cult, the

Rajneeshees, who had built a extensive compound, called Rajneesheepuram, on a 64,000 acre parcel of land in Wasco County, some 84 miles from The Dalles. The Rajneeshees, so called because they were followers of their spiritual leader, Bhagwan Shree Rajneesh, soon controlled the nearby town of Antelope, forcing a name change to Rajneesh.

The Rajneeshees had sprinkled their salmonella "salsa" on lettuce, added the salmonella to coffee creamers, and scattered it over fruits and vegetables at salad bars in the effort to win control over county government by making non-Rajneeshees too sick to vote in upcoming November elections.

The number of patients who became ill due to the salmonella poisoning grew to 751, overwhelming Mid-Columbia Medical Center, the local hospital. "For the first time ever, all of Mid-Columbia's 125 beds were filled; some patients had to be kept in corridors. Many were angry and hostile, and very frightened; doctors had difficulty treating them. Violent patients and their families demanded their test results; some even threw stool and urine samples at the hospital's doctors and technicians."[70]

Furthermore, the case revealed some serious problems with the relationship between law enforcement and the scientific and medical communities. "Information was not shared; opportunities were missed. It proved difficult to establish a crime had been committed. Even to trained eyes, a natural outbreak and a germ assault look much the same: large numbers of people become violently ill...Investigators cracked the case only after members of the cult came forward and confessed their crimes."[71]

In the final analysis, under the direction of Ma Anand Sheela, who ran the cult commune, and Ma Anand Puja, who was in charge of germ warfare, the Rajneeshees had purchased the salmonella from VWR Scientific Products in West Chester, Pennsylvania. Other dangerous pathogens, including the sometimes fatal *Francisella tularensis*, a universally recognized agent for bioweapons, were obtained from American Type Culture Collection, then headquartered in Rockville, Maryland. (As mentioned, ATCC has since relocated to Manassas, Virginia.)

Both U.S. companies *and* the U.S. government, in effect, contributed to the poisoning spree. VWR Scientific and ATCC sold the germs to the Rajneeshees because the cult operated a quasi-medical corporation. Oblivious to the potential danger, neither the state of Oregon nor the federal government had regulations in place to restrict such sales.

Fortunately, with of prosecution of the Bhagwan, Sheela and Puja, the residents of Antelope were eventually able to take their town back.

Sheela and Puja were sentenced to prison (they are now out), while the Bhagwan received a suspended sentence, paid a fine, and was deported.[72] He died in 1990 after changing his name to Osho.

Anthrax Mailings of September and October 2001

The more serious bioterror attack occurred in the wake of September 11th with the mailing of four letters containing anthrax, two on September 18 and two on October 9, 2001. The four letters were addressed to Democratic Senator and Majority Leader, Tom Daschle; Democratic Senator from Vermont, Patrick Leahy; NBC news reporter Tom Brokaw; and the "Editor" of the *New York Post*. Apparently, three other letters were mailed as well, but were destroyed before their significance was known. The letters most likely contained anthrax and were sent to American Media, ABC, and CBS, as was evident from the fact that people at those locations got sick from anthrax poisoning.

The intent of the anthrax letters may have been to "warn" the media and the Senators, since a couple of the letters either identified the powder as anthrax or instructed the recipient to take penicillin. Despite the warning, and particularly because anthrax spores seeped through the envelopes and contaminated mailroom processing machinery, as well as other mail, five people died and 13 others became ill.

Many of the mistakes made and inadequacies indicated by the scenario at the beginning of this chapter, and suggested by the CDC and GAO reports, came to life during the government's response to the anthrax attacks. As the *New York Times* reported, the handling of the anthrax outbreak was "marked by a catalog of miscalculations, missteps and misunderstandings about bioterrorism in general and anthrax in particular."[73]

Much of the blame for misinformation stems from the fact that non-medical people were in charge of disseminating information. For example, when Department of Health and Human Services (HHS) Secretary Tommy G. Thompson first reported that Robert Stevens, who worked for a supermarket tabloid in Florida, had inhalation anthrax, he suggested to the American people that it was an isolated case and did not have any connection to bioterrorism. He went on to imply that Stevens had become infected by drinking water from a stream, even though experts had indicated that such a means of infection would be unprecedented.[74] Either Secretary Thompson was confused, or he purposely misled the public. Either way, significant damage was done.

While such misinformation permeated news reports and government press conferences, the Centers for Disease Control and Prevention (CDC), for its part, was left out in the cold.

"Soon…it became clear that the CDC was desperately needed as a spokesperson for this outbreak, but by that time we were in a reactive state," explained Dr. Julie L. Gerberding, acting deputy at the CDC's infectious disease center. At the time, the CDC was operating under the Federal Emergency Management Act. The decision was made to leave the CDC out of the loop with respect to communicating to the public.[75]

While ill-informed government officials continued to spread misinformation, evidence suggests they also withheld information critical to the health of the American people. During a hearing before Congress, Secretary Thompson testified that he was "frustrated at times," in his efforts to obtain and disseminate information on anthrax. According to the *New York Times*, Secretary Thompson said he "could not disclose all the information that might be important to public health because some was classified and some was restricted by the Federal Bureau of Investigation." In other words, the government withheld information that could have saved lives.[76]

"I would give us as a government a 'D' on communication – both within the government, and between the government and the public," said Dr. Tara O'Toole, deputy director of the Civilian Biodefense Studies at Johns Hopkins University in Baltimore, Maryland. "There were a lot of mistakes, a lot of missed connections, a lot of misjudgments."[77]

Despite the fact that Secretary Thompson told the American people that the United States is prepared to handle "any contingency, any consequence that develops from any kind of bioterrorism attack," these "mistakes" put the public in a state of panic that overwhelmed the public health system, even when considering the relatively small scale of the outbreak.[78]

Laboratories were overrun with a landslide of nasal swab samples, most of which were taken from individuals who did not have the disease. Hospitals were deluged with patients, most of whom were healthy, wanting to be tested. And "federal state and local governments were unprepared for the close collaboration required in an investigation that combined the medical and the criminal."[79]

In the end, however, the most disturbing lesson learned from the anthrax crisis is not that government officials made honest mistakes, but rather that they may have purposely mislead the American people. More than a month before Stevens took ill, White House personnel were given doses of the antibiotic Cipro. On the night of the September 11th attacks, The White House Medical Office dispensed Cipro to staff accompanying Vice President Dick Cheney as he was secreted off to the safety of Camp David.[80]

And while the government took great pains to ensure the good health of powerful individuals like Vise President Dick Cheney, rank and file government workers were not so fortunate. U.S. Postal Service workers were not treated with antibiotics for anthrax exposure at a mail facility at Brentwood, resulting in two deaths. They were told by the CDC that it was not necessary to test workers, even though the anthrax-laced letter to Senator Tom Daschle traveled through the Brentwood facility.

"It's like our lives are not as important," said Melvin Thweatt, an employee at the Brentwood facility, in an interview with CNN.[81]

In terms of the government's investigation of the matter, today we are no closer to determining the source of the anthrax – and the killer – than we were when the first anthrax-laced letters were received by Tom Brokaw of NBC and the *New York Post*. The U.S. Postal Service has failed utterly in its response to the anthrax attacks as well. From October 2001 through August 2002, the Postal Service has spent nearly $500 million and has provided the public scant protection from another bioterrorist attack through the mail. Instead, it keeps pushing back dates for implementing new safeguards, to include anthrax detection and decontamination machines, while telling the public there is no problem.

Conclusions

Among the problems identified by Dark Winter, the salmonella and anthrax attacks and the above scenario:

1. A biological attack launched against the United States could lead to massive casualties, civil chaos, and a loss of confidence in government officials. Such a scenario would most certainly compromise national security.

2. There is no "surge capacity" in the public health system, or the pharmaceutical and vaccine industries. As exemplified in our scenario, hospitals were overwhelmed and were rendered ineffective, while vaccine stocks could not be replenished quickly enough to contain the disease and reassure the public.[82]

3. "Major 'fault lines' exist between different levels of government (federal, state and local) between government and the private sector, among different institutions and agencies, and within the public and private sector."[83] "Dark Winter…demonstrated how poorly current organizational structures and capabilities fit with the management needs and operational requirements of an effective bioterrorism response," Margaret Hamburg, an Assistant Secretary with HHS under Clinton, testified before the Committee on Government Reform.[84] These organizational deficiencies could exacerbate the problem leading to greater loss of life.

4. Information management and negotiations with the media are important to maintaining public composure. Misinformation not only undermines public confidence and can lead to greater loss of life as was demonstrated by the Brentwood postal facility incident and, in our scenario, by the HHS Secretary's false information regarding the effectiveness of smallpox vaccines administered before 1972.

5. U.S. leadership is unfamiliar with the characteristics of biowarfare and how to effectively assess policy options in the midst of a crisis.

6. The actions of individual citizens will be crucial in helping contain the spread of disease, yet of the $10 billion spent on public health infrastructure, not one dollar is allocated to programs that educate the public on BW.[85]

7. The vast majority of communities in the United States are untrained and unprepared for a biological attack. Furthermore, of the 120 cities scheduled to receive training from the federal government to prepare for a bioterrorist attack, only 51 have received this training.[86]

8. Political elites in Washington are willing to withhold information from the American people and protect themselves at all costs. They cannot be trusted.

The Greatest Threat: A Web of Corruption

It is clear that mistakes in foreign policy and the ill preparedness of our public health system have left our nation vulnerable to a biological attack. But in the end, the greatest threat to the lives of American citizens may just be the cancer of corruption from within our own government, coupled with a tangled web of suspicious relationships among prominent laboratories and companies in the United States and Great Britain.

In 1989, two years before Dr. Ken Alibek defected to the United States, Dr. Vladimir Pasechnik, head of the Institute of Ultra-Pure Biopreparations for the Soviet Union, defected at a meeting in Paris, France. After unsuccessfully approaching both the French and Canadian embassies, Pasechnik was welcomed with open arms by Great Britain.

While in the Soviet Union, Dr. Pasechnik reported to Dr. Alibek; and understandably, there was great apprehension all the way up to Mikhail Gorbackev when Pasechnik defected. Pasechnik was able to provide the West with specific and shocking information about the Soviet Union's offensive bioweapons programs, outlawed by the 1972 Biological and Toxic Weapons Convention.[87]

One of Dr. Pasechnik's projects was the modification of cruise missiles for the delivery of biological agents. During strategy meetings, top officials of the KGB and Biopreparat tried to figure out how to control the damage of his defection, and consideration was given to assassinating Pasechnik. The proposal was rejected by Dr. Alibek.[88]

Though he escaped being eliminated in the days following his defection, death ultimately caught up with him. Dr. Pasechnik died on November 22, 2001 from a "stroke." What is strange about the event was that, with the exception of his obituary in the *New York Times* a week later, his death went unreported for a full month. Moreover, the person who informed the *New York Times* about Pasechnik's death was Christopher Davis, MD, the former MI6 intelligence officer for the British who debriefed Pasechnik when he defected 13 years prior. Dr. Davis called the *Times* from his home in Virginia, where he now resides.[89]

In Russia, the *National News Service* commented: "The chief developer (while in the Soviet Union) of the military grade plague as well as several successful types of binary weapons died, according the *New York Times* obituary, from a stroke, although the fact that the newspaper quotes a former member of British intelligence rather than the doctor, makes people believe in other versions of death of the person who knew too much."[90]

While his death alone is enough for many to raise questions, four other top microbiologists died under relatively suspicious circumstances during a 31-day period stretching from November 12 to December 13, 2001. All apparently had some connection with Pasechnik. The five scientists and the sequence of these deaths are as follows:

- November 12, 2001 – Dr. Benito Que, a cell biologist working on how infectious diseases like HIV could be engineered into a biowarfare program, was found comatose outside his laboratory at the Miami (Florida) Medical School. Early in the afternoon, Que had headed for his car; and according to police (as reported by the *Miami Herald*), he was possibly the victim of a mugging. At the time, also according to the *Miami Herald*, Que had no wallet on him. Family members believe Que was attacked by four men, at least one being armed with a baseball bat; yet, police maintain there was a lack of visible trauma to Que's body. Que's death has now been officially ruled "natural," caused by cardiac arrest. Both the Dade County Medical examiner and the Miami police refuse to comment on the case, stating that it is closed. No explanation has been provided as to why Que did not have his wallet on him. Dr. Que had met with Pasechnik on several occasions at biomedical conferences.[91]

- November 16, 2001 – Dr. Don C. Wiley, a Harvard biochemistry and biophysics professor and one of the foremost infectious disease researchers in the United States, was declared missing while attending St. Jude's Children's Advisory Dinner in Memphis, Tennessee. His car was found on the Hernando DeSoto bridge over the Mississippi with a full tank of gas and keys in the ignition. The bridge was in a direction opposite to where he was staying. His body was later found 300 miles down river, and his death was declared an accident.[92]

  According to the *New York Newsday*, "Because Harvard University biologist Don C. Wiley's work involved such deadly microbes as influenza, HIV and the Ebola virus, the FBI and Memphis police are pursuing his disappearance as possibly linked to bioterrorism… The FBI is not discounting the possibility that someone targeted Wiley because they thought he might be a source of either microbes or vital information about dangerous viruses."[93] Though nothing discovered by investigators contradicts this theory, it was eventually dropped in favor of a less likely, albeit less sinister, scenario.

  The Shelby County Medical Examiner theorized that Dr. Wiley accidentally fell over the edge when he got out of his rental car to inspect the damage resulting from a collision with a construction sign on the bridge. (Investigators maintain the vehicle had yellow paint marks on it and a missing hubcap.)[94] However, in order for Wiley to have fallen over the rail, three things must have occurred almost at the same time: 1) Wiley must have had one of the two or three seizures he had per year due to a rare disorder known only to his family and close friends; 2) a passing truck must have created a massive blast of wind and/or a significant amount of "roadway bounce"; and 3) Wiley must have been standing on the curb flush against the guardrail, which would have come to his mid-thigh.

Importantly, there were no witnesses to corroborate the story that Dr. Wiley had a car accident or stopped his car on the bridge at all, despite the fact that police had been regularly patrolling the bridge. Also, the bridge had been restricted to one lane because of construction, which means a truck is not likely to have been speeding over the bridge. Finally, no reports exists as to which construction sign Wiley hit; and no explanation has been given as to why the police would consider Wiley missing, if, in fact, there was clear evidence of a car accident. (Early police reports made no mention of paint marks or the missing hubcap.)[95]

Dr. Wiley did his research at the prestigious Howard Hughes Medical Institute, and was noted for his work with Ebola, the Marburg virus, and Q fever. He had shared some of his research with Dr. Pasechnik.[96]

- November 21, 2001 – Dr. Vladimir Pasechnik, as indicated, died of a stroke. According to Dr. Leonard Horowitz, a U.S. specialist in the field of toxic poisons, a number of nerve agents can be employed to mimic a stroke and leave no traces. In the last weeks of his life, Pasechnik had turned his research on anthrax over to the British government, in the aftermath of the terrorism attacks on America.[97]

- December 12, 2001 – Dr. Robert M. Schwartz, a distinguished biophysicist who had worked closely with Dr. Pasechnik on DNA sequencing, was found murdered at his remote farmhouse near Loudoun County, Virginia. He had been stabbed to death. Three teenagers involved in witchcraft were arrested in the case. While a connection between the teenagers and the doctor's daughter has been explored, the case has not yet been

147

sufficiently explained, and professed motives need to be challenged.[98]

- December 13, 2001 – Dr. Set Van Nguyen, who was a microbiologist at Australia's Animal Health Laboratory, apparently died in an airlock chamber while entering a low temperature storage area where biological samples are kept. Supposedly, nitrogen had leaked into the chamber, making it impossible for him to breath. Nitrogen, however, is not a deadly gas, and is a component of air. An extreme over-abundance of nitrogen in a person's immediate atmosphere would cause shortness of breath, lightheadedness, and fatigue – conditions that a biologist would certainly recognize. Nguyen would have had time to exit the chamber, unless he was somehow locked in.

  Dr. Nguyen had been part of a team led by Drs. Ron Jackson and Ian Ramshaw, working on an extremely virulent strain of mousepox, a cousin of smallpox. The journal *Nature* announced in January 2001: "Australian scientists, Dr. Ron Jackson and Dr. Ian Ramshaw, accidentally created an astonishingly virulent strain of mousepox, a cousin of smallpox, among laboratory mice. They realized that if a similar genetic manipulation was carried out on smallpox, an unstoppable killer could be unleashed."[99] While no direct connection has been made, Dr. Nguyen was known to follow the research performed by Dr. Pasechnik. (Dr. Jackson has been postulated as the intended target instead of Dr. Nguyen.)[100]

Adding to these questionable deaths is the fact that MI6 and other intelligence services are looking into the backgrounds of five microbiologists who died on October 4, 2001 on a regularly scheduled commercial flight from Tel Aviv to Novosbirsk in Siberia. The aircraft was "accidentally" shot down by a Ukrainian surface-to-air missile that was 100 miles off course.[101]

Other mysterious deaths include the following: Dr. Tanya Holzmayer, a Russian-born genomic scientist, who co-invented a tool that has helped find hundreds of molecular targets to combat HIV, was reportedly shot by a China-born former colleague in February 2002;[102] and Dr. Stephen Mostow, one of the United States' leading infectious disease and bioterrorism experts, was killed in a twin-engine Cessna plane crash on March 24, 2002. National Transportation Safety Board investigators said that weather did not appear to be a factor in the crash.[103] Dr. Larry Ford, a research scientist with known ties to South African bioterrorist, Wouter Basson, and the U.S. government, "committed suicide" on March 2, 2002, three days after his business partner, James Patrick Riley, was shot by a masked gunman outside the pair's Biofem Pharmaceutical office in Irvine, California. Police reportedly found barrels full of hazardous biological materials buried in Ford's back yard.[104]

According to Gordon Thomas, an award-winning foreign journalist and author of the book *Seeds of Fire* (which is about China's possible involvement in the September 11th attacks on the World Trade Center and the Pentagon) British and U.S. intelligence are exploring a possible Communist Chinese connection to the deaths of at least some of the microbiologists mentioned. Thomas maintains that MI6 and the CIA are attempting to establish whether or not China has sent "killer" squads from its own secret service to eliminate scientists it had approached and who had declined to work for China.[105] Pasechnik told Davis that China had attempted to recruit him for its own bioweapons program, but he refused.[106]

A Tangled Web

In Great Britain, Dr. Pasechnik was employed by Porton Down until he launched his own venture, Regma Biotechnologies Ltd., in November 2000, under the auspices of Porton Down and on Porton Down property. He was working "to provide alternative forms of treatment to replace antibiotics in cases where they are no longer effective."[107]

In the 1980's, a significant part of the civilian component of Porton Down, the Centre for Applied Microbiology and Research (CAMR), was privatized as Porton International. Porton International is owned by Speywood Holdings Ltd., which, in turn, is owned by I&F Holdings NV, a corporate shell in the Netherlands owned by Fuad El-Hibri, a Lebanese Arab with citizenship in both Germany and the United States, and his father, Ibrihim El-Hibri.[108] El-Hibri had tried unsuccessfully for years to obtain an anthrax vaccine from the United States for Saudia Arabia. His conquest of Porton Down provided him with such an opportunity. When El-Hibri took over the privatized company, he arranged for the delivery of biotech defense products to Saudi Arabia.

According to the *Washington Post*, Porton Down is one of five labs that received the Ames strain of the anthrax virus from the U.S. Army Medical Research Institute of Infectious Diseases (USAMRIID) at Fort Detrick, Maryland. (Actually, at least nine laboratories, including

USAMRIID, are known to have worked with the Ames strain.*)[109]

More than a decade after the establishment of Porton Down, privatization of a public laboratory occurred for a second time – this time, in the United States. Ibrahim and Fuard El-Hibri, who had previously gained control over Porton International, joined with Admiral William J. Crowe, President Clinton's Ambassador to Great Britain, to establish Bioport Corporation. They did so by orchestrating a scheme to take control of the State of Michigan's Biological Products Laboratory, and then secured a contract increase of $24.1 million with the Department of Defense (DOD) to supply anthrax vaccine less than a month later.[111] The new agreement included an advance payment of $18.7 million.

Even though Bioport did not yet have FDA approval to sell the vaccine, the DOD agreed to increase the per-dose price paid from between $4.36 and $2.26 (the amount previously charged by the State of Michigan) to $10.64.[112] At the same time, the number of doses under the contract was reduced from 7.9 to 4.6 million.

According to ABC News Reporter Howard L. Rosenberg, Bioport Corporation was created solely to take over the assets of Michigan Biologic Products Institute (MBPI) by Admiral Crowe (who received his share in the venture as a "gift" from El-Hibris), his partners in a company called Intervac, LLC and a group of former managers of the Michigan-based institute.[113]

Multiple media reports have also linked the Carlyle Group also with ownership of Bioport. The Carlyle Group is an investment firm known for

---

* According to the *Hartford Courant*, two current and former scientists at Fort Detrick told the newspaper that controls at the lab were so lax, little could have been done to prevent an employee from smuggling the ingredients for biological terrorism out of the country's premier biodefense lab. Not only that, "biological agents were exchanged with other labs through the mail" without effective checks to ensure "the recipient of a package was a bona fide researcher with a legitimate reason to have the material."[110] All of this, of course, leads back to the anthrax mailings, and suggests that the source for the anthrax is likely to be a U.S. or British laboratory or an individual who once worked in one of the labs.

The seven laboratories, in addition to USAMRIID and Porton Down are: 1) Dugway Proving Ground in Utah; 2) Naval Research Medical Center/Armed Forces Institute of Pathology in Maryland; 3) Battelle Memorial Institute in Ohio; 4) Duke University Medical School in North Carolina; 5) VA Medical Center in North Carolina; 6) U.S. Department of Agriculture Laboratory and Iowa State College of Veterinary Medicine in (Ames) Iowa; and 7) Louisiana State University College of Veterinary Medicine in Louisiana.

making quick and substantial amounts of money for its clients in the U.S. defense industry. Among those associated with Carlyle is President George H. W. Bush. Other top Republicans associated with the Carlyle Group include former Secretary of State, James A. Baker, former Defense Secretary and Deputy CIA Director, Frank Carlucci, and former Clinton-Gore administration Defense Secretary William Perry.[114]

Bioport Corporation is the only company in the Unites States currently licensed to produce and supply anthrax vaccine. The company, however, has failed two FDA inspections and is mired in manufacturing and financial difficulties.[115] Due to pressure from the military, the Pentagon abandoned its controversial mandatory anthrax vaccine program, thus depriving Bioport of substantial revenue.

Broken Promise

PROMIS (PROsecution Management Information Systems) was developed in the 1980's by a Washington DC-based company called Inslaw, founded by Bill and Nancy Hamilton. Hamilton had begun work on case management software for the government in the 1970's with financing from the now defunct Law Enforcement Assistance Agency (LEAA). The Justice Department (DOJ), under President Reagan's Attorney General (and long-time associate) Ed Meese, bought an original version of PROMIS software from Hamilton for $10 million.[116]

According to Hamilton, as soon as the DOJ took delivery of the 1980's version of PROMIS, Meese reneged on the contract and withheld payments, forcing Inslaw into Chapter 11 bankruptcy.[117] The DOJ then launched what Hamilton called "a covert effort" to completely liquidate Inslaw (which would give the asset to the DOJ without the need for payment). Inslaw retaliated by suing the DOJ in U.S. Bankruptcy Court. After a three–week trial, Judge George Bason ruled that officials of the DOJ "stole" 44 copies of PROMIS *through trickery, fraud, and deceit*," and then tried to drive Inslaw out of business. The award was for more than $7 million.[118] (Reportedly, according to a DOJ source, the Inslaw case was "a lot dirtier for the DOJ than Watergate had been, both in its breadth and its depth.")[119]

A federal appeals court later overturned the decision on technical grounds (the lawsuit had been brought in the wrong jurisdiction).

Hamilton's problems began in 1983, when he received a phone call from Dominic Laiti, then chairmen of Hadron, Inc. According to Hamilton,

151

Laiti wanted to buy out Inslaw, as Hadron was seeking a monopoly in law enforcement software. When Hamilton indicated that he was not interested, Laiti reportedly said "We have ways of making you sell."[120]

Hadron has been around for 30 years, and is the company that Ken Alibek ultimately went to work for (as mentioned, he is President of Advanced Bio Systems, Inc, a subsidiary of Hadron, Inc.). However, there is no known, or suspected, connection between Dr. Alibek and the Inslaw affair.

The owner of Hadron, Inc. several years ago was Dr. Earl Brian, who was a good friend of Meese and was Secretary of Health for Ronald Reagan when he was Governor of California. Brian had owned a number of companies that folded, and spent time in jail on unrelated fraud charges. Apparently, neither Laiti nor Brian are involved with Hadron today. Hadron itself had been struggling until Meese became Attorney General, at which time the company managed to secure lucrative contracts with the DOJ.[121]

After delivering the original version of PROMIS to the government to meet his contractual requirement, Hamilton developed an enhanced VAX VMS version that he intended to sell privately.[122] In order to get its hands on the upgraded version, the DOJ delayed payments owed to Inslaw for the original version and demanded the new improved version. Hamilton yielded, but still did not get paid. Instead, he ended up being audited by the IRS and was forced into U.S. Bankruptcy Court.[123] The DOJ kept the enhanced version of the software and eventually turned it over to Brian. Brian then had a computer expert, Michael Riconosciuto, adapt the software for intelligence purposes.

Brian's purpose in appropriating PROMIS was to use it to gain the inside track on a $250 million contract to automate DOJ litigation divisions.[124] During Meese's confirmation hearings, it was revealed that Ursula Meese, his wife, had borrowed money to buy stock in Brian's Biotech Capital Corporation, which, at the time, controlled Hadron, Inc.[125]

Once Brian turned the upgraded version of PROMIS over to Riconosciuto, he and others soon involved the Cabazon Indian Reservation (located near Indio, California) and a company called Wackenhut, a private security firm, in the rewriting of the software. [126] Once rewritten as intelligence software, PROMIS was sold to Israel and Canada. (According to some accounts, Israel created a "backdoor" for penetrating the computers of unsuspecting foreign companies that had been provided the software.) Ultimately, the FBI spy, Robert Hanssen, who was responsible for installing PROMIS at the FBI, stole the software and sold it to Russia and possibly as many as 80 nations and groups, including Iraq.[127]

Reports are that Russia subsequently sold the software to Osama bin Laden. Also, according to Gordon Thomas, "MI6 and CIA have told me that PROMIS has now been modified by Chinese intelligence, CSIS," to allow it to tap into the databases of scientists involved in biological research and development, including Pasecknik.[128]

Future Climate for Bioterrorism

On July 12, 2002, scientists at the State University of Stony Brook announced their latest medical achievement while at the same time providing rogue terrorists with a blueprint for the production of a biological weapon. They created an infectious poliovirus from scratch using chemicals they had acquired from a scientific mail order house, and then published the formula in the journal *Science Express*.

According to the *Washington Post*, armed with the details of the Stony Brook report, this scientific feat, which once seemed impossible, is now "within the skill range of many molecular biologists today and could be done with perhaps as little as $10,000 worth of equipment."[129] If true, the proliferation of biological agents would become a non-issue as any terrorist group with a few dollars in the bank account could manufacture any bioagent it wished.

In 2001, another wake up call was issued in February when Australian scientists at Canberra's Research Center for the Biological Control of Pest Animals genetically altered the harmless mousepox virus and turned it into a killer. They, too, published the details of their efforts, this time in the journal *Science*.[130]

In his testimony before the Senate Committee on Government Affairs, Dr. Thomas V. Inglesby, Deputy Director of the Center for Civilian Biodefense Strategies, cataloged a series of breakthrough medical techniques already being used in labs around the world. "Already present on the planet are examples of biological knowledge that are disturbing," Dr. Inglesby testified. "The methods for making new influenza strains never before seen; the directions for making Ebola virus from non-living fragments of genetic material; the techniques to make anthrax or plague resistant to many or even all available antibiotics; attempts to combine a set of genes from viruses that cannot spread to viruses that can; biological aerosols that might once have harmlessly floated away can be stabilized in the environment and altered to make them more easily inhaled."[131]

Not mentioned by Dr. Inglesby, but equally important, were the accomplishments of Soviet Union's scientists in the early 1990's. In a project known as Bonfire, these scientists discovered a "new class of weapon."[132] Through genetic engineering, they were able to create biological agents from chemical substances naturally produced by the human body. Such compounds, which are not prohibited by the Biological Weapons Convention, can "damage the nervous system, alter moods, trigger psychological changes, and even kill."[133] Furthermore, they are untraceable. The Soviet Union had developed a way to inject these compounds, or toxins, into *Yersinia pestis*, or plague, creating a new version of one of mankind's most virulent bacterial enemies. While medical professionals were busy treating the disease, the toxins would be fast at work killing the victim regardless. It is not too far of a leap to suggest that scientists could find a benign delivery system, one that is not, unlike plague, prohibited by the BWC. As such, a wholly new, 100 percent fatal and 100 percent "legal" biological weapon will have been created.

As disturbing as today's reality is with respect to biological weapons, it cannot compare to what lies ahead. A United Nations Office of Drug Control report claims that advances in genetic biotechnology have set the stage for the development of "ethnic bullets" — bioweapons specially designed to target members of specific ethnic groups. Such a weapon, the UN concluded, would remove a major concern for those who ponder the use of biological weapons – the risk of infecting one's own people. While the technology today resides just on the outer edge of the capabilities of science, the report suggests such a procedure "could be a reality within 10 years."[134]

So, this is the future of biological warfare. Genetically altered, or in some cases, artificially manufactured disease agents for which we have no defense. Agents custom designed for ethnic cleansing campaigns. Agents created from compounds that occur naturally in the human body. The question remains, how will we defend against it?

Recommendations for Defending the United States Against Bioterrorism

U.S. preparations for defending the country against terrorism in general, and bioterrorism in particular, have escalated considerably since the events of September 11th. In December 2001, the U.S. House of Representatives approved legislation authorizing spending $2.5 billion to fight biological terrorism. In May 2002, the amount was upped to $4.6

billion and passed by both the House and Senate. The bill includes funding for states and health care facilities to improve response capabilities, and for expansion of vaccine and medicine stockpiles, $640 million being devoted to producing and stockpiling smallpox vaccines.[*][135]

Much attention is being given, at least verbally and in print, to ways of improving the ability of hospitals, clinics, laboratories, and first responders to recognize and respond to a biological event. Today, the "3R's," an expression once known to generations of school children, has taken on a new meaning. Instead of "Reading, wRiting, and aRithmetic," it now stands for *Recognize It*, *Report It*, and *React To It*.

Yet, despite our attempts to become more aware of symptoms, link databases so as to be able to share information across the country in the case of a disease outbreak, and have action teams in place to contain the disease and provide almost immediate, front-line treatment, the United States will continue to remain extremely vulnerable to a determined terrorist with a few grams of powder in his (or her) pocket. With 100 or more al Qaeda operatives estimated to be in this country, and who knows how many hundreds of others planning a terrorist act, a significant biological attack is a strong possibility for the near future. The problem, of course, is complicated by the easy access to the United States from Canada and Mexico; and according to David Harris, former chief of strategic planning for the Canadian Security Intelligence Service, "We have the most generous refugee system in the world." In a seven month period following September 11th, Canada accepted 15,000 refuges, 2,500 of which arrived from terrorist countries. Included among the 50 known terrorist organizations finding a haven in Canada, are such radical groups as Hezbollah, Hamas, al Qaeda, and the IRA. [137, 138]

What this suggests is the need to be proactive in protecting Americans by implementing a cost-effective means of identifying and tracking non-citizens. Fingerprinting of immigrants by the INS has been suggested as one possibility, though doing so will be no easy task, as some 35 million people visit the United States each year.[139]

Specific challenges facing the United States and strategic

---

[*] The bill also includes funding for assessing the vulnerability of water systems, improving food inspections, and upgrading CDC facilities. A separate bill creating a $38 billion Department of Homeland Security, in which 170,000 employees from 22 agencies are to be shifted into a single, massive department, is pending passage – and probable modification – by the U.S. Senate.[136] The "pros" and "cons" of centralization are certain to be debated over the coming months and years.

recommendations for defending against bioterrorism are as follows[*]:

1. As has been discussed, the incubation period for smallpox being seven to 17 days, a person infected with the virus could, in turn, expose dozens of people through conversation and contact. Adding to the problem is the fact that the disease is not likely to be recognized when the initial symptoms appear; the person may even be diagnosed with the flu and sent home. The disease, therefore, could be widespread, with many people beyond help by the time a smallpox outbreak is recognized. Also, because we live in a highly mobilized society, circling an infected person with a "ring" of immunized people is not likely to work as it has in the past. According to William Patrick III, "with old-fashion natural smallpox, you can bring a society to its knees."[140]

    Full immunization of the population, and immunization of people deemed to be at risk, are possible solutions being weighed by The White House and Congress. Full immunization is actually a misnomer, because the process would be voluntary and as much as 40 percent of the civilian population would choose not to be vaccinated because of the risk, especially to those with suppressed immune systems (estimated to be about 30 percent of the population in the United States).[141]

    Recommendation: 1) Produce sufficient quantities of the vaccine and make it available to the public on a voluntary basis[*], and 2) vaccinate health care workers exposed to the

---

[*] The need for devising and implementing state and federal action plans has been widely discussed in the media and is not considered in depth.

[*] The availability of sufficient quantities of smallpox vaccine [as well as vaccine immunoglobin (VIG), used to treat complications related to the vaccine] no longer appears to be an issue. (Distribution is more likely to be a problem than availability.) Evidently, the estimated 15.4 million doses of Dryvax manufactured by Wyeth-Ayerst Laboratories 30 years ago, can be diluted to produce five times the doses without losing effectiveness. More notable is the fact that the HHS awarded a $428 million contract in November 2001 to Acambis Inc. to produce 155 million doses of smallpox vaccine by the end of 2002. This is reportedly in addition to the $343 million September 2000 contract with Acambis to produce 40 million doses by 2004, since renegotiated to become 54 million doses by late 2002. DynPort Vaccine Company LLC is scheduled to develop and manufacture 17 different vaccines and antidotes for the Joint Vaccine Acquisition Program (JVAP) office of the Pentagon. Smallpox vaccines head the list.[142]

disease. Most important, efforts should be focused on developing an effective and safe antiviral drug that can be administered after symptoms appear.

2. The Russians were successful in producing a strain of anthrax that resisted conventional antibiotics, including tetracycline. Such progress has likely been repeated by other nations, such as China and Iraq.

    Recommendation: Attention should be given to developing new, effective, and inexpensive multipurpose antibiotics.

3. While radical groups cannot be overlooked, the primary danger to the United States concerns state terrorism, in other words, rogue nations with sophisticated laboratories capable of producing anthrax and variola major, as well as other agents, in a spore size that can cause widespread infection and harm.

    Recommendation: Russia should be pressured into helping to identify who the missing scientists are, what their knowledge base is (areas of expertise), and where they have gone. The role of U S. intelligence, especially the CIA, is crucial in this arena.

4. Conceivably, the most significant ultimate danger to the United States could involve peptides (compounds containing two or more amino acids), not only because their devastating effects would be attributed to natural causes, but also because such an attack would be arguably outside the provisions of the 1972 Bioweapons Convention.

    Recommendation: Again, pressure is essential on Russia to divulge the status of such research and the scientists involved.

5. According to William Patrick III, with regard to the possibility of a national inoculation program, "I don't think that vaccines will ever be the answer." His reasoning is based on two factors. First, for protection against some diseases, such as tularemia and smallpox, a live, attenuated vaccine must be used, which is dangerous for women who are pregnant, and can cause severe adverse reactions in others. Second, the possibility exists that the terrorist group would use a "cocktail of agents," which would mean that a vaccine developed for a single organism would be ineffective against the combined agents. "It seems to me that the way to protect against a BW attack may lie in some of the research being directed today toward immuno-

modulators, which stimulate the immune system against not one organism but against all organisms."[143]

Recommendation. Research should be expedited on developing multivalent vaccines to achieve a means of creating superimmunity against a broad range of pathogens. Of particular note is the gene vaccine research being conducted under the auspices of the U.S. Defense Advanced Research Projects Agency (DARPA), an arm of the Pentagon. Two DARPA research programs are notable: a) gene research being conducted by Maxygen, Inc. to produce an enzyme capable of neutralizing the most deadly viruses and bacteria;[144] and b) progress being made by Ken Alibek at Advanced Biosystems, Inc. to develop a spray that, when inhaled, boosts the immune system so as to provide short-term protection against various infectious agents.[145]

The intent of the latter vaccine is to provide enough time for the infectious agent to be identified and proper treatment to begin.

Appendix I: Bioagents[*]

As was mentioned in the *Future Trends* section of this chapter, perhaps the most dangerous biological agent is one that, as yet, does not exist. Genetic engineering has provided mankind with the morbid opportunity to mix and match diseases in an attempt to maximize their deadly potential. At the same time, even without further manipulation, there are a number of biological agents that could wreak significant havoc were they to be used as weapons of terror.

The following bioagents are listed by the CDC as "Category A Diseases/Agents." As such, they are considered to be high-priority agents that pose a risk to national security because they meet some or all of the following requirements:

- They can be easily disseminated or transmitted from person to person;

- They can result in high mortality rates and have the potential for major public health impact;

- They might cause public panic and social disruption; and

- They require special action for public health preparedness.

Anthrax (Bacillus anthracis)

Symptoms of anthrax vary depending on how the disease was contracted. *Cutaneous* anthrax infection occurs when the bacterium is deposited under the skin through a cut or abrasion. It presents with a raised itchy bump resembling an insect bite. Within 1-2 days a lesion appears followed by a painless ulcer, approximately 1-3 cm in size, with characteristic dead black skin in the center. Lymph glands around the area of infection may also swell. Roughly 20 percent of untreated cutaneous cases will result in death. The mortality rate for *Inhalation* anthrax is near 100 percent. Onset of the disease is gradual with symptoms generally beginning one to six days after infection. Initial symptoms resemble a number of different viral, bacterial and fungal infections, making diagnosis difficult. They include fever, malaise and fatigue, followed by respiratory distress and shock, with death following shortly thereafter for those who are not treated. A third type of anthrax infection, *Intestinal,* occurs by way of

---

[*] Primary Source: CDC website: www.cdc.gov, Atlanta, GA: HHS. (Exceptions noted in reference section.)

the consumption of infected meat. Symptoms are similar to those experienced during a bout of food poisoning and include nausea, loss of appetite, vomiting, fever and abdominal pain. Death follows in 25-60 percent of the cases. Anthrax can be treated with antibiotics and it is not spread person-to person.

Potential Threat: Inhalation anthrax, in particular, provides a potent biological weapon. A lethal dose is considered to be 10,000 spores. Less than one millionth of a gram will kill the victim within five days of exposure. "According to an estimate by the U.S. Congress's Office of Technology Assessment, 100 kilograms of anthrax, released from a low-flying aircraft over a large city on a clear, calm night, could kill one to three million people."[146]

Botulism (Clostridium botulinum)

Botulism toxin belongs to the family of Clostridial neurotoxins – the most toxic substances known to man.[147] It is normally encountered when food has been cooked, canned or preserved improperly, but it is also extremely effective as a biological agent. Single cases of Botulism may be confused with other neuromuscular disorders, making it more difficult to diagnose. Classic symptoms, which generally occur 24-36 hours following exposure to Botulism, include double vision, blurred vision, drooping eyelids, slurred speech, difficulty swallowing, dry mouth and muscle weakness. Botulism can result in death due to respiratory arrest. Today, mortality rates are at roughly 8 percent for those who get treatment. Some patients who do recover may require ventilator assistance and intensive medical care for several months following exposure to the toxin. Fatigue and shortness of breath can continue for years.

Potential Threat: "Botulinum toxin is one of the most potent compounds known; it is 100,000 times more toxic than sarin."[148] If used as a bioweapon, the toxin would likely be transmitted by aerosol or through the contamination of food and water supplies.[149]

Plague (Yersinia pestis)

Yersinia pestis has ravaged mankind for centuries and is perhaps the most recognized and feared bacterial agent in human history. There are two main types: bubonic and pneumonic. In the bubonic form, infection comes by way of a flea-bite which causes a painful swelling of the lymph gland.

Fever, chills, headache and extreme exhaustion follow. Skin lesions and pustules may develop along with black patches on the skin. (Hence the name, "Black Death"). An incubation period of two to 10 days makes bubonic plague an idea biological agent. The pneumonic form of plague results from the inhalation of the organisms and is easily transmitted from one person to another by way of cough droplets containing the disease. The victim will experience malaise, high fever, chills, headache, aching muscles, and a cough that expels bloody sputum. The disease can then progress quickly to death as the patient's respiratory functions begin to collapse. If untreated, death results in 50 percent of all cases of bubonic plague and 100 percent of all cases of pneumonic plague. Patients can be treated with antiobiotics if such treatment commences within 24 hours of infection. However, there is no guarantee of recovery.

Potential Threat: Due to the highly infectious nature of plague and the potential for secondary transmission, it is considered a most dangerous biological agent. In a bioterrorist attack, the plague could be delivered via contaminated fleas, which would lead to the bubonic type or via aerosol causing the pneumonic type.[150] Dr. Ken Alibek, who operated the former Soviet Union's offensive biological weapons program, claims the Soviet Union had developed strains of plague resistant to all forms of antibiotic treatment.[151]

Smallpox

At one time, smallpox, the most notorious of all the pox viruses, wiped out as much as 30 to 40 percent of entire populations during outbreaks. It was not until 1977 – 1978 that the disease was considered eradicated. Only two storehouses of the virus remained in the entire world– Atlanta, USA and Koltsovo, Russian Federation. Today, however, given the reality of proliferation, it is unclear as to how many nations and/or terrorist states have access to the disease. Smallpox is considered an ideal biological agent for two reasons. First, it can withstand an explosive blast dissemination (it can survive an explosion). Secondly, it is easily transmitted. The virus may spread through the air when an infected person breathes, talks, laughs or coughs. Given the 12-14 day incubation period, the potential for mass infection is enormous. The onset of the disease is marked by 2-3 days of high fever and extreme tiredness accompanied by severe backache and headache. Then, the rash develops. It begins with a few red spots on the face and forearms and in the mouth. It then spreads to the trunk and legs. By the fourth day, the red spots have turned to blisters, and then to pus filled lesions. Smallpox skin sores are deeply embedded in the skin and feel like firm round objects in the skin. By the fourteenth day, they begin to crust and develop scabs. There is no known cure for smallpox. It is possible to lessen the severity of the illness or to prevent it by administering the vaccine within four days of infection. However, given the similarity of symptomology between smallpox and the flu, diagnosis is difficult within that time period. The death rate remains at roughly 30 percent.

   Potential Threat: Smallpox is highly infectious and has a long incubation period, which increases the potential for mass casualties during a biological attack. In fact, "some estimates suggest that as many as a million people could die following a major smallpox outbreak in an urban area."[152] Weaponization is made easier by the fact that the disease can survive a large explosion.

Tularaemia (Francisella tularensis)

There are several routes of infection for Tularaemia. The bacteria may enter through an abrasion in the skin, blood or tissue fluids from infected animals, through insect bites and, less commonly, inhalation or ingestion.[153] Depending on the route of infection, symptoms can include skin ulcers, swollen and painful lymph glands, inflamed eyes, sore throat, oral ulcers or pneumonia. If pneumonia results, the patient might develop chest pain, difficulty breathing, bloody sputum, and respiratory failure. If the bacteria were inhaled, symptoms would include fever, chills, headache, muscle aches, joint pain, dry cough, and progressive weakness. The death rate for the lung form of the disease is as high as 40 percent.

Potential Threat: Tularaemia "is a highly potent BW agent as it resists freezing and can also remain viable for weeks in water, soil, carcasses, and hides."[154] The bacteria is easily aerosolized and only a small number of organisms (10-50) are needed to cause the disease.

Viral Hemorrhagic Fevers

(Arenaviruses, Lassa Fever, LCM, Rift Valley Fever, Filoviruses, Ebola, Marburg)

Viral Hemorrhagic Fevers are a group of illnesses that are caused by several different families of viruses. At the same time, there are similarities. The survival of VHF's is dependent on an animal host and with a few exceptions there is no cure or treatment. While some symptoms depend upon the specific VHF diagnosed, there are also some initial signs and symptoms that are common to all of them, including high fever, fatigue, dizziness, muscle aches, loss of strength, and exhaustion. Serious VHF cases can also be marked by bleeding under the skin, in internal organs, or from the eyes, mouth and ears. Patients may also present with compromised nervous systems, shock, coma, delirium, seizures and, with some VHF's, renal kidney failure. Perhaps the most dangerous VHF's with respect to bioterrorism are those that can easily be transmitted. Ebola, Marburg and Lassa, three such examples, are passed on through close contact with infected people, their bodily fluids, or with objects that have been exposed to bodily fluids.

Potential Threat: According to a recent report by the Journal of the American Medical Association, an unannounced aerosol attack using VHF's would pose a "serious risk" as a biological weapon.[155] Due to the lack of accurate laboratory tests for VHF's and clinicians' unfamiliarity with these diseases, diagnosis would be difficult.[156] At the same time, the potential for mass casualties exists given the infectious nature of some of these viruses and the fact that cures and treatments are virtually non-existent.

Category B Agents:
Brucellosis (Brucella species)
Epsilon Toxin of Slostridium perfringens
Food safety threats (e.g. Salmonella)
Glanders (Burkholderia mallei)
Melioidosis (Burkholderia pseudomallei)
Psittacosis (Chlamydia psittaci)
Q fever (Coxiella burnetii)
Ricin toxin from Ricinus communis (castor beans)
Staphylococcal enterotoxin B
Typhus fever (Rickettsia prowazekii)
Viral encephalitis
Water safety threats (E.G. Virio cholerae)

Category C Agents:
Hantaviruses
Multidrug-resistant tuberculosis
Nipah virus
Tickborne encephalitis viruses
Tickborne hemorrhagic fever viruses
Yellow fever

[1]   Preston, Robert, "The Demon in the Freezer," *The New Yorker*, July 12, 1999.

[2]   Smallpox attack scenario and production of spores based on input provided by William Patrick III.

[3]   Preston, Robert, "Annals of Warfare: The Bioweaponeers," *The New Yorker*, March 9, 1998.

[4]   Alibek, Ken with Stephen Handelman, *Biohazard: The Chilling True Account of the Largest Covert Biological Weapons Program in the World ? Told from the Inside by the Man Who Ran It.* New York: Dell Publishing, a division of Random House, Inc., 1999, pg. 278.

[5]   Preston, Robert, "The Demon in the Freezer," *The New Yorker*, July 12, 1999.

[6]   Alibek, personal communication, May 20, 2002.

[7]   Alibek, Ken with Stephen Handelman, *Biohazard: The Chilling True Account of the Largest Covert Biological Weapons Program in the World ? Told from the Inside by the Man Who Ran It.* New York: Dell Publishing, a division of Random House, Inc., 1999, pg. 154-155.

[8]   Patrick, William III, personal communication, April 16, 2002.

[9]   Department of Justice, *Five-Year Interagency Counterterrorism and Technology Crime Plan*, unclassified edition, Washington DC: Government Printing Office, 1999, pg. 36, as reported in *A Survey of Biological Terrorism and America's Domestic Preparedness Program* by Gregory D. Koblentz, September 2001,pg. 1.

[10] Mangold, T., Goldberg, J., *Plague Wars: The Terrifying Reality of Biological Warfare.* New York: St. Martins, 1999, pg. 56.

[11] Ibid, pg. 54.

[12] Ibid, pg. 61.

[13] Ibid, pg. 56.

[14] Ibid, pg. 57.

[15] Miller, Judith, Stephen Engelberg, and William Broad, *Germs: Biological Weapons and America's Secret War.* New York: Simon & Schuster, 2001, pgs. 63-64, 71. Also, Alibek, Ken with Stephen Handelman, *Biohazard: The Chilling True Account of the Largest Covert Biological Weapons Program in the World ? Told from the Inside by the Man Who Ran It,* pgs. 7, 19, 140-145.

[16] Ibid, pg. 62.

[17] Preston, Robert, "Annals of Warfare: The Bioweaponeers," *The New Yorker*, http://www.geocities.com/mrostov/subpages/bioweaponeers.htm, March 9, 1998, web pg. 9.

[18] Mangold, T., Goldberg, J., *Plague Wars: The Terrifying Reality of Biological Warfare.* New York: St. Martins, 1999, pg. 94.

[19] Ibid, pg. 102.

[20] Ibid, pg. 62.

[21] Ibid, pg. 64.

[22] Ibid, pg. 66.

[23] Ibid, pg. 76.

[24] Ibid, pg. 85.

[25] Ibid, pg. 86.

[26] Ibid, pg. 89.

[27] Preston, Robert, "Annals of Warfare: The Bioweaponeers," *The New Yorker*, http://www.geocities.com/mrostov/subpages/bioweaponeers.htm, March 9, 1998, web pg. 10.

[28] Ibid, Web pg. 11

[29] Mangold, T., Goldberg, J., *Plague Wars: The Terrifying Reality of Biological Warfare*. New York: St. Martins, 1999, pg. 213.

[30] American Foreign Policy Council, "Russian Military Still Developing Anthrax, Smallpox, Plague Weapons," *Russia Reform Monitor*, No. 422, http://www.afpc.org/rrm/rrm422.htm, March 31, 1998, web pg. 2.

[31] Alibek, Ken, personal communication, May 20, 2002.

[32] Preston, Robert, "Annals of Warfare: The Bioweaponeers," *The New Yorker*, http://www.geocities.com/mrostov/subpages/bioweaponeers.htm, March 9, 1998, web pg. 1.

[33] Brand, David, "CU's Vogel: Russian Biological Warfare Plants Still Pose a Global Threat, *The San Francisco Chronicle*, www.news.cornell.edu/Chronicle/01/2.22.01/AAASVogel.html, February 22, 2001, web pg. 1.

[34] Pincus, Walter, "GAO Critical of Program Aimed at Jobs for Russian Scientists," *The WashingtonwPost*, www-tech.mit.edu/V119/N7/gao.7w.html, February 23, 1999, web pg. 1.

[35] PBS, Interview with Richard Butler, www.pbs.org/wgbh/pages/frontline/shows/gunning/interviews/butler.html, October 2001, web page 5.

[36] Mangold, T., Goldberg, J., *Plague Wars: The Terrifying Reality of Biological Warfare*. New York: St. Martins, 1999, pg. 287.

[37] PBS, Interview with Richard Butler, www.pbs.org/wgbh/pages/frontline/shows/gunning/interviews/butler.html, October 2001, web page 1.

[38] Mangold, T., Goldberg, J., *Plague Wars: The Terrifying Reality of Biological*

Warfare. New York: St. Martins, 1999, pg. 291.

[39] Ibid, pg. 292.

[40] PBS, Interview with Richard Butler, www.pbs.org/wgbh/pages/frontline/shows/gunning/interviews/butler.html, October 2001, web pg. 1.

[41] Shribman, David, "Russia, France Offer Gauge for Iraq Policy," *The Boston Globe*, www.globalpolicy.org/security/issues/iraq/2002/0312france.htm, March 12, 2002, web pg. 2.

[42] Smith, Jeffrey R., "Did Russia Sell Iraq Germ Warfare Equipment," *The Washington Post*, www.washingtonpost.com/wp-srv/inatl/longterm/russiagov/stories/germ021298.htm, February 12, 1998, web pg. 1.

[43] Ibid, web pg. 2.

[44] Butler, Richard, *The Greatest Threat: Iraq, Weapons of Mass Destruction, and the Growing Crisis of Global Security.* New York: Public Affairs, 2000, pg. 107.

[45] Government White Paper, "Iraq Weapons of Mass Destruction Programs," www.fas.org/news/iraq/1998/02/13/whitepap.htm, February 13, 1998, web pg. 1.

[46] Butler, Richard, *The Greatest Threat*: Iraq, Weapons of Mass Destruction, and the Growing Crisis of Global Security. New York: Public Affairs, 2000, pg. xxiv.

[47] Alibek, Ken, personal communication, May 20, 2002.

[48] Cole, Leonard A., "The Specter of Biological Weapons," *Scientific American*, http://web.elastic.org/~fche/mirrors/cryptome.org/biowar-cole.htm, December 1996, web pg. 1.

[49] Alibek, Ken with Stephen Handelman, *Biohazard: The Chilling True Account of the Largest Covert Biological Weapons Program in the World Told from the Inside by the Man Who Ran It.* New York: Dell Publishing, a division of Random House, Inc., 1999, pg. 273-277.

[50] "U.S.: Cuba Sharing Bioweapons Technology," CNN.com, www.cnn.com/2002/WORLD/americas/05/06/cuba.weapons/?related, May 6, 2002, web pg. 1.

[50] Gedda, George, "Cuba May Have Bio Warfare Program," *Associated Press*, www.canf.org/News/020506newsb.htm, May 6, 2002, web pg. 1.

[51] Alibek, Ken with Stephen Handelman, *Biohazard: The Chilling True Account of the Largest Covert Biological Weapons Program in the World Told from the Inside by the Man Who Ran It.* New York: Dell Publishing, a division of Random House, Inc., 1999, pg. 273-277.

[52] Gedda, George, "Cuba May Have Bio Warfare Program," *Associated Press*, May 6, 2002.

54   Alibek, Ken, personal communication, May 20, 2002.

55   Canadian Security Intelligence Service, "Biological Weapons Proliferation,"
      Report #2000/05, www.csis-scrs.gc.ca/eng/miscdocs/200005_e.html, June 9,
      2000, web pg. 3.

56   Ibid, web pg. 3.

57   Ibid, web pg. 5

58   Ibid, web pg. 6.

59   Ibid, web pg. 5

60   Federation of American Scientists Website, "Chemical and Biological
      Weapons," www.fas.org/nuke/guide/china/cbw/, web pg. 2.

61   McCormick, E., Williams, L., "Did bin Laden Buy Bioterror? 1999 Testimony
      Says He Did," *San Francisco Chronicle*,
      www.freerepublic.com/focus/fr/553162/posts, October 21, 2001, web pg. 2.

62   Mangold, T., Goldberg, J., *Plague Wars: The Terrifying Reality of Biological
      Warfare*. New York: St. Martins, 1999, pg. 289.

63   Ibid.

64   Dolan, J. and D. Altimari, "Anthrax Missing From Army Lab," *Hartford
      Courant*, www.commondreams.org/headlines02/0120-05.htm, January 20, 2002,
      web pg. 1.

65   Office of the Press Secretary, "Joint Statement on U.S.-Russian Cooperation
      Against Bioterrorism," www.whitehouse.gov/news/releases/2001/11/20011113-
      7.html, November 13, 2001, web pg. 1.

66   Center for Civilian Biodefense Strategies, Johns Hopkins University, "Shining
      Light on "Dark Winter,"
      www.journals.uchicago.edu/CID/journal/issues/v34n7/020165/020165.html,
      February 19, 2002, web pg. 9.

67   "Invisible Enemy, Simulation Shows U.S. Unprepared for Bioterrorist Attack,"
      ABC News.com,
      http://abcnews.go.com/sections/wnt/WorldNewsTonight/bioterrorism010723feat
      ure.html, July 23, 2001, web pg. 2.

68   Weiss, R., "Bioterrorism: An Even More Devastating Threat," *The Washington
      Post*, http://www.mercola.com/2001/sep/26/bioterrorism.htm, September 17,
      2001, web pg. 2.

69   Ibid, web pg. 2.

70   Miller, Judith, Stephen Engelberg, and William Broad, *Germs: Biological
      Weapons and America's Secret War*. New York: Simon & Schuster, 2001, pg. 19.

71   Ibid, pg. 33.

[72] Ibid, pgs. 15-33. Also Török, Thomas J., M. D. et al, "A Large Community Outbreak of Salmonellosis Caused by Intentional Contamination of Restaurant salad Bars,"*JAMA*, Vol. 278 No. 5, August 6, 1997.

[73] Altman, L., Kolata, G., "Anthrax Missteps Offer Guide to Fight Next Bioterror Battle," www.nytimes.com/2002/01/06/health/policy/06ANTH.html, *The New York Times*, January 6, 2002, web pg. 1.

[74] Ibid, web pg. 3.

[75] Ibid, web pg. 4.

[76] Judicial Watch, Press Release, "HHS Secretary Tommy Thompson Forced to Admit That Key Information Kept from Public About Anthrax Crisis," October 25, 2001.

[77] "Expert Gives Feds a 'D' on Anthrax Response," CNN.com, www.cnn.com/2001/HEALTH/conditions/11/06/anthrax/, November 6, 2001, web pg. 1.

[78] Hardy, D., McNulty, M., "Ready for Bioterror? Hardy and McNulty Explain Federal Role in Disaster Control," *WorldNetDaily.com*, January 7, 2002, pg. 1.

[79] Altman, L., Kolata, G., "Anthrax Missteps Offer Guide to Fight Next Bioterror Battle," *The New York Times*, www.nytimes.com/2002/01/06/health/policy/06ANTH.html, January 6, 2002, web pg. 2.

[80] Judicial Watch Press Release, "The Government is Lying About the Full Extent and Source of Anthrax Attacks," October 24, 2002.

[81] "Postal Workers Angry over Response," CNN.com, http://fyi.cnn.com/2001/US/10/22/dc.postal.workers , October 23, 2001, web pg. 1.

[82] Anser Institute for Homeland Security, "Dark Winter," www.homelanddefense.org/darkwinter/index.cfm, web pg. 3.

[83] Ibid, web pg. 3

[84] Hamburg, Margaret, Testimony before the Subcommittee on National Security, Veterans Affairs and International Relations, http://www.house.gov/reform/ns/107th_testimony/testimony_of_margaret_a.htm, July 23, 2001, web pg. 2.

[85] Center for Civilian Biodefense Strategies, Johns Hopkins University, "Shining Light on "Dark Winter," http://www.journals.uchicago.edu/CID/journal/issues/v34n7/020165/020165.htm, February 19, 2002, web pg. 20.

[86] Taylor, Eric R., "Are We Prepared for Terrorism Using Weapons of Mass Destruction? Government's Half Measures," Washington, DC: Heritage Foundation, November 27, 2000.

87 Alibek, Ken with Stephen Handelman, *Biohazard: The Chilling True Account of the Largest Covert Biological Weapons Program in the World — Told from the Inside by the Man Who Ran It*, pg. 144.

88 Ibid, pg. 145.

89 Rarey, Jim, "Investigation into Responsibility for Recent Anthrax Incidents," World Newsstand, www.worldnewsstand/mediumrare/7.htm, December 13, 2001, web pg. 8.

90 National News Service, Moscow, November 27, 2001, 08:58 as reported in Ibid, web pg. 8.

91 Thomas, Gordon, Globe-Intel, "MI6-CIA Probe Into Deaths of Top Scientists in Bio-defense Programs...," March 18, 2002, web pg. 3; Kidd, Devvy, "The Deaths of Five Microbiologists: Murder, Suicide, Accident?," December 31, 2001, web pgs. 1 and 2.

92 Court TV report by Kidd, Devvy, "The Deaths of Five Microbiologists: Murder, Suicide, Accident?," www.courttv.com/news/2001/1221/body_ap.html, December 31, 2001, web pg. 14.

93 *Newsday*, "Probing Disappearance Of Infectious Disease Expert," http://www-tech.mit.edu/V121/N62/ish62_wn_shorts_1.62w.html, November 27, 2001.

94 Davidson, Michael and Michael C. Ruppert, "Microbiologist Death Toll Mounts," Wilderness Publications, www.Rense.com, March 7, 2002, web pgs. 3 and 4.

95 Ibid, pg. 4.

96 Thomas, Gordon, Globe-Intel, "MI6-CIA Probe Into Deaths of Top Scientists in Bio-defense Programs...," www.gordonthomas.ie. March 18, 2002, web pg. 4.

97 Kidd, Devvy, "The Deaths of Five Microbiologists: Murder, Suicide, Accident?," www.courttv.com/news/2001/1221/body_ap.html, December 31, 2001, web pg. 3.

98 Maria Glod, "Three Charged in Va. Scientist's Fatal Stabbing," *Washington Post* December 13, 2001, pg. B01.

99 Kidd, Devvy, "The Deaths of Five Microbiologists: Murder, Suicide, Accident?," www.courttv.com/news/2001/1221/body_ap.html, December 31, 2001, web pg. 20.

100 Ibid, web pg. 37.

101 Thomas, Gordon, Globe-Intel, "MI6-CIA Probe Into Deaths of Top Scientists in Bio-defense Programs...," www.gordonthomas.ie, March 18, 2002, web pgs. 4 and 5.

102 Webby, Sean and Lisa Krieger, "Pizza Delivery May Have Been Ambush," *The Mercury News*, February 28, 2002.

[103] Piper, Jeannie, Web Producer, "Victims Identified in Fatal Plane Crash," www.9news.com, (K*USA TV Denver), March 26, 2002, web pg. 1.

[104] Rarey, Jim, "Investigation into Responsibility for Recent Anthrax Incidents," World Newsstand, www.worldnewsstand/mediumrare/7.htm, December 13, 2001, web pg. 6 and 7.

[105] Thomas, Gordon, Globe-Intel, "MI6-CIA Probe Into Deaths of Top Scientists in Bio-defense Programs...," www.gordonthomas.ie, March 18, 2002, web pg. 1.

[106] Ibid, web pg. 2.

[107] Kidd, Devvy, "The Deaths of Five Microbiologists: Murder, Suicide, Accident?," www.courttv.com/news/2001/1221/body_ap.html, December 31, 2001, web pgs. 35 and 36

[108] Rarey, Jim, "Investigation into Responsibility for Recent Anthrax Incidents," World Newsstand, www.worldnewsstand/mediumrare/7.htm, December 13, 2001, web pg. 8 and 9.

[109] Rosenberg, Barbara Hatch, "Analysis of the Anthrax Attacks," Federation of American Scientists, www.fas.org./bwc/news/anthraxreport.htm, February 5, 2002, web pg. 9.

[110] Dolan, Jack, Dave Altimari and Lynne Tuohy, "Anthrax Easy to Get Out of Lab," *Hartford Courant*, www.ctnow.com/news/specials/hc-detrick-122001.story?coll=hc%2Dheadlines%2Dhome, December 20, 2001, web pgs. 1 and 3.

[111] Cooper, David E., Associate Director, Defense Acquisition Issues, National Security and International Affairs Division, United States General Accounting Office, "DOD's Anthrax Vaccine Manufacturer Will Continue to Need Financial Assistance," GAO Publication GAO/T-NSIAD-00-140, April 14, 2000, pg. 3.

[112] Ibid, pg. 3.

[113] Rosenberg, Howard L., "Anthrax Cloud's Silver Lining," www.abcnews.com, March 12, 2001, web pg. 2.

[114] Gurney, Ian, "Vaccine-Maker BioPort and bin Laden - A Profitable Symbiosis?", www.rense.com, December 19, 2001, web pg. 3.

[115] Cooper, David E., Associate Director, Defense Acquisition Issues, National Security and International Affairs Division, United States General Accounting Office, "DOD's Anthrax Vaccine Manufacturer Will Continue to Need Financial Assistance," GAO Publication GAO/T-NSIAD-00-140, April 14, 2000, pg. 1.

[116] Brooks, Jack B., Chairman, Committee on the Judiciary, United States House of Representatives, "The Inslaw Affair," Investigative Report Together with Dissenting and Separate Views Based on a Study by the Full Committee, September 10, 1992, web pg. 1.

[117] Ibid, web pg. 2.

[118] Richardson, Elliott L., "A High-Tech Watergate, *The New York Times*, op-ed section, October 21, 1991, web pg. 1.

[119] Ibid, web pg. 2.

[120] Mahar, Maggie, "Beneath Contempt, Did the Justice Department Deliberately Bankrupt INSLAW?", *Barron's National Business and Financial Weekly*, first article of two-part series, March 21, 1988, web pg. 4.

[121] Mahar, Maggie, "Rogue Justice, What Really Sparked the Vendetta Against INSLAW?", *Barron's National Business and Financial Weekly*, second of two-part series, April 4, 1988, web pgs. 14 and 15.

[122] Hamilton, William A., "The Largest Global Software Theft in History," luncheon address at World Computer and Internet Law Congress: Managing the Global Digital Information Technology Explosion, Monarch Hotel, Washington, D. C., May 3, 2001, web pg. 4.

[123] Mahar, Maggie, "Beneath Contempt, Did the Justice Department Deliberately Bankrupt INSLAW?", *Barron's National Business and Financial Weekly*, first article of two-part series, March 21, 1988, web pgs. 1 and 2.

[124] Richardson, Elliott L., "A High-Tech Watergate, *The New York Times*, op-ed section, October 21, 1991, web pg. 1.

[125] Mahar, Maggie, "Rogue Justice, What Really Sparked the Vendetta Against INSLAW?," *Barron's National Business and Financial Weekly*, second of two-part series, April 4, 1988, web pg. 15.

[126] Riconosciuto, Michael, Affidavit, United States Bankruptcy Court for the District of Columbia, in re: Inslaw, Inc., Case No. 85-00070 (Chapter 11), Adversary Proceeding No. 86-0069, March 21, 1991. web pgs. 1 - 4.

[127] Thomas, Gordon, "Intelligence Briefs," January - August 2001, (www.gordonthomas.ie), September 2001, web pg. 5.

[128] Thomas, Gordon, *Seeds of Fire: China and the Story Behind the Attack on America*, Dandelion Books, 2001.

[129] Weiss, Rick, "Polio-Causing Virus Created in NY Lab," *The Washington Post*, July 12, 2002, pg. A01.

[130] Regush, Nicholas, "Future Fears, The Potential of Genetically Engineered Viruses and Bacteria," ABC News.com, http://abcnews.co.com/sections/living/SecondOpinion/secondopinion011116.html, web page 1.

[131] Inglesby, Thomas V., "The State Public Health Preparedness for Terrorism Involving Weapons of Mass Destruction: A Six Month Report Card," Congressional Testimony, Committee on Government Affairs, http://www.senate.gov/~gov_affairs/041802inglesby.htm, April 18, 2002.

171

132 Alibek, Ken with Stephen Handelman, *Biohazard: The Chilling True Account of the Largest Covert Biological Weapons Program in the World ? Told from the Inside by the Man Who Ran It*. New York: Dell Publishing, a division of Random House, Inc., 1999, pg. 164.

133 Ibid.

134 United Nations Office for Drug Control and Crime Prevention, Terrorism and Weapons of Mass Destruction, http://www.undcp.org/terrorism.weapons.mass.destruction.page002.html, July 31, 2002.

135 "Senate Approves $4.6b Bioterror Bill," *Boston Globe*, May 24, 2002, pg. A8.

136 "House Ok's Homeland Security Bill," *Boston Globe*, July 27, 2002, pg. A1.

137 "Al-Quaida in Canada?," *60 Minutes*, www.cbsnews.com, April 25, 2002. web pg. 1.

138 "CSIS Head Labels Canada as a Haven for Terrorists," *The Online Edition Windsor Star*, www.southam.com/windsorstar/news/020427/92130.html, April 27, 2002, web pg. 1.

139 "Plan for More Fingerprinting Highlights Past Problems," *Boston Globe*, June 6, 2002, pg. A29.

140 Preston, Robert, "Annals of Warfare: The Bioweaponeers," *The New Yorker*, http://www.geocities.com/mrostov/subpages/bioweaponeers.htm, March 9, 1998, web pg. 14.

141 Brown, David, "Limited Smallpox Vaccine Use Eyed," *Washington Post*, June 21, 2002, pg. A01.

142 "HHS Awards $428 Million Contract to Produce Smallpox Vaccine," *HHS News*, U. S. Department of Health and Human Services, November 28, 2001, multiple pgs.

143 Patrick, William, "The Threat of Biological Warfare," Washington Roundtable on Science and Public Policy, February 13, 2001, www.marshall.org/PatrickRT.htm, web pg. 6.

144 Miller, Judith, Stephen Engelberg, and William Broad, "Future Germ Defenses," PBS Online, www.pbs.org/wgbh/nova/bioterror/germs.html, web pg. 4.

145 Alibek, Ken, personal communication, May 20, 2002.

146 Federation of American Scientists, *Special Weapons Primer*, www.fas.org/nuke/intro/bw/agent.htm, web pg. 2.

147 Mangold, T. and J. Goldberg, *Plague Wars: The Terrifying Reality of Biological Warfare*. New York: St. Martins, 1999, pg. 387.

148 New York City Department of Health Bureau of Communicable Disease,

Medical Treatment and Response to Suspected Botulism: Information for Health Care Providers During Biologic Emergencies, www.nyc.gov/html/doh/html/cd/botmd.html, July 2000, web pg. 4.

[149] Ibid, web pg. 2.

[150] Federation of American Scientists, *Special Weapons Primer,* www.fas.org/nuke/intro/bw/agent.htm, web pg. 12).

[151] Alibek, personal communication, May 20, 2002.

[152] BBC News, "Smallpox vaccine 'could kill hundreds,'" http://news.bbc.co.uk/1/hi/health/1973070.stm, May 8, 2002, web pg. 1.

[153] Mangold, T., Goldberg, J., *Plague Wars: The Terrifying Reality of Biological Warfare.* New York: St. Martins, 1999, pg. 383.

[154] Ibid.

[155] Journal of the American Medical Association, "Hemorrhagic Fever Viruses as Biological Weapons," http://jama.amaassn.org/issues/v287n18/ffull/ist20006.html, Vol. 287, No. 18, May 8, 2002, web pg. 2)

[156] Ibid, web pg. 3.

Nuclear and Chemical Terrorism: The Next Wave of Attacks?

*"The most urgent unmet national security threat to the
United States today is the danger that weapons of mass destruction
or weapons-usable material from Russia could be stolen, sold to
terrorists or hostile nation states and used against American troops
abroad or citizens at home."*[1]

> Former Senator Howard Baker
> Former White House Counsel Lloyd Cutler:
> "A Report Card on the Department of
> Energy's Nonproliferation Programs with
> Russia"
> January 10, 2001

*"An international team assembled by the ISEA will begin a search today
for two abandoned Strontium 90 generators in a ca. 550 sq km area of
western Georgia. About 80 people, mostly Georgian nationals, will take
part in a two-week search beginning Monday, June 10. Radiation experts
from the IAEA, India, France, Turkey and the U.S. are also part of the
team, which will set out on horseback, foot and car."* [2]

> "Search Begins for Missing Radiation
> Sources in Republic of Georgia":
> International Atomic Energy Agency
> Press Release
> June 10, 2002

Nuclear Terrorism

Once reserved for Tom Clancy novels and Pentagon "doomsday"
war gaming scenarios, the notion of a terrorist strike against a U.S. target
involving a nuclear or chemical weapon is now the subject of daily press
reports. The possibilities that al Qaeda might acquire the materials and the
knowledge for building nuclear weapons or "dirty bombs" or might attack
commercial nuclear-power facilities to trigger a nuclear meltdown are an
immediate concern to the American public.

During his State of the Union Address in January 2002, President George W. Bush stated: "We have found diagrams of American nuclear power plants and public water facilities, detailed instructions for making chemical weapons, surveillance maps of American cities, and thorough descriptions of landmarks in America and throughout the world." The American public will not get a clearer, more urgent warning of planned terrorist attacks.

On November 12, 1972, three hijackers re-routed a Southern Airlines DC-9 and threatened to crash the plane into the research reactor at a military nuclear research center at Oak Ridge, Tennessee. The hijackers settled for $2 million dollars and a trip to Cuba. In light of the September 11th attacks, the November 1972 hijacking is an eerie precursor that lends itself to a brief discussion of reactor containment facility structural integrity. Most commercial power plants cannot withstand an aircraft crashing into them. David Kyd, spokesman for the International Atomic Energy Agency, confirmed the plants' vulnerability, stating: "[Reactors] are built to withstand impacts, but not that of a wide-bodied passenger jet full of fuel . . . These are vulnerable targets, and the consequences of a direct hit could be catastrophic."[3] The extreme vulnerability of such nuclear sites resulted in the decision of the French government to station permanent anti-aircraft missile batteries and air defense radars to protect nuclear plants and reprocessing facilities. The U.S. government has not reportedly taken any such precautions.

Besides a nuclear weapon detonation or aircraft attack on a nuclear facility, nuclear terrorism also includes the use, or threat of use, of fissionable radioactive material in an attack designed to cause extensive, or perhaps even irreversible environmental damage that would render large areas uninhabitable for generations – the so-called "dirty bomb," that is also known as a "Radiological Dispersion Device," or "RDD."

Nuclear blackmail and the government's ability to react to the terrorists' threat of a strike, without knowing the actual likelihood of a detonation, is one of the "worst nightmares" facing the Bush-Cheney administration. The terrorists' "threat of use" should not be underestimated for the potency of its psychological and economic effects on the United States. When Attorney General John Ashcroft announced the arrest of Jose Padilla for allegedly planning a "dirty bomb" attack in the United States, the New York Stock Exchange took an eighty point dive after struggling to rebound from "soft" economic indicator figures. Imagine the crippling effect on the American economy if terrorists announced on a Monday morning that a nuclear weapon was somewhere in New York harbor and was set to explode within a certain time period.

Terrorists can also simply launch a conventional weapon, such as a truck bomb, against one of the many nuclear reactors around the world, damaging the reactor enough to release radioactive material into the atmosphere and thereby endangering the surrounding area. Nuclear power plants maintain enormous quantities of radioactive materials in spent fuel pools. Normally, these pools contain up to five times as much material as in the actual reactor core, and they are housed in ordinary utility buildings that are even more vulnerable to attack than the reinforced structures characteristic of a reactor containment facility.[4]

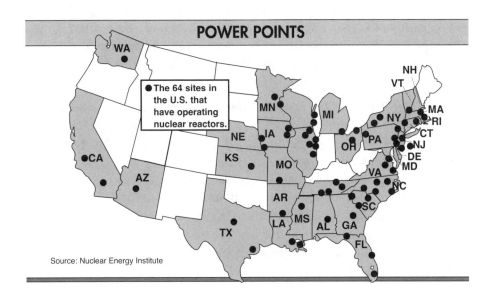

POWER POINTS

● The 64 sites in the U.S. that have operating nuclear reactors.

Source: Nuclear Energy Institute

The attacks of September 11th demonstrate for the American public and the world that al Qaeda is prepared to inflict civilian casualties on a scale that is consistent with the use of a weapon of mass destruction (WMD). Terrorists do not subscribe to the same moral code as the United States and its allies, and thus they do not fear a nuclear response or damage to their international interests as a result of using a WMD – a fear that deterred sovereign states from using those types of weapons throughout the post-World War II period.

Al Qaeda may attempt to obtain fissionable materials or a nuclear bomb through the black market – particularly from sources in Eastern Europe or the Former Soviet Union (FSU). There is clear evidence that al

Qaeda agents have made unsuccessful attempts to procure enriched uranium in the mid-1990's, and that bin Laden has consistently expressed his desire (he would call it his "duty") to have a nuclear weapon.

At the trial of the four men convicted of planning the U.S. embassy bombings of 1998 in East Africa, al-Qaeda informant Jamal Ahmed al-Fadl testified to his role in helping to arrange a 1993 deal in which bin Laden attempted to pay $ 1.5 million for a cylinder of South African uranium. Al-Fadl saw the cylinder, but he wasn't present to see when – or if – money and material changed hands.[5]

In December 1994, Czech police seized 4 kg of highly enriched uranium. Later in 1994, the German police seized more than 400g of plutonium.[6] In October 2001, Turkish police arrested two men with 1.16 kg of weapons-grade uranium.[7] During the same period, the Russian Defense Ministry reported two incidents of terrorist groups attempting, unsuccessfully, to gain access to nuclear storage sites.[8]

Since 1993, the International Atomic Energy Agency has reported 175 cases of nuclear trafficking, with 18 of those cases reportedly involving highly enriched uranium or plutonium.[9] During the Cold War, the Soviet Union built an unknown number of portable nuclear explosives, small enough to be carried in a suitcase or backpack. After the Iron Curtain came down, Russia claimed to have secured all nuclear weapons, but many analysts have doubts. In 1996, Russian General Alexander Lebed maintained that his government had lost 134 backpack nukes, and stories have circulated that bin Laden himself bought 20 of them from the Chechens for $30 million and two tons of opium.[10]

Besides hardware and fuel issues, there remains the "human factor." It is unlikely that the terrorists themselves would construct a radiological device. The specialized know-how, training and education required to successfully produce a nuclear weapon is not a skill developed quickly or easily. Al Qaeda appears to have had a volunteer to assist them in their radiological ambitions. Since 1998, Sultan Bashiruddin Mahmood, one of Pakistan's leading nuclear engineers and part of the team that developed Pakistan's nuclear arsenal, traveled in and out of the Taliban stronghold of Kandahar, where he has helped the Afghans construct a complex of buildings he describes as "flour mills."[11] Al Qaeda is certainly ready to accept technical assistance from ideological and religious allies, but that is not necessarily a requirement for the consulting job. FSU and former East Bloc scientists are available for a price, and money has never been a stumbling block for Al Qaeda.

Meanwhile, the worldwide hunt for unaccounted-for sources of radiological material continues. The two "orphaned"* Strontium 90 radiothermal generators (RTGs) being sought in the Republic of Georgia contain the heavy metals that, while not used to make nuclear weapons, could be used by terrorists with a conventional explosive to create a devastating RDD. The RTGs are self-contained power sources that convert radioactive energy into electricity. They were used in remote areas to power radio equipment, navigational beacons, and antennae assemblies. The devices themselves are between two to four feet long and can weigh over one ton – although the capsule containing the Strontium 90 is only the size of a flashlight. The rest of the unit consists of shielding and lead cladding.[12] Exposure to the highly radioactive core of the RTG containing the Strontium 90 can give a fatal dose of radiation in two minutes.[13]

The search for the RTGs and other devices like them (poorly accounted for after the collapse of the Soviet Union and available on the black market for a price) should be of paramount concern to the Bush-Cheney administration. Overshadowed by domestic affairs and treated with only passing interest by defense and security analysts, the January 2001 "Report Card on the Department of Energy's Nonproliferation Programs with Russia," by Howard Baker and Lloyd Cutler, under the auspices of the Secretary of Energy's Advisory Board, painted a very grim picture of the nuclear state of affairs relative to potential acts of terrorism by a well-organized, well-financed, terrorist organization such as al Qaeda.

The Bush-Cheney administration needs to reexamine the nuclear terrorist threat. At an absolute minimum, two things need to happen immediately: 1) Air defense radars and weapons should be stationed at all of the country's nuclear facilities and, 2) Commercial nuclear power plants should have their guard forces rigorously tested outside of the typical "canned" training scenarios, and augmented by National Guard troops.

Chemical Terrorism

While nuclear terrorism poses problematic technical and logistical issues that, to some degree, may limit or reduce the probability of a terrorist nuclear attack on U.S. soil, chemical terrorism is far easier and more practical. The best known chemical attack by terrorists in recent history was in 1995, by members of the "Supreme Truth" cult, against various targets including the subway systems of Tokyo and Yokohama, Japan. Despite the high toxicity of the material released by the terrorists and the subsequent panic that set in among the subway passengers, the casualty figures were, fortunately, relatively low.

The use of chemical weapons by conventional armed forces dates back to the Peloponnesian War. Fire and smoke remained the principal chemical weapons up until the 19th century, when advances in science, chemistry, engineering, and the advantages of the Industrial Revolution led to the development (and use during World War I) of devices such as the flamethrower, tear gas grenades, and artillery shells with chlorine, phosgene, and mustard gasses. The United States entered World War I in April 1917, completely unprepared for chemical warfare: no organization, no equipment, and no personnel trained for chemical warfare. The Army scrambled and under the direction of the American Expeditionary Force commander, General John J. Pershing, the Chemical Corps was created. Throughout World War II, poison gas was not used by any of the warring states against uniformed combatants (the notorious exception, of course, being Nazi Germany's gassing of millions of civilian Jews in concentration camps). The flamethrower and the smoke generator were the chemical weapons most used in both theatres of World War II. Since World War II, chemical weapons have been used sporadically, but most notably in the Middle East and Southwest Asia:

- In 1963, the Egyptians used mustard gas against Yemeni royalists in the Arabian Peninsula.

- The Soviets used chemical warfare agents in their Christmas 1979 invasion of Afghanistan, most probably mustard gas and a nerve agent.

- In the 1980's, Iraq used mustard gas and a nerve agent against Iran in their eight year long war.

- Iraq used hydrogen cyanide and a nerve agent against its own Kurdish minority population in 1988.

- Some U.S. Gulf War veterans question whether they were subjected to Iraqi chemical (or perhaps biological) attack, due to a variety of medical ills and conditions ("Gulf War Syndrome") connected with their service during that conflict.[14]

Chemical attacks by terrorist organizations can be categorized into two methods. The first aims to cause mass devastation in congested population centers, seeking to create as many casualties as possible. The horror of thousands of dead or injured people speaks for itself. The second method is a true "terror" attack meant to induce fear, panic, and suspicion, or create conditions for political blackmail and/or economic sabotage. The objective is not on inflicting casualties, *per se*, but on terrorizing the public's psyche with fear of "what might be next." Success in this method of terrorism erodes public support and confidence in its leaders and government. A series of relatively simple, pinprick attacks on civilian population centers could make the government appear to be a blind, muscle-bound giant – groping about frantically and ineffectually. Such terror attacks do not lend themselves to counterattacks by F-16s and Marines. They would highlight the country's woefully inadequate civil defense, emergency public health system, and counterterrorism law enforcement programs.

For the terrorists, chemical attacks are simple and effective. Most of the chemical substances or ingredients necessary for a devastating attack are available in supermarkets and hardware stores. The processes needed to manufacture the toxic chemicals can normally be accomplished in a garage, basement, storage shed, or almost any location the terrorist selects that has a reasonable degree of privacy and security. A bright high school chemistry student possesses the degree of technical knowledge required to prepare the terrorists' chemical weapons. Instances when terrorists have been intercepted before carrying out their planned chemical weapons attacks are noteworthy by the fact that due to their own missteps, the terrorists compromised their operational security and called attention to themselves, terminating their illegal operations – not proactive counterterrorism or law enforcement actions. The mastermind of the 1993 WTC bombing, Ramzi Yousef, and his comrade-at-arms, Abdul Hakim Murad, accidentally set fire to their Manila apartment on January 6, 1995, while brewing chemicals intended for a phosgene gas attack on then-President Clinton. When Murad attempted to reenter the building after the fire to retrieve Yousef's laptop computer, Philippine National Police arrested him. The contents of Yousef's computer yielded a treasure trove of information for counterterrorism investigators.[15]

Many state-sponsors of terrorism, including Iran, Iraq, Syria, Libya, North Korea and others, have ample supplies of very sophisticated chemical weapons at their disposal. The transfer of particularly complex or sophisticated binary chemical weapons from a state-sponsor of terrorism to a terrorist organization is certainly a possibility, particularly for a high-profile, mass casualty terror strike, where the terrorists are looking to maximize both the damage and the resultant media coverage of the attack. The advantage for the sponsoring state is the plausible deniability afforded by the terrorist organization acting as its surrogate.

Technological advances have made the development of chemical terror weapons easier to transport and increased the lethality of small amounts of weaponized chemical agents. A small jar containing a few hundred grams of a chemical agent, when deployed in the right conditions, can cause mass casualties and contaminate large areas or entire facilities – such as a subway system. On top of the actual physical reaction to the weapon, there is the added terror factor that tends to rip through the general public. Fanned by hysterical media reporting, news of a chemical weapon attack can trigger widespread panic, and undermine or hinder both the government's ability to effectively respond to the attack with appropriate medical and public safety countermeasures, as well as the apprehension of the perpetrators by law enforcement.

There is little doubt al Qaeda has plans for the use of chemical weapons. Videotapes obtained by CNN and CBS show al Qaeda evidently testing chemical agents on animals.

Chemical weapons are normally divided into three classes of agents: nerve agents, such as "Sarin;" blister agents, such as "mustard gas;" and choking agents like phosgene and chlorine.

Direct and severe exposure to a nerve agent results in involuntary muscular twitching; labored, shallow and rapid respiration; profuse bronchial secretions and salivation; abdominal cramps, followed by involuntary defecation and urination; and eventually cardio respiratory arrest, followed by death.

Blister agents burn and blister the skin and other exposed tissue on contact. They act on the eyes, mucous membranes, skin and lungs. They sear the respiratory tract when inhaled and cause vomiting and diarrhea when ingested. The blisters formed on the skin by the chemical agent are necrotic and extend beneath the surface to underlying tissue. The damaged tissues are extremely susceptible to infection. The only protection from blister agents is full chemical agent protective clothing, including a respirator "gas mask."

Choking agents attack the lungs and cause pulmonary edema (the excessive build-up of fluid in tissue spaces or a body cavity). Phosgene is typical of most choking agents, in that it is a colorless gas. Eighty percent of all chemical fatalities in World War I are attributed to Phosgene. As its name suggests, the effects include choking, coughing, nausea, vomiting, and headache. The onset of pulmonary edema is not apparent for anywhere from 2 to 24 hours – but begins with renewed coughing, shallowness of breath, feeble, rapid heartbeat, and frothy sputum. Patients develop shock-like symptoms (e.g., pale, clammy skin), but if they survive more than 48 hours, they usually recover.[16]

Little or nothing has been done by the Bush-Cheney administration, or any previous administrations going back to Eisenhower, to educate and prepare the American public for the possibility of a chemical attack. As part of the government's overhaul and re-invention of its counterterrorism and civil defense programs, a public education campaign on the effects of chemical weapons must be instituted immediately. The public has been left with the false and misleading notion that should anything like a terrorist chemical attack occur, then rescue and medical workers will suddenly materialize and "fix" everything. This could not possibly be further from the truth. Americans, for the most part, are going to be "on their own" because of the extremely limited resources available to respond to a major terrorist chemical attack. Responsible city and county governments should be holding public classes and seminars for concerned citizens on conducting decontamination procedures and administering first aid to terror victims. The response from all levels of government – federal, state and local – is akin to the proverbial ostrich.

Merely hoping that terrorist chemical and nuclear attacks will not occur provides no measure of prevention or security. The U.S. government, as well as state, county and local governments have an affirmative obligation to protect and inform the public. When it comes to terrorist nuclear and chemical strikes, these governments have been, and remain, negligent in educating and preparing the public for terrorism – particularly in metropolitan areas and population centers that are the likely targets of terrorists. The time for an aggressive, realistic public education and training campaign is now. Anything less, including the current complacency, could cost American lives on the scale of the September 11th attacks – or worse.

---

[1] US Department of Energy, Secretary of Energy's Advisory Board, "A Report Card on the Department of Energy's Nonproliferation Programs with Russia," Howard Baker and Lloyd Cutler, Co-Chairs, Russia Task Force, January 10, 2001.

[2] International Atomic Energy Agency Press Release, "Search Begins For Missing Radiation Sources in Republic of Georgia," June 10, 2002, http://www.iaea.org/worldatom/Press/P-release/2002/prn0208.shtml.

[3] Transcript, *Moneyline*, CNN, September 18, 2001.

[4] Tiwari J., *Vulnerability of U.S. Nuclear Power Plants to Terrorist Attack and Internal Sabotage*, Washington, DC, PSR Center for Global Security and Health, 2001.

[5] Jeffrey Kluger, "Osama's Nuclear Quest," *Time*, November 12, 2001.

[6] G.T. Allison, O.R. Cote, R.A. Falkenwrath, S.E. Miller, *Avoiding Nuclear Anarchy*, Cambridge, MA; Center for Science and International Affairs, Harvard University, 1996.

[7] *Reuters*, "Turkish Police Detain Suspects Selling Uranium," November 6, 2001.

[8] G.T. Allison, "Could Worse Be Yet To Come?," *Economist*, November 1, 2001.

[9] International Atomic Energy Agency Press Release, "Calculating the New Global Nuclear Terrorism Threat," November 1, 2001, http://www.iaea.org/worldatom/Press/P-release/2001/nt_pressrelease.shtml.

[10] Jeffrey Kluger, "Osama's Nuclear Quest," *Time*, November 12, 2001.

[11] Jeffrey Kluger, "Osama's Nuclear Quest," *Time*, November 12, 2001.

[*] "Orphaned" is a term use by the International Atomic Energy Agency (IAEA) to describe nuclear/radiological devices no longer under the control or accountability of the government that created the item(s). It is used most often with devices created by the Soviet Union and former East Bloc countries.

[12] Joby Warrick, "Making a Dirty Bomb," *Washington Post*, March 18, 2002.

[13] *Interfax*, "Radiation Source in Remote Area of Western Georgia Remains Active," FBIS Document CEP200020108000169, January 8, 2002.

[14] Robert J. T. Joy, M.D., F.A.C.P., "Historical Aspects of Medical Defense Against Chemical Warfare," *Textbook of Military Medicine: Medical Aspects of Chemical and Biological Warfare*, U.S. Army Medical Research Institute of Chemical Defense, Office of the Surgeon General, Department of the Army, 1997.

[15] Reeve, Simon, *The New Jackals*, (Northeastern University Press, Boston 1999), page 87-90.

[16] Federation of American Scientists, "Chemical Warfare Agents," *Special Weapons Primer*, http://www.fas.org/nuke/intro/cw/agent.htm.

Cyber-Terror

The advent of the Information Age and the overwhelming reliance of all sectors of American society on computers, as well as the Internet, has boosted productivity and opened new technological and commercial horizons. The downside to our dependence on automation, complex information systems, electronic communications and the Internet is their potential vulnerability to disruptive and destructive attacks by terrorists. The nature and scope of these attacks can range from relatively innocuous, nuisance attacks that merely inconvenience businesses, government and the general populace, to potentially devastating acts against the information systems and networks at key strategic targets, resulting in massive casualties and a breakdown not just in computing and communications, but in civil order.

Cyber-terrorism might include cyber-attacks ranging from economic loss (virus attacks, disruption in online banking, etc.) to possible violence (triggering an explosion, disrupting air traffic control systems, aircraft collisions, etc.). For example, a "worm" that struck last year, Code Red, is estimated to have caused $2.62 billion in damages worldwide, and planners fear is it only a matter of time before another one causes hardship for millions of private citizens.[1]

As far as the threat of an al Qaeda cyber-attack is concerned, technical competence remains the only barrier to their launching an electronic strike on U.S. interests. The vulnerabilities, "back doors," and exploitable weaknesses in our nation's information systems architecture exist – as evidenced by any number of "hacker" stories receiving press coverage over the last 15 years or so.

The U.S. government is in fact, well aware of its vulnerability – as are leaders in the information systems and Internet industries. In 1997, the U.S. Department of Defense conducted an exercise, code-named "Eligible Receiver," wherein a team of 35 government contracted hackers, were successful in breaking into the power grids of nine American cities, disrupting their 911 emergency systems. The hackers also achieved "root access" in some of the Pentagon's computer networks, meaning they were able to take absolute, or universal, control over the networks and their subordinate systems. The exercise demonstrated severe weaknesses in the Defense Department's information infrastructure and proved that motivated hackers could indeed compromise national security. It also demonstrated that despite the United States being undoubtedly the most wired nation in the world, it is also the most vulnerable to Information Warfare. Even more disturbing is the fact that Defense Department information systems and networks have a more advanced security system precisely because of the classification and sensitivity of the information processed. No wonder it is extremely wary of the "asymmetric threat" posed by terrorists and non-state actors targeting the United States.[2]

Al Qaeda operatives have been exploring U.S. Internet sites and probing the electronic infrastructure of American companies in search of ways to disable power and water supplies, disrupt phone service and damage other parts of critical infrastructure.

Ron Ross, who heads a new group formed by the NSA and the National Institute of Standards and Technology, told the *Washington Post* that immediately after the September 11th attacks, air traffic controllers oversaw the safe landing of every commercial plane in the air.

"If there had been a cyber-attack at the same time that prevented them from doing that," Ross said, "the magnitude of the event could have been much greater. A cyber-attack can be launched with fairly limited resources. It is not science fiction."[3]

There is evidence that al Qaeda is pursuing precisely the sort of terrorist attack Mr. Ross envisioned. The increasing power of commercially available off-the-shelf computers, programs and specific engineering and technical applications, as well as the ability to gain high-speed access to the Internet through a variety of means and from almost any location on earth, no matter how remote, raises the specter of sophisticated cyber-terrorism strikes launched by almost anyone, from virtually anywhere. Money and technical know-how are the two critical components – certainly both are readily available to al Qaeda and like-minded allies, whether they are state sponsors of terrorism or individual cells, operating independently.

A computer seized in January 2002, by the U.S. military from an al Qaeda office in Afghanistan, contained models of a dam, made with structural architecture and engineering software that enabled the planners to simulate its catastrophic failure. According to the FBI, the computer had also been running Microstran, a tool for analyzing steel and concrete structures.[4]

"We were underestimating the amount of attention [al Qaeda was] paying to the Internet," said Roger Cressey, a long-time counterterrorist official who became chief of staff of the President's Critical Infrastructure Protection Board in October 2001. "Now we know they see it as a potential attack vehicle. Al Qaeda spent more time mapping our vulnerabilities in cyberspace than we previously thought. An attack is a question of when, not if."[5]

The vulnerability of U.S. information systems to information attacks for the purpose of disrupting our economy, infrastructure and public safety is enormous. The possible scope of a crippling attack on our systems, networks and communications – both private and government, military and civilian – leaves virtually no sector of our society immune from such a terror attack. Other than an occasional news article and technical or professional discussions of our vulnerabilities to cyber-terror, the Bush-Cheney administration has done very little in the way of public education or increasing America's awareness. A concerted effort needs to be made by the administration to correct that shortcoming and to "harden" the nation's information systems – public, defense, private and commercial – before we face what has been referred to as a "Cyber Pearl Harbor." A side benefit to such cyber-preparedness would be the enhancement of individual privacy on the Internet, consistent with the Bill of Rights.

---

[1] Ross Kerber, "Cyber-Structure Still At Risk Effort To Prevent 'An Electronic Pearl Harbor' Is Lagging," *The Boston Globe*, June 25, 2002.

[2] "Al Qaeda's Threat Extends To The Information Frontier," *Financial Express*, July 14, 2002

[3] Jovi Tanada Yam, L@wyer.com;Al Qaeda and Cyber-Terrorism, *BusinessWorld*, July 18, 2002.

[4] "U.S. Fears al-Qaeda Cyber-Attack: Control of Dams, Nuclear Power Plants Possible, FBI says," *National Post*, June 28, 2002.

[5] Barton Gellman, "Cyber Attacks by al Qaeda Feared," *Washington Post*, June 27, 2002.

Al Qaeda: Alive & Well

Despite the best efforts of the U.S. military, its allies and "friendly" Afghan warlords, by mid-December 2001, nearly 1000 members of al Qaeda, including most of the terrorist organization's leadership, fled to safety in Pakistan. While few believe him dead, many military and intelligence analysts think that Osama bin Laden himself was among the group that U.S.-backed Afghan mercenaries allowed to successfully slip out of the al Qaeda and Taliban stronghold of Tora Bora to freedom. Since their escape into Pakistan, only one al Qaeda notable, Abu Zubaydah, has been captured by Pakistani security forces.

Al Qaeda's scattering to the four winds to rest, rearm, reorganize and plan the next wave of attacks poses an additional degree of difficulty on those trying to target the terrorist organization's operatives and actions. The dispersal of the terror cells and their leadership actually makes their identification and neutralization even more difficult for U.S. military and intelligence analysts. Al Qaeda faces its own new challenges. In addition to the loss of some senior leaders and the disruption of its communications, al Qaeda has typically depended on sanctuary in "safe havens" such as Pakistan (1970's), Sudan (1980's) and Afghanistan (1990's) in order to operate effectively and plan for coordinated large-scale attacks. When al Qaeda was headquartered in Afghanistan, the organization, its leaders and operations developed a "signature" or recognizable pattern to intelligence organizations skilled at detecting such operational profiles. A centralized base of operations in a known area is easier to monitor and analyze than small groups scattered across two dozen countries in an arc half-way around the world. There are likely scores of semi-autonomous al Qaeda cells, cautiously reconstituting themselves and planning another series of strikes against U.S. targets, since it is estimated that 8,000 to 10,000 potential operatives passed through al Qaeda training camps.

Certainly, in the Southwest Asian theatre of operations, the U.S. military faces a much greater unconventional threat now than in October 2001, when organized Taliban and al Qaeda forces first engaged U.S. ground and heliborne forces. Understanding the financial costs, level of military effort, and tempo of operations is important in appreciating the degree of damage inflicted upon al Qaeda. At the height of operations, over 70,000 U.S. military personnel were committed to the theatre, including two Navy carrier battle groups. Fifteen other nations provided troops of some description – mostly in the fields of medical, administrative and logistics support. British forces were the allies chiefly engaged in ground combat alongside U.S. troops. American and coalition air forces have flown more than 36,000 sorties in support of Operation Enduring Freedom, 21,000 of which were flown over Afghanistan. Pentagon estimates calculate that the war costs between $2 billion to $2.5 billion each month.

Closer to the Beginning, Rather than the End

The Bush-Cheney administration's decision to rely heavily on Afghan militia, and not U.S. forces, to close off escape routes in the mountains of Tora Bora last December compromised an opportunity for a clear cut military victory, when a number of intelligence indicators put bin Laden and his top lieutenants within striking distance of U.S. forces. Michael Swetnam, a counterterrorism expert at the Potomac Institute for Policy Studies, has stated, "Roughly 70 percent of the Qaeda leadership apparently escaped our campaign unharmed, and there is evidence they are trying to reconstitute the organization."[1]

The U.S. military's operations in Afghanistan and that country's border region with Pakistan are constrained, in part, due to the sensitivities and vulnerabilities of Pakistan's "president," General Pervez Musharraf, who has pledged the cooperation of the government of his Islamic nation which, for the most part is the source of support for the radical Islamist fundamentalists the United States is hunting. Musharraf presides over a nation aware that he is in great political and physical danger. The presence of U.S. forces in Pakistan is highly sensitive. Officially, the United States will not admit they are there, but as many as 100 are working alongside the Pakistani army. Tribal warlords in Pakistan's western provinces are extremely resistant to compromising the fruits of their local madrassas to the joint, U.S. Special Forces – Pakistani Army patrols hunting the Taliban and al Qaeda. Tribal leaders will now only continue to cooperate with the search for Al Qaeda on condition that no U.S. forces are involved. They also demanded that Pakistani authorities inform them in advance of the locations for raids, which observers said would guarantee the escape of any fugitives.[2] And, General Musharraf has to answer difficult questions from his Islamic countrymen concerning the "religious justification" of soldiers injured or killed on patrols with U.S. forces against other Islamists.

Our "Allies" In The "War on Terror"

Pervez Hoodbhoy, one of Pakistan's leading pro-democracy advocates, teaches physics at Quaid-e-Azam University, Islamabad, and in a recent newspaper editorial he explained one of Musharraf's vulnerabilities, "To die in Kashmir officially qualifies a soldier or officer as a 'shaheed' (martyr). But, is fighting America's war a "jihad," and are soldiers slain by al Qaeda or other former allies also to be justified and revered as martyrs? Since official certification of martyrdom is tied to land grants and compensation to families, this question carries very real material significance."[3] Does dying for "infidel Americans," who are hunting Islamist brothers, gain the soldier paradise and his surviving family a land grant and annuity? The answer to that question, as well as the other political and religious pressures Musharraf faces, apparently has great weight with the Bush-Cheney administration.

Another example: In what can only be described as a "stunning" interview with Phillip Smucker of the *Christian Science Monitor*, Mohammed Muslim, the Kashmiri regional chief of Pakistan's powerful Interservices Intelligence (ISI) agency, stated:

> "The US government destroyed the World Trade Center so that it would have an excuse to destroy Afghanistan," he says, drinking tea in the office of the regional police chief, who nods in full agreement. "After that, the US military killed tens of thousands of women and children in Afghanistan."
>
> * * *
>
> Asked if he agreed that Al Qaeda was a terrorist group, Muslim chuckled and said that Osama bin Laden has been wrongly vilified through CIA-produced fake videos of him talking about the World Trade Center attack. He added: "We don't have to agree with Musharraf here. He is the leader of our country, but he is not an elected leader."[4]

Ironically, to a large degree, the political fate of President George W. Bush, is tied to that of General Musharraf. Indeed, Musharraf's political viability and the stability of nuclear-armed Pakistan, as well as fear of political fallout from U.S. casualties provided justification for President Bush deciding not to allow U.S. forces to engage in a "hot pursuit" of al

Qaeda and the Taliban into the safe haven of Pakistan. It defined the limitations on the U.S. military's mission and netted the short-term, unsatisfactory results that could leave President Bush with vulnerabilities that could become more acute over time, despite early, strong poll numbers.

Back in December 2001, the Bush-Cheney administration's plan called for Afghan militias to drive al Qaeda fugitives out into zones where U.S. troops could neutralize them as an effective fighting force, through either capture or combat. There were simply not enough U.S. troops (approximately 1300, not all of whom were acclimated to the altitude of the two mile high mountain passes) to cover all of the possible escape routes, and the Pakistani border proved to be too porous.

Eventually, Musharraf moved two brigades of Pakistani troops along the Parachinar Salient, but his attention was diverted by having to shift resources and personnel to the Indian border as a result of a December 13th attack by (Pakistani based and al Qaeda allied) Kashmiri separatists on the Indian Parliament. Within three days Tora Bora fell, and the remaining al Qaeda holdouts fled to Pakistan, essentially unimpeded.[5]

The Ones That Got Away . . .And Their Supporters

The surviving remnants of al Qaeda have not yet launched a large scale terrorist act since the attacks of September 11th, but they, or their sympathizers, have continued to lash out at U.S. and Western interests on almost a monthly basis:

January, 2002 – Kidnapping and murder of American journalist Daniel Pearl.

March, 2002 – Grenade attack in Islamabad, Pakistan, that killed four Protestant International Church congregants, including a U.S. Embassy employee and her daughter.

April, 2002 – Truck bombing of a synagogue in Tunisia that killed 19 people, including 14 German tourists.

May, 2002 – Bombing of a bus in Karachi that killed 14 people, including 11 French engineers.

June, 2002 – Bombing of the U.S. Consulate in Karachi, Pakistan, that killed 12 Pakistanis.

August, 2002 – Two attacks in Pakistan – against a Christian missionary school and a Christian hospital, killing 10 people.

The April 2002, truck bomb attack on a synagogue in Djerba, Tunisia, is the sole attack since September 11th that U.S. intelligence agencies believe is attributable directly to the remnants of al Qaeda. The other attacks in Pakistan on Western targets appear, so far, to be the work of sympathetic militants, not of al Qaeda itself, officials say. The United States also believes other al Qaeda operations were averted by arresting suspects and tightening security measures.[6] While small scale, the frequency and persistence of the attacks launched by al Qaeda sympathizers demonstrate both the scope and depth of support for the terrorist organization throughout Pakistan.

The whereabouts of Osama bin Laden remain a mystery, and he has not been taken "dead or alive," as President Bush once boasted. Defense Secretary Donald Rumsfeld claimed no knowledge concerning bin Laden's condition or location when testifying before Congress on July 31, 2002. Various foreign intelligence and diplomatic sources provide unconfirmed and conflicting tidbits of rumor, innuendo and speculation about al Qaeda's symbolic figure, hero, financier and founder. The unconfirmed stories are often reported by both print and electronic media, along with various anecdotal claims by Afghani or Pakistani "local guides." No reports concerning bin Laden's health or whereabouts have been independently confirmed.

Two things are certain: 1) the war in Afghanistan is by no means "over," and 2) the administration of Afghan leader Hamid Karzi is, at best, unsecured. U.S. forces still encounter hit and run raids and ambushes in remote areas of the country. Karzi is guarded by U.S. Special Forces soldiers within the city limits of his own capital – Kabul. On August 20, 2002, Pakistani President Musharraf warned that the al Qaeda network may be regrouping in Afghanistan because of the weakness of the Afghan government, raising new questions about the success of the U.S.-led war on terrorism.[7] Musharraf, who has an interest in minimizing his country's responsibilities, said the failure of U.S.-led forces and the Afghan administration to establish control outside Kabul since the fall of the Taliban militia meant conditions were ripe for al Qaeda to regroup. If this is the state of affairs in Afghanistan, thanks in large part to the help of our Pakistani allies, one wonders what the future may hold for the Bush-Cheney administration, and the American public when it comes to a possible U.S. experience in Iraq. And the failure to capture or kill bin Laden, al Qaeda, and Taliban leaders holds ramifications for U.S. homeland security.

[1] Siobhan Gorman, Sydney J. Freedberg Jr., Neil Munro, Peter H. Stone, James Kitfield , "Preventing New Attacks," *The National Journal* , August 10, 2002.

[2] Liz Sly, "Tribal Defiance Thwarts U.S. Hunt For Al Qaeda; Pakistanis In West Hinder Operations," *Chicago Tribune*, June 26, 2002.

[3] Pervez Hoodbhoy, "Musharraf and Jihad Industry," *Bangkok Post*, August 18, 2002.

[4] Phillip Smucker, "Al Qaeda thriving in Pakistani Kashmir," *Christian Science Monitor*, July 2, 2002

[5] Rod Nordlund, Sami Yousafzai and Babak Dehghanpisheh, "How Al Qaeda Slipped Away," *Newsweek*, August 19, 2002.

[6] David S. Cloud and Ian Johnson, "Hunt for al Qaeda Misses The Likes of Nizar Nawar," *Wall Street Journal*, August 20, 2002.

[7] *Singapore Straits Times*, "Al-Qaeda Regrouping in Afghanistan?," August 20, 2002.

<u>**Conclusion**</u>

A Demand for Accountability

There is little concept of both personal and official responsibility in government, and particularly in our nation's capital. Politicians and high ranking government bureaucrats posture, offering platitudes and "sound bites" for the television cameras, rather than accepting the consequences and responsibility for the years of fatal neglect that left America wide open to a terrorist attack. Sadly, these government officials are never *really* called to account for their derelictions and gross negligence. The American people are owed a full accounting from the public servants who have failed their nation and betrayed the public trust – the elected officials and government bureaucrats who allowed September 11th to happen.

The consequences of U.S. government corruption become painfully acute in light of the attacks of September 11th. It is the type of corruption that erodes our faith in our constitutional republic and corrosively destroys our ability to defend ourselves. This sort of corruption is the easy, lazy, indifference of rationalization and moral pilferage that incrementally robs the nation of its vitality, unity and sense of purpose. It is a corruption that taints not just the offices of government, but that infects the American national character and metastasizes to the point where citizens surrender their heritage of rugged individualism, self-sufficiency and individual liberty in order to satisfy themselves squabbling over the amount and degree of government entitlement, subsidy and allowance.

For the last 20 years, Americans have listened to government officials talk about "accepting responsibility," but rarely are there any substantive results.

While the Clinton-Gore administration is largely to blame for allowing our nation's security apparatus to atrophy, the Bush-Cheney administration's response to the terrorist attacks has been incomplete and contradictory. Osama bin Laden has not been taken dead or alive. And domestically, rather than taking concrete, precise steps to shore up on-going intelligence and law enforcement inadequacies at the CIA and FBI, the administration "merely" announced the largest reorganization of government in 50 years.

Accountability and responsibility require action. The following steps must be taken by the government now in order to restore the faith of the American public, gain justice for those murdered on September 11th, and ensure the defense of the American public:

Fire and/or take legal action against the government officials who allowed September 11th to happen.

Create a National Counterterrorism Agency designed, manned and equipped to proactively identify, locate and destroy terrorist threats to the United States, wherever they may be located.

Establish a Blue Ribbon Commission, as proposed in this book, to identify the government's September 11th related failures, and develop a corrective plan for implementation (that specifically addresses Homeland Security).

Modify the current plan for a Department of Homeland Security and concentrate the intelligence and law enforcement resources of the federal government on: 1) current, on-going investigations and operations of the FBI, CIA, *et al*.; and 2) the creation of a National Counterterrorism Agency.

Station air defense weapons at all nuclear facilities in the United States.

Make greater use of the states' National Guard units to augment security along the U.S. border (to include our waterways and ports), at nuclear facilities, and for nuclear, biological and chemical countermeasures and first aid training at the county level, particularly in metropolitan areas.

Solve the mystery of the anthrax attacks. Failure to do so is an injustice to the families and friends of those who died and became seriously ill, as well as a tacit endorsement of the incompetent law enforcement and biomedical investigations to date. Should a large scale attack be launched against the United States, many would perish. The government's apparent indifference is appalling.

Take other corrective measures as new information emerges about U.S. national security and homeland defense inadequacies.

The tragedy of September 11th can serve as the opportunity for a rebirth of government accountability, national character and respect for our heritage and institutions. What is required of our political leadership and the country as a whole, is the considered, mature, and honest commitment to the founding principles of our constitutional republic and the unflagging pursuit of responsibility from our elected representatives. If told the truth and openly challenged, Americans are still capable of responding in a manner reminiscent of World War II's "Greatest Generation." That sort of leadership and honesty in government requires a radical departure from the last 40 years of corruption and falsehood. And in the end, if our leadership and our citizenry do not take this terrorist threat seriously, America's future is in jeopardy and we may well find ourselves on the path already trod by such defunct civilizations as Ancient Greece and Rome. If we continue to allow the barbarians – this time Islamist radicals – to slip past our sentries, the United States will cease to exist as the beacon of liberty.